COMBAT SWIMMER

Praise for
COMBAT SWIMMER

"Bob Gormly tells his story with remarkable wit, wisdom, drama, and grace. *Combat Swimmer* is a superb and fascinating story about the U.S. Navy SEALs, from one of the best of the breed."

—Hans Halberstadt, author of *U.S. Navy SEALs, U.S. Navy SEALs in Action*, and *Inside the U.S. Navy SEALs*

"*Combat Swimmer* is a 'from the ground up' story, taking the reader from fire ants to firefights, from compelling patriotism to government failures, all told by a survivor of the most dangerous kind of combat."

—Roger C. Dunham, author of *Spy Sub: Top Secret Mission to the Bottom of the Pacific*

"*Combat Swimmer* is a gripping, stroke-by-stroke, firsthand account of Navy SEALs."

—Gerald Astor, author of *The Mighty Eighth* and *Crisis in the Pacific*

"Gormly is a warrior for the working day . . . . In a harsh world, it will comfort many to know that men with Gormly's spirit, character, and patriotism wear this company's uniform."

—*Publishers Weekly*

"Gormly tells it like it was, not hiding his mistakes and the tragedies that go hand in hand with combat and military training . . . a quick, fun read."

—*Soundings*

COMBAT SWIMMER

MEMOIRS OF A NAVY SEAL

CAPTAIN ROBERT A. GORMLY, USN (RET.)

NAL Caliber
Published by New American Library,
a division of Penguin Group (USA) Inc.,
375 Hudson Street, New York, New York 10014, USA
Penguin Group (Canada), 90 Eglinton Avenue East, Suite 700, Toronto,
Ontario M4P 2Y3, Canada (a division of Pearson Penguin Canada Inc.)
Penguin Books Ltd., 80 Strand, London WC2R 0RL, England
Penguin Ireland, 25 St. Stephen's Green, Dublin 2,
Ireland (a division of Penguin Books Ltd.)
Penguin Group (Australia), 250 Camberwell Road, Camberwell,
Victoria 3124, Australia (a division of Pearson Australia Group Pty. Ltd.)
Penguin Books India Pvt. Ltd., 11 Community Centre,
Panchsheel Park, New Delhi - 110 017, India
Penguin Group (NZ), 67 Apollo Drive, Rosedale, North Shore 0632,
New Zealand (a division of Pearson New Zealand Ltd.)
Penguin Books (South Africa) (Pty.) Ltd., 24 Sturdee Avenue,
Rosebank, Johannesburg 2196, South Africa

Penguin Books Ltd., Registered Offices:
80 Strand, London WC2R 0RL, England

Published by NAL Caliber, an imprint of New American Library, a division of Penguin Group (USA) Inc. Previously published in Dutton and Onyx editions.

First NAL Caliber Trade Paperback Printing, August 2010
10 9 8 7 6 5 4 3 2 1

Set in Electra
Designed by Ginger Legato

Printed in the United States of America

For the people who made it all possible:
the SEALs with whom I served, and especially Becky.

CONTENTS

PART 4 · FIRE THREE: SEAL TEAM SIX

PART 5 · FIRE FOUR: A NEW WAY OF DOING BUSINESS

COMBAT SWIMMER

PREFACE

Since I retired, many of my former SEAL shipmates have asked me when I was going to write a book. Other former SEALs have written accounts of their careers, but only one has offered a commanding officer's perspective. I want to provide the reader not only with "war stories" but with serious analyses of events in the evolution of SEALs into the best fighting force in the U.S. military. My story in many ways mirrors the story of the Naval Special Warfare program. I have been fortunate enough to participate in the forefront of what has become one of the most sought-after officer career programs in the Navy.

The Vietnam War is forever etched in the minds of my generation. Reflecting back, I think our cause was just, but the way we went about it was flawed. SEALs who fought in Vietnam were professional military men, not draftees; the war just didn't affect us as it did others. I'd like to illustrate what we professionals achieved in the Vietnam War.

The complete story of SEAL Team Six has not yet been told; it may never be. Much has been written about the command in the years since it was formed. For three years I commanded SEAL Team Six, and I think the brave and dedicated men I served with deserve recognition.

I was fortunate enough to have four SEAL command tours. Timing, not talent, was responsible for that. I also commanded two SEAL platoons and a SEAL team in combat, and was lucky to have survived a number of close calls. I like to tell people who hear me groan every time I move that if I had thought I'd live this long, I'd have taken better care of my body when I was young!

Any success I had during my SEAL career was a direct result of the truly outstanding people I worked with and for. Most SEALs I've known were not Rambo types. The ones who thought they were usually fell by the wayside. Instead, most SEALs were hardworking, highly trained, extremely motivated men who did dangerous jobs well but never thought of themselves as particularly special. I've tried to make this their story as much as mine, describing as well as I can remember who participated in various events. If I've included anyone who wasn't with me at a particular time, or excluded anyone who was, I apologize for the oversight. Also, in some cases I've chosen to not use the full names of certain people still involved in SEAL activities.

Some key people have helped me in this effort. My wife, Becky, and my son, Kevin, provided much-needed proofreading, and suggestions that have improved the quality of my work. My daughter, Anne, provided encouragement and support. My agent, Andrew Zack, gave me guidance and assistance beyond that normally expected of an agent, and my editor, Todd Keithley, brought my sometimes disjointed thoughts into focus. Hans Halberstadt, a friend and fellow author, provided encouragement and advice when I was about to throw up my hands in frustration. One of my former officers and a good friend, Lieutenant Commander MacKenzie (Mac) Clark, USN (Retired), provided initial editorial assistance and advice. Commander Tim Bosiljevac, author of *SEALs: UDT/SEAL Operations in Vietnam* and a hard-charging SEAL officer, provided me copies of many of the Mission Reports I wrote during my Vietnam deployments. I used these "Barndance Cards," as they were called, to verify my memory.

Despite all the help I've received writing this book, I take full responsibility for the content. *Combat Swimmer* is my recollection of what I consider the most significant events in my naval career. I've tried to be as accurate as possible, and any errors of fact are unintended.

PART 1

Lock and Load

"Lock and load" is a command used on all U.S. military firing ranges. Literally, it means "Get ready to fire," but lock and load is more than that; it's a mind-set. It is the realization that you have to be ready to go into combat at a moment's notice. You stay ready—you stay locked and loaded.

For SEALs, combat comes in many forms and at any time—often when no other U.S. forces are committed. The lock-and-load mind-set begins the day a prospective SEAL steps across the threshold of our basic training facility. SEALs stay locked and loaded as long as they're in a SEAL Team. Most military units train for combat under as realistic conditions as possible, but most don't have the sense of urgency found in SEAL Teams. There's one difference between SEAL training missions and actual combat: we don't kill the enemy in training.

1

"WATER, WATER EVERYWHERE . . ."

February 1966

In *Sea Lion*'s forward torpedo room, I had just finished briefing my men for the mission. U.S.S. *Sea Lion* was a World War II–vintage fleet submarine that had been converted for swimmer operations. It was gliding through the water at six knots, thirty feet below the surface, maneuvering to our launch point.

I looked around the room at the twenty-four other men from Underwater Demolition Team 22. Dressed like me in black wet suits with Mark 6 diving rigs on our backs, they were standing close together between two racks of torpedoes. We all held swim fins and face masks. Over our diving gear each of us wore a rolled-up life jacket with an emergency flare attached. Around our waist was a weight belt loaded with thirty pounds of lead weights. On one leg we each wore a diving knife. None of us had firearms. We wouldn't need them on this mission. If we had to shoot someone, the mission would fail. We'd pick up the rest of our mission equipment from external storage lockers on the submarine deck after we locked out. The forward escape trunk, through which we were exiting the sub, was barely big enough to handle a pair of swimmers and the trunk operator.

The forward torpedo room was designed to accommodate six men, who loaded the torpedoes into the forward tubes. We filled the space and then some. Sweat filled my wet suit and dripped off my face. Our suits would keep us warm once we were in the water, but now, as we waited for the submarine to reach the launch point, they were about to dehydrate us.

The trunk operator was already standing by in the chamber. The submarine dive supervisor stood by the entrance to the forward escape-hatch ladder, waiting to receive the word from the submarine commanding officer in the conn. I knew my commanding officer, Lieutenant Commander Dave Schaible, was standing right next to him, making sure his boys were launched at the right place.

I was at the bottom of the ladder, going over in my mind all we were about to do. My swim buddy, Petty Officer Second Class Tom McCutchan, stood next to me, checking to see if all the men were ready to go. I knew they were. I could see it in their eyes. My men were all aggressive warriors, and they were well prepared for the mission. Adrenaline levels were high, and confidence levels even higher. All they wanted to do was get off the damn submarine before they sweated to death.

Suddenly, we all leaned slightly forward as the *Sea Lion* slowed to three knots. It was time to start. The first dive pair headed up the ladder and squeezed into the small forward escape trunk to begin the lockout cycle. The dive supervisor carefully lowered the bottom hatch and shut it tightly. Pressing the call switch on the 1MC internal communications system, he told the conn, "Ready to commence lockout."

Through the speaker I heard, "Commence lockout."

The loudspeaker squawked again as the trunk operator said, "Undogging side door." Then, "Opening flood, opening vent."

I heard the rush of water and the roar of escaping air as the trunk operator opened the flood and vent valves to fill the escape trunk with water. I watched through the small window in the bottom of the hatch as the seawater filled the trunk.

"Water at waist level, swimmers okay," the trunk operator said.

"Roger," responded the dive supervisor, located just under the escape trunk. "Continue the flood."

I watched as the two swimmers washed their masks in the water, spat in them to reduce fogging, and put them on.

"Water at chest level, closing vent!" yelled the trunk operator.

"Side door opening." I heard a clunk. Through the hatch window I saw the door swing open as the pressure in the trunk equalized with the pressure outside the submarine.

"Swimmers leaving trunk" came through the speaker.

I watched as my men escaped the cramped trunk for the freedom of the night ocean. They disappeared from my sight through the trunk's accessway below the main deck of the submarine. It was just after two in the morning and very dark.

I pictured the first swim pair moving aft toward the sail, holding on to lines that were strung along the deck to guide them to the small "cigarette deck" halfway up the sail. There each man would swap his mouthpiece for one attached to the submarine's air supply, so as not to deplete his Mark 6 gas supply while waiting for his teammates to arrive.

As soon as the second swimmer's fins cleared the entranceway, I watched as the trunk operator closed and dogged the side door.

"Opening blow, opening drain," said the operator as he opened the blow and drain valves. That slightly increased the pressure in the trunk and forced the water out into a holding tank in the bilge area of the submarine.

"Roger," replied the dive supervisor.

"Water at bottom hatch," said the operator. "Securing drain and opening vent." As he secured the valves, he cracked the vent to bring the trunk back to the "surface"—in other words, to make the air pressure equal to that inside the submarine.

When the gauges indicated the trunk was "on the surface," the dive supervisor said, "Stand clear, opening hatch," and pushed open the bottom trunk hatch.

The next pair of swimmers climbed up the ladder into the trunk to repeat the cycle. That first cycle had taken nine minutes—a good but not great time. We repeated the process until, 117 minutes later, only my swim buddy Tom McCutchan and I remained in the submarine.

I turned to Tom. "You ready?"

"Let's get the hell out of here," he replied.

Up the five-foot ladder he went, me behind. Tom leaned forward as he got to the hatch opening. I reached up and guided his diving rig as he wiggled inside. When I got to the hatch opening Tom reached down, grabbed the top of my rig, and helped me wedge my frame through. It was a tight fit.

I am about six feet, one inch, and I weighed 205 pounds in those days. Tom was equally tall but not quite as heavy. Together, we more than filled the escape trunk. We wriggled around as the dive supervisor gingerly closed the bottom hatch, trying not to catch one of our feet. As we moved, the fiberglass coverings on our diving gear bumped against the piping in the trunk. We had to be careful not to bang them too hard. We also had to be careful not to snag one of the canvas-covered rubber breathing bags or our breathing hoses, crammed against our chests. The Mark 6 was a somewhat fragile rig. It wasn't designed for locking out of submarines.

As the water flooded into the trunk and began to creep up my legs into my wet suit, a feeling of calm came over me. It was time to do the mission. The rising water began to relieve some of the weight I carried. Fully immersed, we would be almost neutrally buoyant. When the side door opened, I put in my mouthpiece, hunched down, and eased into the short accessway to the main deck. Tom was right behind me. We both stopped and put on our swim fins. From this point on there would be little need for talk.

We swam along the deck, careful not to look around too much. We didn't want the water flow from the moving submarine to rip off our face masks. The submarine was highlighted in an eerie blue-green glow as the sea's microscopic organisms contacted the hull and signaled their existence with phosphorescence. I could see about twenty feet along the submarine deck as we held the guideline and swam upward toward the sail.

As the cigarette deck came into view, I saw that my men had retrieved and distributed all our equipment from the external storage areas. They appeared ready to go. Tom and I slipped over the railing and settled in next to the men.

After checking with my assistant platoon commander, Lieutenant Junior Grade John Hennigan, I swam to the small, air-filled "Bubble" attached to the sail, stuck my head in, and pulled out my mouthpiece. "We're ready to launch," I told the sub CO through the loudspeaker.

"Roger," he replied. "We'll be at the drop-off point in five minutes."

I signaled to John and waited for the CO's signal to go. I could see John's baby face peering at me through his face mask . . . we kidded him about his young looks, but he was tough as nails. I could see he'd done his usual good job getting things organized outside the submarine.

"Thirty seconds to launch" came through the speaker in the Bubble. "That was a quick five minutes," I thought.

The men spat out the mouthpiece from the air regulators attached to the manifold on the cigarette deck and went back on their Mark 6 rig. They were hovering at the top of the railing around the cigarette deck, holding on to the "Lizard Line," the long rope that keeps SEALs together during submerged operations.

At precisely 0400, the submarine CO said over the speaker, "Course to Point Alpha same as planned—*go!*"

"Roger. See you in about five hours."

"We'll keep the coffee hot," Dave said, giving us his personal send-off.

I gave the hand signal to push off. The lead pair swam into the boat's flow stream and set a course toward the beach, while I positioned myself next to Tom on the Lizard Line and started kicking to get clear of the submarine. Looking back along the line, I saw the latter half of my team falling into formation as the sub slowly disappeared into the murk.

My best navigators were the lead pair, and I knew they would guide us to the target beach. We swam in double file, each pair holding a loop spliced into the Lizard Line. Tom, swimming at my side, appeared to hang suspended as we moved effortlessly through the water, and in front of me the fins of the swimmers gave off a bioluminescent glow.

The trip to Point Alpha was going to take about an hour and a half. On long swims, like this one, it was hard for me to keep from going into a trance. Swimming always relaxed me, and the water was wonderfully warm. The slight current created by my swimming cooled me as the wet suit got more comfortable.

We were on our way to an enemy beach on a small island in the Caribbean, where we would prepare the way for an amphibious landing by a large naval force. We had to reconnoiter the beach without being seen, which meant we had to stay underwater. A submerged swimmer reconnaissance is the most complicated operation I ever ran as a SEAL officer, and it took more than three hours to conduct the mission briefing. Once we left the submarine, we weren't going to be able to talk things over: all communication would be in sign language. Every man had to know not only his own assignment but everyone else's so he could take over any role if we had casualties.

Today's mission was straightforward. We had to give the amphibious force commander the location of every man-made and natural obstacle that might impale a landing craft. We had to locate and mark mines as well. The commander also needed to know whether the beach sand could support tanks, bulldozers, and other heavy equipment in the landing force. And of course, we had to do it all without the enemy knowing we'd been there.

To accomplish our mission we had to leave the submarine about two miles off the beach. We'd swim submerged all the way. Three hundred yards off the beach, we'd establish a grid reference, "Point Alpha." In designated swim pairs, we'd proceed along assigned lanes within the grid system, recording the water depth and any natural or man-made obstacles we encountered. After assembling back at Point Alpha, we'd swim back to sea, to a submarine rendezvous point. All of this had to be done underwater, much of it at night. Each man would spend about seven hours submerged—if all went well. We were trained as well as any UDT Platoon could have been, but it would still be a tough mission.

None of us wanted to face our commanding officer, Dave Schaible, if we blew it.

I felt the line slow and looked at my watch. It was 0530 and we had arrived at Point Alpha. It was still dark. Tom and I swam to the front of the line, where one of the men was already screwing the first of his reference augers into the sandy bottom, twenty-five feet beneath the surface. It looked like the right place. To make sure, I drifted slowly toward the surface, with Tom below me holding on to my weight belt. When my depth gauge read five feet I signaled Tom, and he remained at that depth keeping a close eye on me. I oriented myself to a compass heading that would have me facing the beach, then gently rose until my face mask broke the surface. I quickly scanned the beach and saw no enemy activity. Maybe they were all still asleep.

I lined up my compass board in the predawn light with a hill about 300 yards to my right front and checked the bearing, then quickly turned left to see the jagged outcrop of rocks that marked the left flank of our target beach. I took another bearing and headed down. My face had been above the surface about thirty seconds—not bad. It would have been almost impossible for anyone to see me amid the light chop of the water. We were close enough to where we needed to be. When we got back to *Sea Lion,* I would adjust the position of Point Alpha and record the data from the new reference point.

We descended to the first auger stake anchoring our survey line, and I gave the signal to begin the reconnaissance. Two of the men snapped their swimmer reel into the auger stake and began a course parallel to the beach, laying out their 500-yard base line. The swimmer reel, a deep-sea fishing reel containing a light nylon line, was used to log distances underwater. Every fifty yards of line was marked by lead shot, so we'd swim a designated number of fifty-yard intervals to get to the right location.

In turn, each swim pair left Point Alpha and swam down the base line until they reached their designated spot. The swimmers assigned to the lane closest to Point Alpha stopped, tied a butterfly knot in the base line, and attached the end of the line from their swimmer reel to the knot. Then they headed for the beach on a course perpendicular to the line.

In the first light of dawn, I watched as each pair moved past to their assigned positions. The lighter it got, the better for us to see—and the easier for the enemy to see us. All the men knew the risks and knew they had to be careful but thorough. There was no margin for error. The information we were gathering was critical, but it was also critical that we not be discovered. Not only were our asses on the line but the entire operation hung in the balance.

Tom and I hooked into the first auger stake and started making our way to the beach. We swam a sinuous course, taking depth readings every twenty-five yards and looking for obstacles. With that technique we could cover about twenty-five yards off our base line, or a lane about fifty yards wide.

Just as we passed the hundred-yard point, Tom grabbed my arm and pointed. To our left front was a large man-made, concrete tetrahedron with a five-foot length of railroad tie sticking out of the top. We took fast measurements, writing them on the plastic board on top of our reel. Water depth eight feet. Obstacle designed to impale a landing craft. No mine attached.

At a four-foot depth I saw two steel tetrahedrons and noted their position. We couldn't get any closer to the beach for fear of being seen. Tom reached down and drove a coring tube into the sand, taking a sample to determine if the beach would support heavy equipment. As he pulled the tube out and capped it we turned and headed back out to sea, reeling in our line. On the way out, we found and recorded two more man-made obstacles and a large coral head that would have to go before landing craft could be brought in.

On our return, Tom tied our reel to the auger stake to let people know we had finished our reconnaissance. Then we started swimming down the base line to check on the rest of the troops. The next pair was just finishing as we passed them. As we swam, I noted that each point on the base line had another line attached, which meant so far all was well.

One of the most difficult aspects of this operation was not knowing how my men were doing. I had the utmost respect for their abilities, and even the weakest swimmer of the bunch was above average. But our diving rigs were somewhat temperamental.

Our Mark 6 semi-closed-circuit, mixed-gas diving rigs could be set to mix gases in different quantities depending on the depth of the dive. On this mission we were using an oxygen/nitrogen mix designed to give us maximum time at the depths we would be swimming—thirty feet to ten feet below the surface. We were using the gear mainly because it gave us the long underwater endurance we needed. As an added benefit, the Mark 6 emitted significantly fewer telltale bubbles than regular civilian scuba.

However, the rigs were old and required careful predive assembly to function properly. For example, if either of the thin rubber non-return valves in the mouthpiece failed to seal, the diver would experience a buildup of carbon dioxide in his system. That, in the worst case, could lead to an oxygen-toxicity seizure and convulsions. By a phenomenon still not completely understood, life-giving oxygen becomes toxic when used to dive deeper than about twenty-five feet. For that reason the Navy allowed us to dive no deeper than twenty-five feet for no longer than seventy-five minutes on pure oxygen. (Since that time we've learned a few lessons from our European friends, and the Navy's oxygen diving rules are much less restrictive.)

I had personally checked that each man had gotten a positive on the dip testing of his rig for bubbles, which would tell of unsuspected leaks. Besides the non-return valve, the CO_2 scrubber had to be properly sealed, or seawater would soak the barilyme (the scrubbing chemical), rendering it useless. Hose connections had to be tight as well. If bubbles appeared anywhere but the pop-off valve plus a few out of the mouthpiece, you had a problem that had to be fixed. Each diver was responsible for his own rig, but dive buddies helped each other.

My platoon chief and diving supervisor, Chief Petty Officer James "Deacon" Criscoe, kept a close watch on all of us. Deacon, who'd been in UDT for over twelve years and was almost as crusty as Dave Schaible, was the perfect platoon chief petty officer. He always supported me but wouldn't let me get into too much trouble. I trusted his judgment completely. Though his role was to make sure we set up each rig correctly, he could have easily taken my place. He was like a hawk, circling the group as we prepared to go. The rigs had to be perfect to begin with, because during the swim, as a diver twisted and turned doing his job, any loose connection could allow seepage. Deacon paid particular attention to each man's oxygen-scrubber canisters, which were made of a fiberglass that was susceptible to warping. If the cover (or the top part of the canister where it mated with the cover) warped, there would be a microscopic break in the seal between the cover and the canister. A small warp wouldn't be noticeable in the predive testing, but would cause problems later because small pressure differentials that occurred during the dive tended to flex the rig's parts and connections.

At the end of my predive briefing I'd told the men that in an emergency they were to surface as a pair and swim to sea. We'd try to pick them up after the rest of us made it back to the submarine, but we probably couldn't get them until after dark. It was all we could do.

Tom and I reached the end of the base line as the last pair was finishing. They gave me a thumbs-up and we headed back to Point Alpha. We passed pair after pair on our way back—no rigs had failed. I was beginning to feel really good, when suddenly I inhaled a mouthful of water—and tasted barilyme.

Had my rig flooded out? Impossible, I thought. I signaled Tom that I had a problem. He gestured toward the surface with a questioning look in his eye. I shook my head no, and signed for him to check my rig. He gave me the once-over and a thumbs-up. That meant he couldn't see any bubbles escaping from my scrubber canister, so if I had a leak it probably wasn't too bad. I swallowed the water and barilyme. We would continue back to Point Alpha to rendezvous.

As we swam I analyzed the situation. I was getting a little water on each inhalation, so there was water in my right breathing hose. It could have a slight leak, which wouldn't be a real big deal, just uncomfortable. I could deal with that. I decided to continue the mission and see what happened. Tom, as he'd been trained, began paying more attention to me to make sure I wasn't exhibiting any of the early signs of CO_2 buildup, such as erratic behavior or labored breathing.

As we approached the group at Point Alpha, I saw Deacon counting heads. I checked my watch: 0715. We had been gone from the submarine for three hours, fifteen minutes. I wanted to be at the rendezvous point with the sub by 0830.

After we pushed off, my situation got worse. I started sucking more and more water-barilyme mix. "Screw it! If it gets to the point where I can't get any gas, I'll surface," I said to myself. Incredibly, no one had had to abort yet. I thought that maybe some of the other guys were experiencing the same thing I was, and I wasn't about to quit on them.

I began experimenting as we swam seaward. By swimming with my head up slightly, I could diminish the problem. Gas at the top of my right breathing bag was apparently keeping the water down. I started getting more gas with each breath. I was going to make it! There was no way I was going to pull Tom to the surface with me and jeopardize the mission. The hell with my briefing!

I slowed the group down on the way out because I couldn't swim horizontally. They knew the situation. Tom watched me closely as we made our way to the rendezvous point. With hand signals, I'd briefed John Hennigan on my situation. I wanted him ready to take charge if things got worse.

We swam on. Out of habit, I tilted forward after about every six to eight kicks of my fins and sucked more of the caustic mixture. Then I got back to a more vertical attitude and breathed good gas. I wasn't feeling any symptoms of a carbon dioxide buildup, but it was only a matter of time.

A lot of things were going through my mind. We'd just completed a good reconnaissance, but if we didn't get back aboard the *Sea Lion* as planned, none of what we'd accomplished would matter. I knew Dave considered us his best submerged-reconnaissance group, and I wasn't about to prove him wrong. The farther we were from the island, the better off we were. Even if something went wrong with the rendezvous, I knew we could surface two or three miles out and wait for our alternate rendezvous time, just after dark. Then the submarine could just surface and pick us up.

Finally, I felt the combined motion of the Lizard Line stop. John swam back and signaled me that we were about where we should be for the pickup. We set up in a line and waited for our submarine.

We had been in the water over five hours, submerged the entire time. The sand bottom was visible below as we intermittently kicked our fins to hold depth.

I signaled Tom that I was going to do a "bounce" dive to make sure that we had at least sixty feet of water beneath us. If not, the submarine wouldn't be able to pick us up, because there wouldn't be enough water under its keel for it to maneuver safely. I was responsible for getting us back on board, and I'd planned to do the bounce dive as part of my routine duty on the mission. I guess my brain forgot about my rig's situation—I couldn't have explained my actions then, and I still can't now.

As I flipped to a head-down position, I was rudely reminded of why I had been carefully swimming almost vertically for the last hour or so. My first inhalation was greeted with the acrid taste of caustic barilyme and seawater. I quickly flipped back, shut the mouthpiece flow valve, took the mouthpiece out, and spat out the barilyme. Reversing the procedure, I inhaled tentatively, relieved to feel the cool breathing mixture back in my mouth.

With my feet down, the salty barilyme soup sloshed to the bottoms of my breathing bags, allowing the gas at the top of my right breathing bag to flow easily. I started down again, this time descending carefully erect, using my arms to push deeper. Tom was right beside me, gesturing toward the surface. I kept on descending. As long as I remained upright, I was fine. I had so much confidence in my ability in the water I knew I could detect the symptoms of CO_2 buildup before it got bad. And I had confidence in my men. If the worst happened, they would pull me up before I drowned.

By the time I arrived at forty feet, about halfway between the surface and the bottom, I could see that we were okay. The sub would have about eighty feet of water depth to maneuver. As I slowly ascended toward the line of frogmen, I signaled the two swimmer pairs with Calypso Sticks. These short lengths of iron pipe were banged together so the submarine's sonar could find us. To the naked ear they sounded too muted to be of any use—merely a faint clicking noise. But to the submarine's sonar operators they sounded like thunderclaps. The submarine would have no problem finding us.

Suddenly Tom jerked my arm, and right ahead of us I saw the bow of *Sea Lion* emerge out of the haze. I'd been dozing; CO_2 was building in my system. The bounce dive probably hadn't helped. I looked at my watch—0910. I watched the submarine move slowly past us and felt the welcome pull on the Lizard Line. We had snagged the periscope. The line swung together behind the sail, and we made our way to the cigarette deck.

The swim pair who had locked out first, some seven hours ago, went directly to the trunk and disappeared. The second pair hovered just outside, awaiting their turn. Tom signaled that I ought to go right in the boat on the next cycle. I signaled no. First out, first in.

The rest of us went "off bag" and on boat air, using the manifold on the deck. For the first time in over two hours I was breathing normally. Deacon swam over to check on me. He looked me square in the eye. I felt great—a slight headache, but that was normal with a CO_2 buildup. I gave him the thumbs-up.

Dave was on the other end of the Bubble. "How'd it go?" he asked.

"Great," I said, and gave him a quick rundown.

"Did you find any minelike objects?" he asked.

"Not that I know of, but I haven't had a chance to debrief the men."

"The first lock-in cycle was completed in under nine minutes," he told me. That was good news. Usually it took longer to lock back into the submarine because the men were cold and tired. Their brains didn't function as well as they had seven hours ago. I wasn't getting any more comfortable, either.

I stayed under the Bubble, and we kept shooting the bull as the cigarette deck slowly emptied of swimmers. Deacon and his buddy left; we were next. I ducked out of the Bubble, put my mouthpiece in my mouth, inhaled, and gagged: no gas, only water. I spat it out again and grabbed a regulator from the manifold to breathe in fresh air.

When Tom looked my way, I passed my hand across my throat and pointed at my rig, then motioned that I was going to "free descend," holding my breath, to the trunk and lock-in. We argued by sign language, and I motioned to the Bubble.

We both stuck our heads under, nose to nose. "Go to the trunk, wait until the side hatch opens and then motion me down," I told him.

"Buddy-breathe with me to the trunk," Tom argued.

"No." Tom's suggestion made sense, but I just didn't want to admit I couldn't handle the problem. Plus, what I was about to do wasn't a big deal. All of us had made many free descents into submarines before. I told Tom to get moving. He went back on bag and left. I left the Bubble, retrieved one of the regulators attached to the sub's air supply, and watched as Tom took a position outside the trunk. The sub's two safety divers were looking up at me, but they didn't move.

When Tom waved, I took a deep breath, slipped over the railing of the cigarette deck, and headed down for the trunk. No problem! I swam right into the trunk, exhaled, stood up, and started breathing from the air cap at the top of the trunk.

The trunk operator asked, "What took you so long?"

"Get this thing drained," I responded. I checked my watch again—1045. Almost nine hours had elapsed since the first swim pair had left the sub.

The bottom hatch opened, and Tom and I went down the ladder. When my head cleared the hatch I saw a large, burly figure at the bottom of the ladder, arms folded across his chest. It was Dave, and he looked pissed. I thought one of my guys had screwed up the lock-in, but he was looking right at me. I figured he couldn't have known what I'd done, but he was obviously angry at Lieutenant Junior Grade Gormly and no one else.

I'd known that Dave was going to be really mad when he saw the condition of my rig. Dave Schaible was a World War II submariner who had been in UDT since 1949. He'd taken over UDT-22 about a year and a half before and had begun a rigorous combat-swimming program. Our submerged reconnaissance was the ultimate level of that program. He was a mustang, meaning he'd come through the enlisted ranks to obtain a commission. So he was older than the average navy lieutenant commander and a hell of a lot more crusty. He had fists the size of ham hocks, and I'd already seen him use them in a bar fight. Man-to-man, he was an imposing gent. He was also one hell of a commanding officer—the best I'd ever had.

"Let me help you break down your rig. You look real tired."

"No, thanks—I'd rather do it myself."

He pulled the Mark 6 off my back, laid it on the deck, handed me a cup of coffee, and went right to the barilyme canister. I watched as he disconnected the hoses, unscrewed the canister top, and dumped the water and barilyme through the bilge grates.

"What the hell did you think you were doing, swimming with the rig in this condition?"

"My job."

"Bullshit—this was a training mission, and you should have surfaced and gotten picked up by the safety boat."

Dave looked at me—hard—put the canister down, and stalked off.

Yeah, it was a training mission—part of a large battle-readiness exercise for UDT-22. We were working out of our winter training base, the submarine base at St. Thomas in the Virgin Islands. We'd go back to St. Thomas, get a good meal and some sleep, and prepare our gear for the demolition mission we'd run early the next morning. Then we'd be back at the target island at 0500, the same way we'd come today, to destroy all the obstacles we'd found. All part of the battle exercise. But I knew that if I had the same problem with my Mark 6 again, I'd handle it the same way. Dave taught us to treat every training mission as the real thing.

Deacon came up to me, and I began to lay into him for telling the CO about what I did. Before I could get two words out of my mouth, he interrupted: "It was stupid for you to keep swimming the rig in that condition, and it was *really* stupid for you to be briefing Tom under the Bubble on your alternate lock-in plan!"

Deacon set a personal record for cumulative words as he chewed me out. And as usual, he was right.

I went to the wardroom after I'd debriefed the troops and we'd cleaned our gear. Dave was pouring coffee. No one else was there, so I figured I was in for a royal ass-chewing.

"Come in and sit down," Dave growled. I walked in and sat down.

Handing me a cup of coffee, he sat across the table from me and said, "Gormly, you're a dumb son of a bitch."

"Thanks for the coffee, Captain."

He told me the platoon had done well on the mission, but he'd had no choice other than to grill me in front of my men. He knew they knew what I'd done, and he wasn't going to tolerate such blatant violations of his diving procedures. Again he demanded, "What the hell did you think you were doing?"

I'd already answered that question, and I couldn't think of anything else to add. Finally, I just looked at him. "What would you have done?"

Dave stared at me for about ten seconds. I figured he was about to reach across the table and rip off my head for being a wiseass. Instead a grin crept onto his scowling face. "Same thing you did."

Figuring I was out of the woods, I looked him in the eye and said, "Gotta train like you're gonna fight—right?"

Dave looked right back at me and said, "Gormly, you're buying the rum and Cokes when we get back to St. Thomas."

I would have many occasions to remember that conversation later in my SEAL career. For one thing, Dave set the tone for me when I later commanded SEAL Teams: never come down too hard on someone who's trying to do his job the realistic way. Another equally important lesson I learned was that if you don't cut corners in training, you're much better prepared for combat.

The difficulties we faced underwater that day in 1966 were good preparation for the tense situations I faced later in Vietnam, Grenada, and other places. Staying locked and loaded was the only way to go.

2

THE ONLY EASY DAY WAS YESTERDAY

A large sign at Basic Underwater Demolition SEAL (BUDS) training tells new students what they can expect: "The only easy day was yesterday." When I went through training, there were no easy days. And as I later learned, the axiom applied to just about everything in the SEALs.

I reported to training, for the second time, in January 1964. Nothing could have deterred me once I started. When something is hard to get, you want it more. As I lay in my bunk that first night, I reflected on how I'd finally made it to this point. It hadn't been easy.

I was born on February 10, 1941, in Long Branch, New Jersey. My father, James Louis Gormly, was from a New York Irish family. He was working on Wall Street in 1929 when the market crashed. That was probably an omen of things to come for the Gormly family, since none of us has ever gotten rich. My mother, Dorothy Percival Gormly, was also from New York. She had been married once before to an electrical engineer, Joseph Leopold. They had one child, my half brother, Joseph Richard Gormly (he took my father's name).

In 1942, when I was eighteen months old, my family moved to Virginia Beach, Virginia. With a partner, my father started a ship's chandlery in Norfolk. He was too old for the military, so, like many others, he got into the wartime shipbuilding industry. His company got some lucrative government contracts to outfit the Liberty ships being constructed at Norfolk-area shipyards. For a few years I guess he did okay, although I was too young to remember. After the war, though, the chandlery went under and he turned to selling cars. My mother spent many years working in real estate. We never had a lot of money, but we did all right. But my father wasn't home much, and in many ways, my older brother, Dick, stood in for him. Dick was twelve years older and was a good influence on me. Thanks to my father's wartime prosperity, he spent three years at the prestigious Virginia Episcopal School in Lynchburg and then went to the University of Virginia. I never held his good fortune against him—I loved Virginia Beach, and never wanted to go to prep school. And my grades were never good enough to get me into UVA!

Both my parents died, destitute, in 1977. My father died in May, the victim of many heart attacks and strokes brought about by hard living. My mother died of a heart attack in December. Both were alcoholics and had smoked heavily for many years. My brother died of throat cancer, brought about by copious consumption of booze, in 1993. After becoming a very successful insurance broker he also died penniless because of poor business and personal decisions. Early in my life, I'd decided to follow a different course.

The summer of 1962 was a pivotal period in my life. I had a big decision to make: what to do after college. After attending Louisburg Junior College in North Carolina for two years, I was finishing my B.A. in history that December at the Norfolk Division of William and Mary. To get through college, I worked thirty-five to forty hours a week at J. C. Penney's. Four nights a week I worked at a Tastee Freeze. Plus, I was taking a course in night school three evenings a week so I'd have enough math credits to graduate. In order to see my future wife, Becky, I would go by her house about two o'clock in the morning, after leaving the Tastee Freeze.

One night I told Becky I was thinking about chucking it all and going to Hawaii to surf for a year. I reasoned I could always come back and finish that last semester in school. I asked her what she'd do if I went to

Hawaii. She said, "Have at it, but don't expect me to be here when you get back." I decided I'd better keep on track instead.

We got married on August 4, 1962. I kid her about her thinking she was marrying Virginia Beach money. In fact, neither family had much. We were determined to make it on our own. Becky had a great job with the local telephone company. In those days Ma Bell was one of the best employers in town, and she made more than I did in both of my jobs.

The turning point came on a warm, sunny day in September 1962. I sat on my surfboard 100 yards offshore, waiting for a good wave and wondering what to do after college. Back toward shore, another surfer was paddling out to the lineup. I knew all the guys who surfed in Virginia Beach, and most of the better surfers from other areas. This guy was a good surfer, but I didn't know his name or anything about him. As he settled in to wait with me, I introduced myself and asked who he was and what he did for a living.

He told me he was Ron Smith and he was in the Navy, stationed at Little Creek, Virginia. And what kind of job did he have that allowed him to surf whenever he wanted? He was the executive officer of an Underwater Demolition Team (UDT). His boss, he said, liked to play tennis, so they had an agreement. If Ron could surf whenever the waves were good, he would watch the shop while his boss played tennis every afternoon.

As we got to know each other better through surfing, he began to talk to me about joining the Navy after I finished college. I was impressed by his character and his willingness to befriend a younger guy. But mostly I was impressed with his job. I figured a job that allowed you to surf anytime you wanted was the job for me.

Ron helped me with the paperwork for getting into the Navy, and I reported to Officer Candidate School at Newport, Rhode Island, in January 1963. I'd hoped to start UDT training that summer, but it didn't work out that way.

I passed the running, swimming, and strength parts of the test easily. All that remained was the pressure and oxygen toxicity test, which I knew nothing about but wasn't worried. However, I made the mistake of listening to the diving corpsman who administered the test. He told us that if we felt the least bit uncomfortable to let him know.

The test was conducted in a recompression chamber. They took us down to 120 feet to see if we could handle the pressure, and then brought us up to 60 feet, where we were to breathe pure oxygen for thirty minutes. This part of the test was designed to see if we were susceptible to oxygen toxicity—a real problem if you wanted to be a frogman.

I had no idea what the symptoms were, and I later found out that the Navy had no real idea why people developed oxygen toxicity, except that it happened sometimes when you breathed pure oxygen under pressure. I began to feel funny after about ten minutes, and I signaled the corpsman. He immediately pulled off my mask and told me to forget about UDT.

We later figured out that I had hyperventilated from the excitement. It didn't matter; UDT wasn't hurting for officers, and I was out of luck. There was no provision for another test. So I finished OCS with the notion that I would do my required three years and get out.

Then a strange thing happened. I got orders to report to UDT training at the Naval Amphibious Base in Little Creek, Virginia, home of the East Coast UDT and SEAL teams. The officials at OCS told me not to question the orders: some doctor probably reviewed my record and decided there was no problem. So I reported for training in June 1963—and the corpsman assigned to the training unit took a look at my record and said, "Sorry, Charlie, you're not qualified—you flunked the oxygen test."

I was pissed, but all my yelling got me nowhere. The Navy sent me to the Naval Amphibious School to await new orders. Because I was a three-year reservist and had a family in Virginia Beach, someone in the Bureau of Naval Personnel probably decided the cheapest thing for the Navy to do was to leave me at Little Creek to do my time with the "Gators." I went to a few training courses and then had the good fortune to get orders to Assault Craft Unit 2 (ACU-2) at the Naval Amphibious Base in Little Creek. There, at a diesel engine maintenance course, I met Tom Gaston, a fellow ensign assigned to UDT-21. Tom convinced the UDT doctor to give me another test. I took it and passed with no problems. I even took a second test to make sure. And in nearly thirty years of diving pure-oxygen and mixed-gas scuba, I never experienced a problem with oxygen toxicity. Thanks, Tom.

In November 1963 I received my orders to report to UDT Replacement Training Class 31, beginning in January. I was a little worried about how the instructors would see me—in those days most people got only one chance at UDT training. But when I walked through the door to the administration building and "instructor's hut" my apprehensions were dispelled. Chief Petty Officer Tom Blais looked up from his desk. "Welcome back, Mr. Gormly. Hit the deck and start doing push-ups until I get tired."

In those days, the first two weeks of training were devoted to physical conditioning as the instructors tried to get all the men who'd been serving on ships in shape for the rigors of "Hell Week," the third week of training. For me the conditioning phase was sort of a pacing period: I'd been working harder on my own beforehand. In fact, throughout the course I found training wasn't as hard for me as for others in the class. First, Ron Smith had done a great job of letting me know what to expect. "Don't quit," he advised, "and you'll make it, because they rarely throw anyone out." Second, I'd had plenty of opportunity to get in shape while biding my time at ACU-2. Third, with a wife and baby depending on me I had plenty of motivation. And finally, I'd had a high school football coach who instilled a never-quit attitude in me. I figured that if I'd survived two-a-day summer practices under his ex-Marine-Corps-drill-instructor tutelage, I could get through anything.

When morning training started, we all got a taste of things to come. With the rest of my fellow trainees, I ran into a hot, stuffy classroom. (We ran everywhere we went.) As we stood at rigid attention, the side door to the classroom slammed open and a large black man in green fatigues roared, "Good morning, class, I am Instructor Bernie Waddell. You can call me Bernie—ha, ha, ha."

"Good morning, Instructor Waddell," we responded in unison. Nobody in their right mind would have considered calling him Bernie.

"Welcome to Class Thirty-one. I'm going to go over a few things you people need to know. How's your spirit?"

"*AAAARH*, Instructor Waddell!" we roared.

"All right. Now listen up, because I'm not going to repeat myself—I say again, I'm not going to repeat myself. Do you people understand?"

"Yes, Instructor Waddell."

He went on to give us the do's and don'ts of getting through training. But I was so intimidated by his presence I didn't hear most of what he said. Chief Petty Officer Bernie Waddell was a legendary instructor, the one most feared, and most respected, when I went through training. Bernie went over all the reasons he had seen people quit. It was a tongue-in-cheek dissertation: "I don't have any clean skivvies"; "I don't have any skivvies"; "My wife doesn't know I'm here"; "I just wanted to get off my ship"; and on and on. What we all got out of that first lesson was this: if you didn't quit, the instructors seldom threw you out. Just what Ron had told me.

The training course was designed to test one's mental toughness. They wanted to see who would quit when the going got tough. The ones who quit, we didn't want on the Teams—on combat missions, the going was always tough.

People started quitting left and right. One particular instance really stunned me. This officer was best in every phase of our two-week preconditioning training. He had the best time on the obstacle course. He was one of the best swimmers and runners, and he had a great attitude. Yet the first night of Hell Week, as we were sitting in the kitchen of the Bachelor Officer Quarters (BOQ), he looked at me and said, "I'm not going back out." We were all cold and wet from head to foot. It was miserable, but we had come through so far and he wasn't hurt. He just didn't want to be cold and wet. Good thing he quit, because we had a lot of cold and wet in front of us.

Our training week ran from 0500 Monday morning to whenever the duty instructor felt like letting us off on Saturday. Usually we'd get liberty by 1400, after the training area had been cleaned to his satisfaction. There was a duty instructor each night, too. He started after the night training exercise and got up the next morning to take muster and lead the morning physical training (PT) and run—all done before breakfast, which we ate at 0700.

For meals the enlisted men had to run a mile and a half to the base mess hall, and we officers had to run just a half-mile to the BOQ. But while enlisted men ate as much as they wanted, officers got only one serving per meal. We never got enough to eat.

Our family was renting a two-bedroom apartment in Virginia Beach, about a twenty-five-minute drive from the training area. I went home on the weekends as soon as liberty went down, eating everything in sight until Sunday night, when I went back to the barracks. A couple of the married guys lived closer to the base and went home every night, but I didn't trust myself to get up in time to drive in for the 0500 muster, so I stayed at the barracks during the week. We had only one car, and it saved Becky from having to get up, bundle up our son, Kevin, and drive me to the base.

Hell Week is the defining period of BUDS. Usually, if you made it through that, you made it through the rest of the training. The instructors did their best to keep us cold, wet, sandy, and miserable for five and a half days. For my class, the winter weather at Little Creek made this easy.

Our Hell Week started at midnight on a Sunday. I had a fever and all the symptoms of the flu, but I kept quiet about it because I didn't want to risk being pulled out of training. I decided I'd just gut it out. The weather cooperated with the instructors. It was in the low thirties and raining—great for the flu, I guess, because by 0900 the first morning I felt fine, even though I was soaked from head to foot and cold. The rest of the week we had the entire gamut of wintertime weather—rain, cold, snow, you name it.

The first thing the instructors did, after rousing us from our racks and screwing around with us a little, was divide the class into boat crews, with an officer in charge of each. Each crew would stay together for the duration of Hell Week, so anyone who quit would draw down on the number of people in his crew, thus making it harder for those who stayed.

Everywhere we went that week we had to carry our Inflatable Boats Large (IBLs), eleven-man rubber rafts that weighed at least a ton. We never had more than six men carrying them. The best way to carry them was on our heads, and we all got shorter, thicker necks that week. One of Instructor Chuck Newell's favorite tricks was to get a running start and jump up into one of the boats as we were running down the road. Chuck stood about six feet, two inches and weighed about 195, all of it muscle. He'd stand up in the boat like Ben-Hur in the chariot, yelling at us to hurry up. Then if the crew didn't pick up the pace (or even if they did), he'd start running around in the boat and jumping up and down. He was a lot of fun.

By the first night of Hell Week, we'd been cold and wet all day long. Around six P.M. we stood at attention in front of the instructor's hut, IBLs on our heads. Out of the hut strode Chief Petty Officer Tom Blais. At five feet, ten inches tall and about 190 pounds, Tom was a sight to behold. We'd already heard how he'd fallen from the top of the fifty-foot "cargo net" on our obstacle course. As he hit the ground back first, he had the presence of mind to take a judo "beat" with his arms to help break his fall. Still, he broke his back. Most men would have been medically discharged from the Navy. Not Tom. He worked hard, rehabilitated himself, and here he was standing in front of us, a raging bull ready to make our lives miserable.

"Good evening, class!" he roared.

"Good evening, Instructor Blais."

"I can't hear yoooou."

"Goooood eeeeevening, Instructor Blais!"

"How's your spirit?"

"*AAAARH!*" we roared. (The instructors were always interested in how we felt—it was so comforting!)

"Tonight," he said, "you're going on a trip around the world."

This dream vacation consisted of a trip around the base and its surrounding waters. We'd travel in and under our trusty IBLs. Because the instructors were so concerned for our comfort, the route offered us many opportunities to get in and out of the water and cross beaches, sand dunes, and roads. That way we wouldn't always be in or on the cold water. They didn't want anyone to get sick!

This being a winter class, we could always count on unpredictable but usually nasty weather, and that night met our expectations. The temperature was in the midthirties, and the wind was blowing about thirty knots out of the northeast. As usual, it paid to be a winner. When your boat crew finished, you could "rest" until the next evolution started—usually right after the last boat crew finished the previous evolution. Any rest was welcome in Hell Week.

As Blais finished explaining the course, Waddell stormed out of the instructor's hut and yelled, "Class, ten-hut."

We snapped to attention.

"Hit the deck."

Sixty bodies slammed onto the wet asphalt, IBLs crashing down on top of us.

"Lean and rest."

Sixty bodies pushed themselves (and the IBLs) up to the beginning position for push-ups: arms extended and locked under your chest, feet straight out behind you. I thought we were going to do push-ups until Instructor Waddell got tired—which might be a long time, since he'd been off all day resting.

"Bernie," Blais said, "what are you doing? I'm in charge of this evolution. You can't just come out here and start giving my men orders."

"Tom, you're being too easy on these pukes."

"Bernie, these guys are tired—they've been working hard *aaaall* day."

As the two instructors went on and on, my arms started quivering. The boat got heavier. And heavier. They did the good-guy-bad-guy routine for what seemed like an hour and was probably no more than three minutes.

Finally: "Okay, Tom, I guess you're right, they do look tired. Class, on your feet," roared Instructor Waddell.

I pulled my feet up under me, urging my men not to drop the boat.

The instructors had already warned us to "take care of your equipment—it will take care of you." We struggled to attention.

"Hit the deck, lean, and rest," Blais yelled. "I'm in charge of you people—*I* give the orders."

And so it went until they got tired. It was great to see the two instructors working in unison. We all appreciated the lesson in teamwork. When they finished playing with us, we hauled ass.

A portion of our trip involved dragging and paddling our boat down a drainage ditch that paralleled the southern boundary of the base. As we came to the road leading in from Gate 5, it appeared we could simply portage our boat across the road and put it back in the ditch on the other side. Not so fast, Ensign. Blais met us at the road and told me that we could portage the boat. But, he said, my boat crew and I would have to go through the drainage pipe to the other side, so we could get the full benefit of the training evolution.

"Not a problem," I thought, but then I went down to look at the pipe. It was high tide and the ditch was nearly full, which made paddling the boat considerably easier than it would have been at low tide. But the high tide also made the pipe considerably fuller than it would have been at low tide. There was barely two inches of clearance between the water and the top of the four-foot pipe. Still, no real problem for future frogmen.

I huddled the boat crew and told them I would lead. We would go through head first, on our backs, with our noses pressed against the top of the pipe so we could breathe. The other side was only fifty feet away. I told them we would take it slowly, and nobody would drown. (I didn't have a plan in case someone panicked in the extremely tight area.)

My main concern was the kapok life jackets we were required to wear throughout Hell Week. Ostensibly, they were for our safety. In fact, though, they were so waterlogged and heavy, I worried that one of the guys might be dragged down as we made our way through the pipe.

After I briefed them, I turned around and started through the pipe with the other six guys close behind me. We acted so quickly that Tom didn't know we had started until I was about halfway through the pipe and all the guys were well inside.

Suddenly I heard Tom yelling at me to get back out of the pipe immediately. Normally we responded to an instructor's orders as soon as they were out of his mouth. But at the moment, we were committed; attempting to turn the train around in the pipe would have been too risky. So I muttered "F— you" in Portuguese, and continued through the pipe to the other side. (Portuguese for "f— you," phonetically "for-doo-say," was our class motto. We'd learned it from the four Brazilians in our class for cross-training, and we yelled it in unison whenever an instructor gave us a command. The instructors loved the spirit we showed. They didn't figure out what we were saying until we'd safely finished training.)

As soon as my head emerged, Tom was in my face, screaming that he hadn't said "Simon says." I told him he had given me my directions, and I had carried them out. Once the last guy came out of the pipe, Tom pulled me aside and calmly explained that he had gotten his neck in the wringer during the previous class because a boat crew had panicked in the pipe and two of the trainees nearly drowned. They had to be resuscitated after the instructors pulled them out. Tom had been ordered by the CO of the Amphibious School not to use the pipe again. So now Tom was only telling the boat crews to go through the pipe to see how many men would quit. Three members of a crew ahead of ours had. I said something like, "No harm, no foul," and dropped for fifty push-ups to pay for my unsuccessful attempt at humor.

One of the evolutions toward the end of Hell Week was a long boat trip. The instructors loaded us into trucks and drove us to Laskin Road in Virginia Beach, about fifteen miles away. We unloaded the boats, and each crew took off in Broad Bay headed for Little Creek. I began to think this might be an easy day. The weather was finally cooperating with the trainees—it had cleared and was in the midforties—and we had a good crew. Soon we were well in front of the other boats. One of the axioms of training was "It pays to be a winner."

The instructors were keeping an eye on everyone from the deck of an outboard-driven Boston Whaler, but our IBLs were spaced so far apart, hours could go by before we saw the instructors.

About noon, though, the Whaler crossed the bay toward us and my guts churned: Petty Officer First Class Herb Clements, a reasonable instructor we'd nicknamed the Trainees' Friend, had been replaced by our resident madman, Petty Officer Second Class Gene Fraley. He circled us, commenting on how far in front we were and how we were going to be standing under hot showers before we knew it.

I was waiting for the ax to fall. I figured Fraley'd tell us we were doing so well we ought to go back and help the next boat. Instead, he pulled up alongside of us and pulled a steel garden rake from the gunwale of the Whaler. I couldn't imagine what he had in mind, but I did know we weren't going to like it.

I wasn't wrong. Fraley took the rake and started hitting our main tube. One of my men—Jerry Sweesy, a huge Sioux Indian from South Dakota—and I tried to fend him off with our paddles. But Fraley succeeded in sinking the tines of the rake in the tube. We began to lose air.

IBLs had two main tubes filled with air, fitted together amidships. Fraley had punctured the one that ran around the stern, and soon we were at water level, paddling our asses off but getting nowhere.

Fraley was cackling like a witch. He said, "Mr. Gormly, your boat seems to be suffering from a lack of oxygen. If you're not careful, it will soon fill with water and be awfully difficult to paddle."

I thanked him for his consultation on the matter and told him to get the hell out of there before he found himself in the same situation. Sweesy was wild-eyed, and I think Fraley saw I meant what I said. He hauled ass, laughing.

Gene Fraley was a hell of a guy. When he left his instructor job and went to SEAL Team Two, he did good work in Vietnam—until he killed himself preparing a booby-trapped flashlight one day in the winter of 1968. I was between tours in Vietnam, and I arranged for a Navy C-1A to fly seven of us (that's as many men as the plane would hold) to East Lansing, Michigan, for his funeral. We had to stand there in the cemetery, freezing, with a forty-knot wind blasting snow in our faces. Just before the bugler blew taps, Tom Blais turned to me, pointed toward the heavens, and said, "I bet Fraley is up there laughing his ass off at us."

After Fraley left, we could hardly move the boat through the water. Other crews started passing, looking at us with not too much sympathy. Someone had to be first, and better them than us. We struggled to the Lynnhaven Inlet bridge, where Lynnhaven Bay empties into the Chesapeake Bay, and encountered a three-knot current from the incoming tide. We could do nothing but tie off to a buoy until the tide changed. The rest of the boats had already been through by now. We were dead last.

The tide changed late in the afternoon, and we got through just after dark. We still had a long way to go, and the final part involved moving the boat across the beach at the base and into a lake for a paddle to the training area. We got to the beach about midnight and manhandled the deflated boat across it and into the lake. By now the temperature had again dropped below freezing, and the lake was almost solid ice.

By the time we reached the shore in front of the training area, we were all pissed and absolutely exhausted. I later found out that when Chief Petty Officer Jim Cook, our senior enlisted instructor, heard what Fraley had done, he told him to stay out of the area until the next day. Good call on Jim's part, because I was ready to strangle the guy. Sweesy wanted to rip off his head and shit in the socket.

Chief Cook was so full of warm and fuzzy thoughts about our plight that he welcomed us at the lake's edge. He took one look at the refuse that had once been a fully inflated IBL and observed that it was full of water. He said, "Mr. Gormly, you'd better dump boat so you can get it out of the water."

I looked at the guys, and as one, we all shrugged. By that time it didn't matter. To "dump boat," all members of the crew stand on one main tube, then reach across the boat and grab the gunwale line on the other tube. Leaning back in unison, they pull on the gunwale line until the boat is tipped over on top of them, inverted in the water. That way all the water inside is dumped out. Next the men move to the other side and reverse the process to get the boat right side up again. Dumping a completely inflated boat full of water isn't easy. Dumping our boat proved to be impossible.

We struggled for the better part of thirty minutes in ice-covered water, breaking the ice with our bodies to begin with, and couldn't get the boat over. Finally Cook thought we'd had enough and told us to just drag the IBL back to the rack and secure it. We got that done just in time to pick up another IBL to start the next evolution, which was already under way by that time. Pays to be a winner.

On "So Solly Day"—the aptly named last day of Hell Week—we had to crawl through an obstacle course set up in the sand dunes behind Beach 7. We conducted much of our training there—demolition, beach reconnaissance, whatever. The beach itself was no more than thirty meters wide, but the dunes behind it stretched about two hundred meters to the south.

The instructors were blowing up explosive charges all around us, standard procedure for So Solly Day. Suddenly Tom Blais stopped the class. I was miserable—wet and cold, with sand completely filling my green fatigues. I was exhausted from the week's activities. My brain was working at half speed from lack of sleep. But I knew the end was in sight. I figured all I had to do was get through the morning and I'd be home free. Blais came to where I was lying facedown in the sand. Without saying anything to me, he started scraping out a hole in the sand just under my face. Then he placed a half-pound block of TNT with a piece of time fuse sticking out of the end two inches from my nose. He lit the fuse and walked away.

"Newell," Blais said, "do you think Ensign Gormly will move before the charge goes off?"

"Damn right," Chuck Newell responded. "He's not stupid."

"Mr. Gormly, do you trust me?"

"Yes, Instructor Blais."

"Do you think I'd just watch as your head departs your body?"

"No, Instructor Blais."

"See, Chuck, he trusts me. Ten bucks says he doesn't move."

"You're on."

Many things went through my mind while the fuse cooked away. I wasn't going to quit, so I reasoned that Tom would do something before the charge went off. But as the fuse got shorter, I began to wonder if my mental acuity wasn't being tested and I was about to fail, big-time! Still, I wasn't going to quit or move.

I watched the fuse burn right into the charge. When it hit the blasting cap, I'd be history. Would the rest of the instructors let that happen? The fuse kept burning and my mind went blank—probably the brain's way of allowing the body to deal with impending death. The pungent smell of cordite filled my nose. Maybe Blais really meant to kill me. The fuse burned and burned, almost into the charge now, and I couldn't have moved if I'd wanted to. Oh, well, I figured—I wouldn't know what hit me. The world grew eerily silent.

"Har, har, har," I heard. "See, Chuck, he *is* that stupid."

"Damn, Tom, you're right—here's your ten."

"Mr. Gormly, you can open your eyes now," Blais said.

I did. I looked where the hole ought to be and saw the charge still sitting there, the fuse no longer smoking. It turned out the "charge" was only the cardboard covering of the half-block of TNT and time fuse. That was a lesson in trusting your teammates. And a little amusement for the instructors. Later on in training, Blais said he couldn't believe I had just lain there. Others he had pulled the trick on had hauled ass. I told him I knew he wasn't about to kill a trainee on purpose, so I hadn't really worried at all—right! Tom and I later served together in SEAL Team Two. He was one hell of an operator in Vietnam.

On July 2, 1964, I graduated from UDT Replacement Training. Our featured speaker was Vice Admiral John S. McCain, Commander Amphibious Forces, United States Atlantic Fleet (COMPHIBLANT), known to all in the Navy as "Mr. Sea Power." The admiral gave a great pitch. He told us we were now part of the cutting edge of the amphibious force—the UDT—and, in a nutshell, we'd be the first to kick ass during war. We loved this—we'd gone through nearly six months of BS to get the opportunity to go to war first. The speech was short and to the point. We *really* liked that. All we wanted to do was get our diplomas and get to the Teams.

In later years when I was called upon to give graduation speeches to BUDS classes, I remembered Admiral McCain's words. I'd simply tell them they had just completed the most rigorous training in the U.S. military. Now it was time for them to go to the Teams and get ready to kick ass.

UDT Training Class 31 was unique because of our extremely high officer-to-enlisted ratio; we had over thirty officers at the start, out of a total class of about one hundred people. Of that starting hundred, ten officers (including two Brazilians) and fifteen enlisted (including two Brazilians) graduated. Seventy-five men didn't make it, but that's average for basic UDT training. Some would say the high officer-to-enlisted ratio was not good, but it didn't matter in UDT basic training because we all did the same things and shared the load equally. That's one reason why SEAL officers and enlisted have close relationships.

The bonds established in our training are much like the bonds formed in combat; rank is not the determining factor. In my view this closeness was one of the things responsible for the combat success of SEALs. Mutual trust and respect among all Team members are givens, and they develop in the basic training course. At first, Yale, Harvard, the Naval Academy, Penn State, and various other institutions of higher learning were represented in our group. At the end of basic training, we were all from the same place: Tom and Bernie's Charm School.

3

DOMINICAN REPUBLIC: FIRST REAL MISSION

I reported to Underwater Demolition Team 22 and was assigned to a platoon to learn the ropes. My instructor was Chief Petty Officer Everett Barrett, who gave me a clipboard with a blank sheet of paper attached. He said, "Always carry this with you, Ensign, and walk fast. The front office will think you're busy."

In those days UDT-22 and UDT-21 rotated platoons with two amphibious ready groups (Navy-Marine contingency forces) in the Mediterranean and Caribbean respectively. When platoons weren't deployed, they were getting ready to deploy. So you were either in the Mediterranean or the Caribbean or training.

I found out that in essence, the basic UDT mission—hydrographic reconnaissance—was pretty basic stuff. So the platoons spent more time trying to learn what I would call SEAL skills, which were different and more fun.

The Teams had a different quality back then. The enlisted men provided all of the continuity or corporate memory and much of the leadership. Once they got in a Team, they seldom left until they retired. They did a great job of instilling unit pride in the junior officers. I doubt we officers pulled our share of the load. In those days, nearly all of us were reservists. We had little concern for anything other than having the most fun possible. We did our time in the Teams and left active duty. The few regular officers who were UDT-qualified and wanted to pursue careers in the Navy had to go to sea to get promoted. After their initial tour, they could expect only one more with the Teams before they became too senior to hold any Team job. That meant the top leadership (CO/XO) usually weren't current on our skills. This became apparent to me when, on my first night-parachute jump with UDT-22, the CO hooked his static line to an electric cable in the plane instead of the anchor cable and almost creamed in before he managed to deploy his reserve chute. To compound matters, he blamed it all on the jumpmaster rather than accept blame for his blunder.

I also found out that being in a peacetime UDT wasn't nearly as exciting as I had thought it would be. We had no immediate expectations of combat. To substitute, we turned to such things as "touch" football. Using no pads, we had about the same amount of contact as in regular football—I never got banged up so bad playing regular football. Everyone who wasn't deployed showed up at each game, cheering those of us who were playing and unmercifully harassing the other team. The games we played against local Marine units were brutal. I think every time we played them there was a fight—the Marines were just as frustrated as we were over the lack of real combat. Despite no "rumors of war," Team morale soared during football season.

When Dave Schaible took over the Team in October 1964, it was a bright day in my career. He was my "Sea Daddy," one of the best leaders I ever had the good fortune to work for, and we had a strong friendship until he died in 1988.

Dave took one look at what the Team had been doing and said, "Boys, you haven't been spending enough time in the water." He had this weird notion that a UDT shouldn't be running around on land trying to be a SEAL team. But I didn't immediately benefit from his new emphasis, because the platoon to which I was now assigned was sent to the Caribbean in March 1965. That turned out not to be a routine deployment. Instead, I had the opportunity to do my first real mission.

* * *

The platoon commander was Lieutenant Junior Grade Gerry Yocum. Ensign Bill Bishop (fresh out of training) and I were his assistants. A country boy from Pennsylvania, Gerry taught me a lot about being a good platoon commander. Bill and I would later serve together in SEAL Team Two. He became an outstanding SEAL platoon commander and was awarded the Silver Star in Vietnam.

Normally there were only two officers per platoon, but Dave wanted us to get as much experience as possible, so he started putting three officers in each deploying platoon. We left Little Creek in March on board the *Ruchamkin*, a converted World War II destroyer. The superstructure had been lengthened and heightened to allow the ship to carry an entire UDT of 100 troops.

We sailed to Vieques Island, off Puerto Rico, in company with the rest of the Caribbean Amphibious Ready Group, and participated in a huge amphibious exercise designed, no doubt, to impress Fidel Castro. After the exercise we moved our gear ashore to begin three weeks of "fun in the sun," i.e., twelve-hour days honing our reconnaissance and demolition skills, and long night swims practicing sneak attacks against ships anchored offshore. We'd been on Vieques three days when we received an emergency back-load—"Get back on board"—order. The ready group was to proceed, at best speed, to a position off the coast of the Dominican Republic. My platoon was to stand by for a landing or to take out U.S. citizens, depending on what Lyndon Johnson decided to do in the wake of a "communist" takeover of the Dominican government. We were going to war—or so we thought.

The Dominican Republic crisis of 1965 has become a footnote in history. The country shares the island of Hispaniola with Haiti, which is located on the western end. The Republic had been ruled for thirty-one years by a ruthless dictator, Rafael Trujillo, who was assassinated in 1961. The country then went through a short period of political upheaval, but made changes by national elections, not by violence. In September 1963, Juan Bosch, the elected president and a former university professor reputed to be "soft on Communism," was overthrown by a military coup, which established a junta. The junta leaders had many of the same economic and social problems that had bedeviled the island republic for years. In early 1965 a series of crises, which the government blamed on Bosch, caused the junta to crack down on Bosch's supporters. The civilian head of the junta, faced with growing rioting and unable to get enough support from his military, resigned. Bosch's supporters took control of the government the next day. Fighting ensued between various factions in the military. Members of the junta asked Lyndon Johnson for help, saying the lives of American citizens in the Dominican Republic were at risk. Johnson in turn ordered U.S. forces to go protect Americans and to escort them out of the country.

UDTs and SEALs had done a few low-risk operations during the Cuban Missile Crisis, but not since the Korean War had the Teams seen combat. We were all apprehensive but eager. We had trained for the real thing, and we wanted a chance to do it.

The *Ruchamkin* could do about twenty-three knots, and we were ahead of the rest of the force when we reached the operations area. We were ready to do a beach reconnaissance just outside the port of Haina on the southern coast, but instead, the *Ruchamkin* got orders to go into port, evacuate the U.S. citizens who had gathered there, take them to Puerto Rico, and return at best speed for an anticipated amphibious landing.

Intelligence about the situation was sketchy, but we thought (correctly) that friendly forces controlled the port. The *Ruchamkin*'s CO decided to put part of our platoon on our Landing Craft Personnel Large (LCPL), a thirty-six-foot steel-hulled craft that was the standard UDT boat in 1965. He ordered the boat to proceed into port ahead of the ship to provide security and line handlers when the ship reached its berth.

Both Bill and I wanted to be in charge of the line-handling party, but Gerry decided to lead it himself. We tied up on schedule, quickly loaded as many people as we could, and set sail for San Juan. The transit was a bit rough, so not only were we sailing "out of harm's way" when we all wanted to be in on the action, but also our ship was covered with puke.

We off-loaded our human cargo as fast as we could and set sail back to the Dominican Republic.

At about 0300 we received notice that the Marine amphibious force was going to land without us first doing a hydrographic reconnaissance of the landing beach. The assault craft were to proceed to the beach single file in order to avoid mines or any other obstacles. We were really disappointed that they could do the landing without our reconnaissance, but it turned out to be a safe operation. We arrived late that morning and did a reconnaissance of the 2,000-yard-wide landing beach to ensure that any follow-on landings would have no problems. My platoon was not authorized to carry weapons, since the Marines already ashore were supposed to provide the firepower. I couldn't understand the "no weapons" order, but at least we got the chance to do something. As it turned out, the only injuries we sustained were healthy sunburns from being in the water all day.

The following morning, we got another mission. This one looked interesting: a day reconnaissance on a small beach just south of the main airport, east of Santo Domingo. The group planners were thinking of using the spot as an evacuation point if needed. They couldn't tell us if the area was under friendly control, so we were to take weapons but not shoot unless shot at. They couldn't provide a gunfire support ship, so we'd be on our own.

Thanks to engine problems we didn't reach the area until well after 1500, about two hours behind schedule. Our plan was to put four swimmers in the water about a thousand meters off the beach. They would swim in to take soundings and sand cores. Because I'd bitched so much about not being allowed to go on the port-entry operation, and also because I was one of the best swimmers in the platoon, Gerry let me take the team in.

Four of us left the boat and swam slowly toward the beach. The water was warm, so we wore just swim trunks and UDT life jackets. A K-Bar knife attached to a web belt, plus fins and face masks, completed our "combat load." We carried lead lines to check the water depth and plastic slates to record the information. Every twenty-five yards we stopped, formed up in a line, let our twenty-one-foot lead lines descend toward the bottom, and wrote the depth on our swimmer slates. Then we'd continue to the next stop point. As we got closer to the beach, the pucker factor went up. We didn't know if there were any rebel forces waiting for us, and in those days UDT swimmers didn't carry weapons in the water because they weren't reliable enough after getting wet to be of any use. So except for the K-Bars, our only defense was our ability to swim fast until our boat provided fire support.

As we approached, we swam lower and lower in the water until just the top half of our face masks was above the surface. I peered anxiously at the top of a low berm that ran along the beach, about ten yards from the water's edge. Low scrub hid from our view anything more than fifteen yards from the water. That meant we were blind, but anyone in the scrub could easily see us, four nicely suntanned targets. Seeing no movement, I signaled to my men to move the final fifty yards to the beach so we could get vital sand samples for analysis. We slithered our way to the beach to fill our sample bottles, making only slight ripples in the blue Caribbean water.

We were almost to the water's edge when a movement in the bushes caught my eye. I looked closer and saw a head and a rifle bobbing up and down as a man came up the back of the berm. As his head cleared the top we made eye contact, and he yelled in surprise and disappeared. I didn't even need to tell my men to head to sea—they had seen the soldier, too.

Just as we cleared the surf zone—with about ten feet of water between us and the coral heads on the bottom—I saw about five men with weapons come over the berm, shouting excitedly in Spanish and pointing in our direction. They aimed their weapons at us. I'd seen enough. I signaled to my men to dive and swim seaward.

If the soldiers started shooting, we'd be hard to hit on the surface. Underwater, the rounds wouldn't penetrate more than a couple of feet. We'd rehearsed this emergency escape procedure many times. The average frogman in those days could hold his breath about two minutes in normal diving conditions. We weren't in a normal situation, though, and I figured adrenaline rush and muscle effort were going to sap our oxygen as we hauled ass out of there. I wanted to gain as much distance as possible before I had to surface for a breath.

Underwater, everything was quiet. I expected to see the bubbly tracks of bullets seeking us out, but I didn't see anything as I kicked furiously toward our boat. When my lungs were about to explode I rose to the surface, rolled over on my back to put my mouth just above the water, and got a deep lungful of precious air. I wasn't up there more than five seconds.

As I rolled back on my stomach and headed for the bottom, I looked right and left. To my right, two of my men were headed back down as well. The man on my left was on his way up. I watched as he did the breathing maneuver, expecting to see bullets hitting the water around him. Since he was the last to go up, I figured he'd draw fire, the other three of us having gotten their attention. But he rolled back toward the bottom. Nothing. We'd covered about a hundred yards on our first dive, and each dive after that would be shorter as we built up an oxygen debt. I figured if we got another hundred yards out we'd be safe.

As I neared the bottom, I heard the unmistakable whine of our boat's engine headed in our direction. I kept kicking and had covered about seventy-five yards when my lungs started burning and my vision began to tunnel: carbon dioxide was building up in my system. This time, instead of going quickly to the surface, breathing, and heading right for the bottom, I decided to take a peek at the beach.

Slowing my ascent just below the surface, I turned to face the beach, exhaled, tilted my head back to expose only my mouth, and slowly drifted above the surface. I gulped a breath of air and tilted my head forward so I could focus through my face mask.

I was at the bottom of a small swell. I let myself ride up with the motion of the wave. As I reached the crest, I saw the berm appear over the top of the next swell. Not a soul was to be seen. I waited on the surface until each man came up and looked around. We all must have had the same idea—not surprising, given our training. I signaled the man to my left, and we swam to join the other two.

I looked shoreward again but still didn't see anything. Our boat was on its way at full speed, men at the .30-caliber machine guns. Others were at the gunwales with M-3 "grease guns," .45-caliber submachine guns capable of killing anything at twenty-five meters. Obviously, the grease guns weren't a threat to anyone on the beach, but they made the men feel better and, I must admit, I liked seeing that hardware rushing to our aid.

Gerry was leaning over the port side, looking for us. I waved, and the boat swerved in our direction. As it got within fifty yards, the coxswain went to full reverse and turned starboard side to the beach, giving the .30-caliber weapons a clear line of fire. We dove and swam toward the boat. As I passed under it, I saw the propeller was not turning—standard procedure when divers are near.

Surfacing just on the port side, I looked down and saw my men coming to the surface right under me. When they were all next to me, I told them to climb into the rubber boat Gerry had put over the side to help us get into the landing craft. Then I pulled myself out of the water and low-crawled in just behind Gerry.

He was more excited than we were. He had been watching us through binoculars when he first saw the five armed men, apparently before I did. Gerry had started yelling to me, but realized there was no way I'd hear him, so he immediately ordered the boat toward the beach and told the machine-gunners to stand by to fire. Under our rules of engagement—the orders fighting men receive before going into a potential combat situation—we couldn't fire unless fired at. As it turned out, the armed men jumped down behind the berm when they saw our boat, and Gerry never saw them come out again.

All of us were breathing hard. We were pumped—we'd just become "combat swimmers." With the adrenaline starting to wear off, we all realized how vulnerable swimmers are in broad daylight. I was proud of the men, and I told them so. They did exactly what they'd been trained to do. Our preplanned emergency procedures had worked. I remember thinking

I never again wanted to swim to a hostile beach without some means of self-defense. Even our .38-caliber revolvers would have been better than nothing. (A revolver works fairly well after being exposed to salt water—all you have to do is make sure the barrel is clear before firing.) Later, when UDTs began doing missions in Vietnam, each swimmer was armed, usually with an M-16 rifle.

By voice radio we reported to our superiors; then, sitting about a thousand meters off the beach, we waited for a reply. About an hour later we were told to head for another beach farther east, and run our boat into it to see if there were any obstacles. Gerry and Bill and I just looked at one another and shrugged.

We didn't get to the new beach until well after dark. Since we hadn't gotten any sand samples on our first reconnaissance, we decided to take the boat in and put people over the side at the beach, under cover of the boat's .30-caliber machine guns. We approached the beach cautiously and got the samples and departed without incident.

It turned out the guys on the first beach had been friendlies. They thought we were part of a Dominican UDT that had defected to the rebels earlier in the day, and the only reason they didn't fire was that we submerged before they could shoot and they were afraid of our boat offshore. I felt a little foolish, but as I was to learn later in Vietnam, friendly fire is just as deadly as hostile fire.

U.S. Army forces stayed in the Dominican Republic for some time. We left in May 1965, our routine deployment finished.

A year after our Dominican Republic adventure, Dave Schaible and I were sitting on the porch of our barracks at the UDT-SEAL training facility in Charlotte Amalie, on St. Thomas in the U.S. Virgin Islands. In the late-afternoon sun we were sipping rum and Cokes, feeling good about what we'd accomplished in the six weeks we'd been there. The Team was finishing a very successful training period in which we'd written the book on submerged reconnaissance. By this time I was a platoon commander and scheduled to take my men on a six-month Mediterranean cruise starting in June 1966. I had other ideas, though. I wanted to become a SEAL.

"Captain," I said to Dave, "I want to go to SEAL Team Two in March instead of taking the platoon to the Mediterranean in June."

"Gormly," he replied, "that's the dumbest thing you've ever said."

Well, that was his opinion, but I think it was one of the smartest.

PART 2

Fire One: First Vietnam Tour

In December 1965, the Navy River Patrol Force CTF-116 was established in the Mekong Delta. Using thirty-two-foot fiberglass river patrol boats, they sought to gain control of the main rivers in the vast delta and contribute to the "pacification" effort against the Vietcong. SEAL platoons started operating in 1966. Based in Nha Be, SEAL Team One established a superb record, interdicting Vietcong sappers who attempted to ambush vessels in the main Saigon shipping channel. Deploying for four months at a time, SEAL personnel in the Rung Sat set a tempo of operations that few units in the war could match. After four months platoons rotated back to their base in Coronado, California, to rest, recuperate, and reconstitute, usually for no more than five consecutive months. Then the men went back to Vietnam to pick up where they had left off—killing Vietcong. SEAL One was so successful that SEAL Team Two was offered the chance to expand SEAL operations into the southern Mekong Delta region.

In 1966, U.S. military strength in Vietnam more than doubled, from 180,000 at the beginning of the year to 385,000 by the end. Yet the U.S. Navy was the only American force represented in the Mekong Delta when SEAL Team Two platoons arrived at Binh Thuy in late January 1967. We were full of piss and vinegar, ready to win the war. Fire one!

4

GETTING READY TO FIGHT

I wanted to join SEAL Two, both for the sake of a change and because Vietnam was heating up; I figured SEAL Team Two was the best way for me to get there. (SEAL One, based in California, offered a better chance of going to Vietnam, but I didn't want to break my ties to Virginia Beach.) In those days, the mid-1960s, you didn't get to join a SEAL Team just because you wanted to. Fortunately, the commanding officer, Lieutenant Tom Tarbox, okayed me.

Back then all SEAL business was classified "Secret." Even people in UDT didn't know exactly what SEALs did. Every piece of paper I saw when I got there was classified Secret, right down to the personnel roster. In fact, SEAL Two was doing very little. From its heyday of the early sixties and the Bay of Pigs, the command had fallen into the doldrums.

SEAL Team Two was small then, ten officers and fifty enlisted; it had no routine deployments, no money, and no real mission. The Naval Operations Support Group Atlantic, which controlled the UDTs, SEAL Team Two, and Boat Support Unit Two, was so unimpressed by its capabilities that, shortly after I arrived, the commodore called me over to his office and chewed me out royally for no other reason than that I had decided to go there. Still, I never thought I had made a mistake in joining

SEAL Two; there, I worked with some of the best people I ever met, and Tom Tarbox was high on that list.

When I checked in, Tom told me I would be assigned to one of the assault groups, as the platoons were called then, and my administrative duty would be as ordnance officer, in charge of the Team's first NWAI, nuclear weapons acceptance inspection.

I replied, "Great. What's that?"

Tom said, "Find out and get back to me." What he didn't say (and didn't have to) was "Don't flunk."

Thanks largely to Chief Petty Officer Bob Gallagher, we didn't. Bob was my "assistant." In his usual diplomatic style, he said, "Lieutenant, you go learn how to be a SEAL, and I'll get the department squared away for the inspection." I took his advice, and we did so well our program was cloned for UDTs 21 and 22 so they could pass their later inspections. Bob Gallagher went on to be probably the most-decorated man ever to serve in SEAL Team Two. On his third tour in Vietnam he was an assistant platoon commander, the only enlisted man from SEAL Two ever to hold that position. During one particularly nasty operation, his platoon took on what they thought was a VC company; it turned out to be a battalion. In the fierce fighting, his platoon commander and many of the men were seriously wounded. Bob's ingenuity and bravery turned the tide. He rallied the platoon, organized a tactical advance away from the enemy, ordered in helicopters, and got all of his men out. He personally carried one of the most seriously wounded men across a rice paddy to waiting helicopters. Then he kept up a deadly stream of fire to cover the rest of his platoon as they boarded. Gallagher was the last man on the last helo to leave the battle zone. He was awarded the Navy Cross, the U.S. Navy's highest decoration, for heroism. If he had been a commissioned officer, he would have been awarded the Medal of Honor.

At the time, though, SEAL Two functioned on a shoestring. It was under the administrative control of COMPHIBLANT (amphibious force), but under the operational control of CINCLANTFLT (Atlantic fleet). That meant the amphibious folks had to pay our bills but didn't get to use us. CINCLANTFLT wasn't using us either, so we were basically dangling in the wind.

For equipment, we were using what the Team had received on its initial outfitting in 1962. Our closed-circuit scubas were badly in need of spare parts. Of course, we couldn't afford to buy spares, so we "cannibalized," using parts from one rig to keep two others going. That's a recipe for disaster, but fortunately our guys were professional enough to pull it off. Even so, we had to cut back on training, especially since the Team was so underfunded we had to pay our own way to training sites.

Things started to get better in August 1966. SEAL Team One, already heavily committed in Vietnam, was being pressured to provide more SEALs in-country. In midsummer we got a new CO, Lieutenant Bill Early, a West Coast SEAL who had just returned from a year tour advising the Vietnamese Linh Doi Nui Nai (their equivalent to SEALs). Bill was acutely aware of the need for more SEALs, so he set about getting his new command involved. After wrangling with Pentagon bureaucrats, Bill convinced the powers that be that we needed to spend some money on training and equipment. In October, the bucks flowed and we got gear.

We had about three months to get ready once the word came that we'd be deploying. Lieutenant Jake Rhinebolt, our detachment officer-in-charge, and the rest of us officers and chief petty officers put our heads together and came up with a schedule we figured would prepare us. We had to polish individual skills and learn new ones—and, most important, we had to learn to work together in our new platoon organization.

SEAL Team One deployed platoon-sized units of two officers and ten enlisted. SEAL Team Two was organized into assault groups of one officer and five enlisted each, so we just combined assault groups to form platoons. SEAL One also operated almost exclusively in squad-sized elements of one officer and five enlisted. The new system was easy to pick up because we had been operating in squad-sized units all along.

My outfit, the 3rd Platoon, was actually two units, each with a different character. Lieutenant Larry Bailey was the platoon commander, and I was the assistant. My squad was the best group of SEALs I had seen up to that point, and I wouldn't trade them for any I've seen since. Meet my "trained killers"!

Chief Boatswain's Mate J. P. (Jess) Tolison was my squad chief petty officer—I worked for him, and he was the best. Quiet, forceful, tough, aggressive, smart, he could do it all. He had more sense and leadership than any officer I've ever worked with, and I trusted his judgment without question. He always seemed to do the right thing. Six feet tall, about 200 pounds, he intimidated a lot of tough SEALs. Jess had blue eyes that seemed to look right through you when he talked—and he always looked you in the eye. When Larry and I picked squads, I stole Jess. The rest of the platoon would go anywhere with him. Sadly, he was killed in a truck accident in 1971. I've buried too many good SEALs, and his funeral was the hardest.

My leading petty officer was Boatswain's Mate First Class Bill Garnett, "Mr. Squared Away." I've never met anyone more organized than Bill. He was also a super operator and, as the second senior enlisted in our squad, the perfect complement to Jess. Bill made sure things got done. He could foresee problems and solve them before they became problems. He was rock-solid dependable, and there was none better under fire. Bill would go on to have a long and distinguished career as a SEAL.

Our "doctor" was Hospital Corpsman First Class Fred (Doc) McCarty, a great field medic and diving corpsman. We'd break 'em, he'd fix 'em. Fred was a Navy First Class Diver, and he had attended many corpsman schools before he came to SEAL Two. He also had a great sense of humor and always seemed to say the right thing when we got in trouble. All SEAL Two corpsmen I saw during the Vietnam era were good, but Fred was the best.

Petty Officer Second Class Charlie Bump was my point man—the first man in the line of patrol—and a superb operator. Long—six feet tall—and lanky—he weighed about 150 (soaking wet)—he could go through mud better than anyone I've seen. He looked like a water bug leading us through difficult terrain. We called him "Mr. Steady," and thanks to his sixth sense in the field, he kept us out of trouble. On a subsequent tour, he was awarded the Silver Star for leading an operation to free American

POWs reputed to be held in the U Minh Forest. Charlie infiltrated the camp with four men, killed a guard, and called in a helo-borne force. They freed about a hundred Vietnamese but just missed the Americans, who'd been moved by the VC only hours before.

Petty Officer Second Class Pierre Birtz was the youngest in the squad and pound for pound the strongest SEAL I have ever seen. He could carry a lot of bullets, so I made him our automatic-weapons man. Of French-Canadian descent, Pierre was the squad dissenter, always "going on record" to make a point. We loved him. His secondary function was to keep me awake on ambushes—he never failed, because he never slept in the field.

I can't imagine being around a better group of people. I cut my fighting teeth with them.

We decided that the best way to get started was to take our detachment away from the home fires for some concentrated training. We went to Camp Picket, an Army Reserve training post about forty miles southwest of Richmond, Virginia, that had everything we needed to get started—weapons and demolition ranges and plenty of woods where we could work on our patrolling techniques.

Jake set up good training problems. He assigned each of the four squads different operating areas; there, we disappeared to set up our base camps. Only Jake knew where all of them were. Each squad was also given a "secret" radio frequency that Jake used to pass us mission orders and set up resupplies. We also each had an emergency frequency, which Jake monitored twenty-four hours a day.

He'd pit one squad against another, usually not telling either group that it had company. We'd be assigned reconnaissance or raid missions, usually five or ten kilometers away from our base camps. Patrolling to and from the targets gave us plenty of opportunities to establish our standard operating procedures and get to know each other, until we came to think of ourselves as one entity rather than six individuals.

After we set up our base camps, we called Jake on the PRC-25 (a rugged, man-portable VHF radio that became our primary means of communicating in Vietnam) to give him the eight-digit grid coordinates for our base camp. Jess suggested it might not be good for Jake to know *exactly* where we were, and I agreed. So I made a "mistake" on two of the numbers, which made it appear we were about a thousand meters from where we really were. Jake never could figure out why Lieutenant Fred Kochey, the 2nd Platoon commander and a whiz with a map and compass, couldn't ever find us.

My squad made shelters with our ponchos and put our sleeping bags underneath. Jess and I talked it over before we went, and I'd opted not to use tents. I wanted to be able to move out in a hurry, because I knew sooner or later Jake would tell each squad where the others were located. This way, when we left on a mission we'd simply collapse the ponchos over our sleeping bags and the gear we weren't using, pile leaves and branches over them, and go. We did such a good camouflage job that we usually had to search for the camp each time we came back.

Chief Bob Gallagher and a couple of other SEAL Two guys helped Jake run the three-week field training. Bob built some quick-reaction ranges for us to shoot on that really improved our close-quarter shooting skills. We figured most of the shooting we'd have to do in Vietnam would be within twenty-five meters because that's what SEAL Team One was experiencing in the Rung Sat Special Zone. Once we got to the Mekong Delta, we found we hadn't been entirely correct; still, it was good training.

We also went to the ranges for controlled shooting with our new M-16s. Each man in my squad was assigned a primary weapon, which would stay with him as long as he was in SEAL Two, or until it broke. We figured a man would take better care of a weapon that was *his* than of one he'd drawn from the armory. Same for our other equipment: each man had his own parachute and Draeger closed-circuit diving gear. As Dave Schaible used to say, "Nobody waxes a rental car."

We all carried the same basic gear: a flashlight with red and green lenses; a medical kit; ammunition pouches; an MK-26 fragmentation grenade;

a K-Bar knife; two canteens; and a butt pack for miscellaneous items. In my butt pack I always carried handheld pop flares to illuminate ambushes after we initiated contact. We always wore, or carried in our butt packs, UDT life jackets; with all the weight we carried, the life jackets were invaluable for crossing canals. They were also handy if we had to get out of a tight situation. Most military forces view water as an obstacle. As long as I was near water I didn't have to worry. SEALs see it as a haven.

We carried the gear on an H-harness attached to a pistol belt, which fastened around our waist. An H-harness distributes the weight evenly on your shoulders and around your waist. We all wore the gear in the same place on our rigs so at night each man could find whatever he wanted on any rig he happened to grab. The grenadier and the heavy-weapons man had different configurations for their ammo, but otherwise we looked pretty much the same. For each mission I would decide what additional weapons or equipment we would carry, and we'd distribute the weight among us; everyone pulled the load.

After his first deployment ended in June 1967, one of the chiefs in Fred Kochey's platoon, Jim Watson, designed a load-bearing vest with a built-in life jacket, magazine pockets, grenade attachment points, and a large pocket in the back that replaced the butt pack. It was a well-thought-out piece of gear. It distributed the weight well, and the magazine pouches were high on the front of the vest to help keep them dry as we waded around in rice paddies. I found I had to wear my knife high on the back of my vest, between my shoulder blades, where I could get to it easily by reaching over my shoulder. The vest resembled one a hunter might wear—appropriately, since we were hunting VC. I liked it and wore one throughout my second tour.

At the end of the three weeks' training we returned to Little Creek much more confident of our capabilities. I'd learned a lot from Jess, and we'd all learned a lot about each other. I never heard any serious bitching (except from Jake when Fred couldn't find and destroy our base camp). Knowing that our lives and the mission would depend on how well we trained, we took no shortcuts. We were determined to train like we were going to fight. That's the only way to go.

Back at Little Creek, we learned for sure we'd be going to the Mekong Delta rather than the Rung Sat. We looked around for someone to talk to about operations there; the terrain was entirely different from the mangrove swamps of the Rung Sat. We found a Navy lieutenant, assigned to the Naval Amphibious School, who'd just returned from a year in the Mekong Delta advising South Vietnam's Junk Force, which used indigenous craft for river operations. Jake and I picked his brain over many a beer, getting a lot of useful information about the river and canal system.

The delta is one of the largest rice-producing regions in the world. It's a landscape of rice paddies, canals, and offshoots of the Mekong River, with trees lining the waterways. Unlike the Rung Sat, the delta was heavily populated, and the VC were fully integrated into the population. Figuring out who was who was a problem throughout Vietnam, but nowhere more so than the Mekong Delta.

With all that open area, we figured we'd better have people trained to direct air, artillery, and naval gunfire, so we took a course at the Naval Amphibious School. We also thought we'd better learn rappelling, a mountaineering technique of rapid descent from heights. In those days we attached ourselves to a rappel line with a simple snap link. The technique involved sliding quickly down the line and braking just before you hit the ground. We practiced many hours on the water tower at the amphibious base until we got damn fast. Then we got helicopter services from a local squadron and taught ourselves to rappel from them, as we'd have to do in Vietnam.

Jake learned that the Marines had a Small Unit Tactics School at Camp Lejeune, North Carolina. We went there to learn from instructors who'd all had a tour in I Corps, the area in northern South Vietnam where most Marine units were assigned. The best things they showed us were their quick-reaction drills. They also helped us modify their small-unit tactics for our *really* small units. Suppose we were ambushed—well, we for sure weren't going to charge our ambushers with six men the way a Marine unit could with forty. We developed tactics to get out of the kill zone as fast as possible and break contact. My squad's basic maneuver was the "leapfrog." If the ambush was to the front or the rear, the closest man to it would fire his weapon on full automatic until he expended a magazine. Then he'd haul ass to the other end of the patrol and reload. As soon as he broke, the next man in line started firing, and so on until we broke contact. If the ambush was on either side of the patrol, we'd do the same thing, only in groups of three. The basic reasoning was to get as much continuous fire as possible. We practiced these drills until we looked like a professional football team running plays. Good thing we did.

By the middle of December 1966 we were ready, and Bill Early wanted to show us off. He arranged for the Secretary of the Navy (SECNAV) to come to Little Creek for a demonstration of our capabilities. We set up a scenario in Desert Cove, a small bay inside the confines of the base. We built two "hootches" (the U.S. military term for the mud-grass huts in which rural Vietnamese lived) in one of the areas designated for explosives on the north side of the cove. From NAS Norfolk, we obtained a CH-46 helicopter, the Navy variant of a heavy-lift helo the Marines used to transport troops and equipment. It had two rotors and two engines—and, most important to us, a stern ramp that lowered to allow easy access in and out of the bird.

We were going to demonstrate an integrated raid on a VC village. Our boats, with the 2nd Platoon embarked, would lay off just outside Desert Cove. My squad would come screaming in at treetop level just as the boats came at high speed down the cove, and we'd hit the hootches as simultaneously as possible, my squad rappelling from the helo as the other platoon attacked. We used blank ammunition in our weapons but put real half-pound charges of C-4 explosives on the hootches. We'd kill the enemy, blow up their hootches, and take off in the boats. Bill told us that all funding flowed from above. Since SECNAV was going to be there, so would CINCLANTFLT and our immediate boss, COMPHIBLANT. We got the picture.

Circling north of the area, I could see that the boats were ready. We got the signal to go, and I had the helo take off across the beach. Jess and I were already hooked into the two rappel lines attached to rings located just above our eye level in the top of the helo. We stood facing in, our heels over the end of the open ramp, ready to go. Between my feet I watched the ground pass rapidly under the helo. My squad came in just over the trees, and the pilot "flared" the helo, coming to a rapid halt over the target.

When the helo tilted forward, the helo crew threw out our two rope bundles, and Jess and I jumped. I had told the guys I didn't want anyone braking until he was just off the ground. That meant we would be almost free-falling down with the line passing through the snap link, one hand wrapped loosely around the rappel line just in front of our face to keep us falling feet first. The other hand would be behind us, also holding the rappel line loosely. To brake we had to bring our lower hand, with the line, across our butts, creating friction on the line as it passed through the snap link. The key to doing it as fast as I wanted was to avoid exerting any pressure on the line with your lower hand until you jerked it across your butt just before your feet hit the ground. If you did this right, you went down fast and landed fairly easily. As soon as your feet hit the ground, you had to open the snap link and pull the rappel line out before the next man could come down the line. Any resistance on the line from below would stop him. We had used ground handlers for safety during training—if a man lost control on the way down, the ground handler could stop him before he crashed. I'd told Bill I wasn't going to use ground handlers for the demonstration because they'd detract from the realness: we wouldn't have ground handlers in Vietnam.

Jess and I fell down the lines side by side, braked at the last instant, and hit the ground together. We quickly disengaged the rappel lines and sprinted to our positions to fire on the hootches. Fred's platoon had thrown smoke grenades, and the smoke was being swirled all around by the downdraft from the helo's rotors. The surrealistic scene was just what we wanted.

I heard a loud thud behind me. Bill Garnett was lying on the ground, with Doc McCarty getting rid of the rappel line. Bill just lay there: he was out. Doc got him off the rappel line, and the last two men, Bump and Pierre, came hurtling down to take positions with Jess and me. The four of us assaulted our "hootch," leaving Fred to tend to Bill. Because there were live demolitions placed on the hootch, which would go off just as we cleared the area for the boats, I wasn't going to leave Bill and Doc where they were.

Instead of going to the boats, we went back to Bill and carried him into the woods behind the hootch area, where we'd be safe when the demolitions went off. Fred's guys saw what we were doing, and left as soon as they hit the boats. The hootches exploded in balls of fire, helped by barrels of diesel fuel placed there beforehand. It was quite a show—and our distinguished guests never noticed that we'd ad-libbed.

As for Bill, he was conscious but dazed. Apparently he'd lost the rappel line with his lower hand about halfway down and had been unable to brake. As he slammed into the ground, his left knee hit his cheek and fractured it. He looked like a pumpkin, but he told me he didn't care what the doctors said, he was going to Vietnam with us. And he did, but the bruise didn't fade completely for three more months.

After our little show was over, the SEALs gathered around the SECNAV to get his pep talk. He was really impressed with what he saw, particularly with how fast "that man came down the rappel line." We said our rear security guy was very conscientious.

In mid-December, we learned we'd be headed to Vietnam in early January. All that remained to be done was pack up our gear and take Christmas leave. Though none of us ever said so, we all wondered if it would be the last Christmas we would be spending with our families. We kissed our wives and girlfriends good-bye on January 12, 1967. After a short stop in Coronado, California, at SEAL Team One, we were bound for Vietnam. Becky was eight months pregnant and not very happy to see me go off to war.

5

FEET WET: BREAKING IN THE TROOPS

January 29, 1967

After a five-day trip in a slow-flying Navy C-121 from California, two hard-charging SEAL Team Two platoons landed in the Mekong Delta at the Binh Thuy Vietnamese Air Force base ninety miles from Can Tho, about ninety miles southwest of Saigon. During our approach to land, I looked out one of the small windows to see what I could see. What I could see was a lot of water, interspersed with heavy vegetation. The Mekong Delta was divided by three branches of the Mekong River: the Bassac (the main branch), the Vinh Long, and the My Tho rivers, which all flowed into the South China Sea. The land was essentially silt that had been deposited over the ages. Innumerable natural and man-made canals spiked off the rivers, and trees lined the canals and riverbanks. At the coast and around the southeastern side of Vietnam, vast mangrove swamps flourished in the brackish water. From a much higher altitude than our plane's, the delta would have looked like a big checkerboard. Most of the land was devoted to rice paddies, which were separated by dikes, and most of the people lived in the tree lines along the canals and rivers. Most of them were farmers, harvesting the vast quantities of rice produced by the fertile land. The Mekong Delta was capable of feeding all of Vietnam, and then some.

From my vantage point all I could see was the Bassac River, a few canals, and some rice paddies. As we passed over the river on our final approach, I was surprised at the volume of boat traffic below me. There were sampans and junks everywhere. How in the hell were we going to sort out the good guys from the bad?

Adrenaline was flowing when we landed and taxied to the apron to off-load. When the door opened, I could taste the heat and humidity. We were all in our combat gear, ready to engage the enemy as soon as we stepped off the plane. Instead, though, friendlies met us. We loaded our gear into waiting trucks and headed for the Navy river patrol force base across the street on the Bassac. We knew the SEAL Team One guys at Nha Be were living on a barge, but we didn't know what to expect at Binh Thuy.

The base had four long one-story cement buildings. One held a mess hall and a small club; the rest were living quarters and offices for the CTF-116 staff and the officers and men of the river patrol. A small pier on the Bassac had a large troop barge tied up alongside, parallel to the shore. The barge, like those at Nha Be, contained offices and repair shops. The whole facility was about the size of two football fields side by side.

Physical security was poor. The perimeter fence was flimsy and ran only ten feet from the building on the airfield side of the base. The main road running parallel to the river was about 200 meters from the fence. Guard towers stood at each corner of the fence, but they offered no protection for the watch, being manned only at night, by not-very-alert sentries. We learned that the base had never been subject to a ground attack but that the VC did mortar them fairly often from a nearby tree line. A few defensive bunkers were scattered in the compound, for protection during a mortar attack. No one seemed to be worried about any of this.

The rooms we were assigned, in the building on the outer perimeter toward the road, weren't bad—pairs of two-man rooms connected by a head with a shower and toilet. Each set of rooms was assigned a "mama-san" maid who cleaned them and washed our clothes. It was better than I'd imagined.

Unfortunately, we apparently hadn't been expected, because CTF-116, the local Navy leadership, didn't have a clue what to do with us. The first thought was that we would ride shotgun on the river patrol boats (PBRs). Some of us did that for a while, but Jake finally convinced the commander that we could best support the CTF-116 mission by operating off the main river, doing what we had trained to do: attacking VC in their safe areas.

At that time there were no U.S. ground forces operating in the Mekong Delta; we were it. Two hundred meters off the main Bassac River was bad-guy country. CTF-116 was reluctant to allow sailors to get away from the main river, on the theory that we'd be killed or captured once out of sight of the boats. This was partly a result of the secrecy surrounding SEAL capabilities. At that time, most senior officers in the Navy had no idea what SEALs could do. Also, the regular Navy's notion was that a sailor ashore was to be avoided the same as a ship ashore. We had to start slow, or we wouldn't be allowed to start at all. Having put our heads together, we decided we'd begin by doing what SEAL One was doing in the Rung Sat (ambushes) even though we sensed our operations area called for different tactics.

CTF-116 was still nervous. Their operations officer thought we ought to send people to the Rung Sat to "learn" how to operate with the proven performers. We knew how to operate, and if they'd just give us a chance we'd prove it. But we swallowed our pride and drew straws for a contingent to go study at the Rung Sat.

I was one of the officers who drew a Nha Be straw. The others were Lieutenants Fred Kochey and Larry Bailey. Ensign Dick Marcinko and his squad stayed in Binh Thuy to watch the gear and learn the river.

Nha Be, which was much larger than our base at Binh Thuy, lay about twenty miles southeast of Saigon, alongside the main shipping channel to the city. As at Binh Thuy, river patrol boats operated up and down the Saigon River and the main estuaries of the Rung Sat. The SEALs lived on a barge tied up at the main pier, but the base itself was a series of Quonset huts set back off the river. I could see many new huts being built and a big, half-finished, warehouselike building that I would later learn would be the new river patrol group headquarters.

Soon after we arrived, the officers huddled to see how we would organize ourselves for the break-in operations. An old friend of mine, Lieutenant Irve C. (Chuck) LeMoyne, was the SEAL One senior platoon commander. He and I had been teammates at UDT-22 from 1964 to 1966, and we had a lot of confidence in each other. He assigned my squad to his.

Chuck's guys exuded professionalism, so although being sent to the Rung Sat had annoyed us, my squad and I were anxious to learn whatever we could from them. Chuck set up an ambush mission to get our feet wet. To keep the numbers down, he included only two people from his own squad. We left base in the detachment mini-battleship, an armored, modified LCM-6. It was slow, but it could take a punch. At low tide, just before dark, we inserted at an ambush site inside the Rung Sat and got settled in. The spot lay on a tributary of the main shipping channel, a favorite avenue of the Vietcong as they traveled to their own ambush sites.

As I've mentioned, the SEAL One mission was to interdict VC trying to ambush shipping headed for Saigon. This was a hit-and-miss proposition at best, but at least we were in the field. As night fell, we sat among the mangrove trees on the canal bank. At this point Chuck introduced us to "stay-awakes"—little green pills guaranteed to keep you from sleeping and missing a firefight.

SEAL One SOP for ambushes called for the squad leader to initiate fire after popping a handheld illumination flare. It also called for one man to be in rear security, about ten meters behind the squad. I didn't like that tactic because I couldn't communicate with the rear guy. But when in Rome . . . I also figured Chuck wasn't going to put us anyplace too likely to see action on our first mission. So I put Charlie Bump in rear security.

We waited and the tide came in. Once just after settling in, we'd thought we heard movement to our rear. Bill Garnett whispered to me that it was probably "Charlie." Now, "Charlie" was not only our man

Bump, but also slang for VC, as in "Victor Charlie." Chuck's two guys overheard, swung to the rear, and took their weapons off safety, ready to fire. I grabbed them—"No, it's Bump." We decided we'd have to start calling Charlie by his last name only!

After four hours the tide was high and we were neck deep in water. I noticed two logs in front of us and pointed them out to Chuck.

"Not logs," he said, "crocodiles."

They went by no more than six feet away. I didn't tell my guys what they were.

Some time later I was staring across the canal, and there was a twenty-foot water buffalo. When I pointed it out to Chuck, he said it was the stay-awakes: they made some people hallucinate. That ended them for me.

The rest of the night was uneventful. We got out of there just before dawn, "experts" at last.

We had one more operation scheduled, but Chuck felt that we didn't need it. Instead, we did what SEALs do when the work is over: we partied. West Coast SEALs and East Coast SEALs found they had more in common than not. After the party, Chuck and I liberated a bottle of scotch from the officer's-club bar, parked ourselves on the ground behind the club, and proceeded to tell lies until about 0500.

At seven in the morning, I was asleep in my bunk aboard the barge. Someone pulled on my shoulder. I did the right thing—I rolled over and took a swing at the intruder. Who was, of course, the messenger of the watch.

Ducking, he yelled, "Hey, Lieutenant, ease up! The Red Cross just sent word your wife had a baby—a girl."

Still bleary-eyed, I said, "Sorry 'bout that."

"No sweat. I took the liberty of ordering flowers in your name. You owe me twenty-five dollars."

I was completely awake in a New York minute. Becky had finally had the baby! Our second child, Anne. I'd felt bad about leaving her in January; but, as usual, she'd understood: duty called.

"Thanks—you're a good man," I told the messenger, feeling like a real asshole. I gave him the money and apologized profusely. I made sure a bottle of his favorite booze found its way to him that night.

We returned to Binh Thuy later that day.

Our main problem before we started operations out of Binh Thuy was how to clear an operations area for ourselves without informing the VC of our whereabouts. At each Vietnamese administrative level there was a U.S. military adviser, and this dual chain of command—half U.S., half Vietnamese—ran all the way to the highest level in Saigon. It was common knowledge that the VC had infiltrated the Vietnamese chain at every level. So we had to figure out a way to inform our chain without the Vietnamese side knowing; otherwise, we'd find artillery and air strikes raining down at the most inappropriate times.

We worked it out that we'd tell the local U.S. military advisers, in general terms, where we wanted to operate. Usually the coordinates we gave them covered about a hundred square miles. They would say nothing to their Vietnamese counterparts, and we would never appear on any map in any operation center. To protect us from inadvertent artillery fire, the U.S. advisers would just tell the Vietnamese not to fire. This worked, for the most part.

While we officers were developing the procedures for putting everyone (including ourselves) in their "comfort zones," the troops got bored. One night Bob Gallagher, the chief petty officer of the 2nd Platoon, took a couple of his men to the Army NCO club at Can Tho Air Field, a Vietnamese base with U.S. Army advisers assigned. Can Tho was also a supply base for the Army Special Forces units who "advised" Vietnamese forces near the Cambodian border. One thing led to another, and Bob's crew got into a fight with the entire club—three against about thirty—and did some serious damage to a couple of Army sergeants. The Army sent a colonel to Binh Thuy to investigate. He came in with fire in his eyes, ready to hang all of us.

"What the hell are you guys doing, letting all your SEALs beat up on our men?"

"Well, sir," Jake explained, "there were only three of our men in the fight."

That was the end of the investigation. Nothing more was said and the colonel left with his tail between his legs. It didn't take long for the truth to spread around Can Tho, and I don't remember us ever having a problem after that. Anyway, once we began to fight the VC, we didn't need other enemies.

Finally, we were able to get to work. We started out just doing ambushes at night along canals known to be VC transit corridors. Sometimes we were successful interdicting VC, but most of the people were curfew breakers or fishermen trying to get an early start. Sure, we were authorized to fire on anyone we saw in the areas in which we operated, but I got no satisfaction out of killing people I didn't *know* were the enemy.

The problem was, our enemy didn't wear uniforms. Often I wasn't sure until we'd already done the killing, and could inspect the sampan, whether we'd hit a good target. If I saw weapons before we opened up, there was no doubt. Sometimes we'd find the weapons after the hit and I'd feel better. Eventually, if I didn't see weapons, I'd call the sampan over to our position. Any hesitation or other indication that the occupants weren't innocent civilians and I'd open up.

Often they'd come over for inspection and we'd find nothing to suggest they were the enemy. Yet I knew that just because we didn't find any contraband didn't mean they weren't Vietcong. Often, the VC would draft villagers as messengers; the villagers would travel unarmed, with the messages in their heads. One night we had about five sampans lined up on the riverbank with us as we continued to wait for the "bad guys." After a while I sent them on their way. No doubt we released some messengers along with the innocent, but I could live with that. I just had to find another way to fight the VC.

The next stage was to patrol in enemy-controlled territory. The Navy intelligence system wasn't set up to provide us the information we needed to go after specific targets, so instead we collected tactical intelligence. I set up many a patrol into VC country with the notion we'd move until we found the enemy, and then we'd attack. Sometimes we found VC, sometimes we didn't, but we learned something new each time we went out. Operating where no other U.S. force had been, we soon knew where to go to get action. Ours wasn't a perfect system, but each time we showed up at a VC's door we created havoc. And every time we went into a new area we provided the river patrol force with another piece of the VC puzzle.

Since we'd been prescribed no strategy from above, we SEAL officers decided our "strategy" should be to kill VC wherever and whenever, terrorizing them by hitting them in their "safe" areas. I chose when and where to operate, and my decisions were based on one goal: to kill as many VC as we could without our missions falling into a predictable pattern.

6

MEKONG AMBUSH: TAKING AWAY THE NIGHT

Mid-April 1967, Lower Mekong Delta

In total darkness on the Bassac River, the twenty-two-foot armored, reinforced-fiberglass SEAL Team Assault Boat (STAB) throttled back, slowed from twenty-five knots to five, and turned toward the riverbank. Six of us crouched expectantly in the boat. My adrenaline meter was pegged.

I put my hand on Bump's shoulder. "Are you all set?"

"Yep." Charlie is a man of few words.

Slowly he lifted the AN PVS-2 night-vision scope to his right eye. "I can't see a damn thing at the insertion point."

"Look to your right, toward the canal."

"Got it. Looks like we're on track."

"Lieutenant," said the coxswain, moving one of the earphones connecting him to the boat radio, "Mr. Baumgart says we need to come left five degrees, and we'll hit the shore two hundred meters from the canal."

"Roger. Do it."

Lieutenant Satch Baumgart, our boat support officer, was in our armored LCPL, cruising near the middle of the Bassac, using the boat's surface-search radar to guide us to our insertion point. Satch and his men from Boat Support Unit One in Coronado ran our specially configured boats. He was lying just off our insertion point, ready to give us fire support if we needed it. We were not using secure radios, because in those days the encryption device for our PRC-25 VHF radio was bigger and heavier than the radio. If we needed to communicate with the River Patrol Force Tactical Operations Center (TOC) at Binh Thuy, Satch would use a code book to "kack up"—encrypt—a voice message.

Bump squeezed my arm. "Take a look at that shit."

I took the night-vision device and put it to my eye. The greenish glow of the scope revealed nothing but a solid wall of vegetation. I knew from the maps that the area near the Long Tuan Secret Zone was covered with thick nipa palm along the rivers and canals, but this was worse than I'd expected. Moving through nipa palm is no fun. The plants grow very close together and the stalks of the plants are solid. I never could figure out if it was a shrub or a tree—not that it much matters.

We'd been operating for more than two months. Our rules of engagement called for us to do our thing in areas that were thought to be inhabited only by the VC. We, unlike other forces on the river, were allowed to fire before being fired upon. The PBR patrols had to take a round or two before they could return fire. Sounds like a strange way to fight a war, but the Mekong Delta was inhabited by many Vietnamese who weren't VC. Unless they fired first or you were in an area designated a free-fire zone, U.S. Navy forces couldn't shoot.

Tonight, our ambush site was on a canal in the western end of the Long Tuan Secret Zone, one of the most hostile areas in the Mekong Delta and a designated free-fire zone. The intelligence guys thought the canal was a major transit point for VC in the area. I knew I wouldn't have to worry about fishermen breaking the dusk-to-dawn curfew.

"We're about a hundred meters out, Lieutenant."

"Roger. Slow down and let's drift for a minute."

As the boat's twin outboard engines went idle, we moved slowly toward the riverbank. We all listened. Ears are better than eyes in complete darkness, and there was nothing darker than the Bassac just before the rise of a full moon. The moon would be up at 2200 that night. It was now 2030.

"I can't hear anything."

"Neither can I, Charlie. Keep looking through the scope." I turned to the coxswain. "Bring her to just above idle and head toward the beach."

Now I could see the riverbank. The tide was ebbing. It would be low in about one hour, leaving a bank about three feet high.

The boat grounded slowly in the river mud, the bank about five meters away. This was the hairy part of the mission. If there were bad guys in the foliage in front of us, they'd have a field day. Even knowing that our operational security was the best didn't keep the big butterflies out of our guts. We were hanging out.

Charlie went over the bow of the STAB, then me. We struggled through the mud to the riverbank. Behind me was Fred McCarty with our radio, followed by Pierre Birtz. Jess Tolison came last, just behind Petty Officer Doyle from SEAL Team One's detachment at Nha Be. He was there to see how we did our thing. By then we'd had quite a bit of success working in the delta, and those guys wanted to have a look.

Near the top of the riverbank, I motioned for the men to form a semicircle perimeter. Behind us, the STAB was backing slowly away. The silenced outboards made no sound. From where I crouched, I could hear only the lapping of water against the hull as the STAB returned to the LCPL.

We sat and listened intently, growing attuned to the night sounds—insects chirping, frogs croaking. A light breeze whispered through the dense nipa palm. No man-made sounds.

I squeezed Bump's shoulder. I didn't have to say anything; he knew what to do. Easing his lanky frame up over the bank, he started slowly toward the canal mouth. I slid silently right behind him. The rest of the men followed, keeping about five meters apart. Rather than trying to walk through the nipa palm, we kept just in front of the riverbank. It would have been stupid to thrash our way through—nobody could move through that stuff without making noise—and from the bank we could easily hear anyone coming our way.

Our feet made a sucking sound as we waded through the mud. I wasn't concerned. The withdrawing tide uncovered holes in the earth, and the noise they made sounded just like someone walking, pulling his feet out of the sticky delta mud. I'd been fooled by it in one of our first ambushes, thinking we were about to be overrun by a large force.

As we neared the canal mouth, Bump held up his hand to stop the patrol. This was another danger area. If the VC were taking any action with a large group tonight, they would probably have a sentry somewhere near the mouth of the canal.

I eased myself up to Bump. "Move back up on the bank and take a look around," I whispered. Meanwhile, I slowly crab-walked toward the mouth of the canal. I wanted to peek around the corner and be in a position to cover Charlie. The rest of the patrol hunkered down and waited.

I reached a spot from where I could see about fifty feet of the bank on the other side of the canal. I couldn't see farther because it was so dark, but I didn't see the telltale shape of a sampan that would have contained the sentry. I looked up to my left, where Bump had crawled along the top of the bank. Lying on his stomach, he peered left, up the canal. After a few seconds he held up his right arm and motioned back and forth. "All clear."

I turned around and gave Fred the same signal; he repeated it. The rest of the guys slowly approached my position. Charlie stayed where he was as we moved up the canal just under him. As we came abreast, Jess climbed up the bank, and Bump slid down just in front of me. Jess covered us as we started up the canal, then he fell in behind.

We slogged through the mud about fifty meters before Bump stopped and turned to me. Into my ear he whispered, "This about right?"

I nodded. We'd gone over the procedure in our mission brief, and everyone knew what I had planned.

I motioned toward the nipa palm above us, watching as each man turned and made his way up the bank. Our patrol order was also our ambush order. I crawled up behind.

At the top we turned and sat, our backs against the thick foliage. As I hunkered into position, I thought this might be fairly comfortable. The relatively soft mud provided a good cushion, and the nipa palm served as a backrest. Sort of like sitting down in front of your TV in your favorite recliner, waiting for your favorite program to come on. My favorite program that night would involve about six sampans loaded with troops moving slowly into our kill zone.

We traveled light, but with a lot of firepower. Now that we'd settled into position, I took a mental inventory. Bump, to my left, had his M-16 rifle, which launched about 900 5.56mm rounds per minute on full automatic fire. I carried an M-16. Doc McCarty, to my right, had an M-16 and the radio. Pierre, just to his right, had a Stoner Model 63 light machine gun that fired more than a thousand rounds of 5.56mm ammo per minute. He had a thousand rounds of ammo with him. Firing in short bursts, he was a killing machine. Doyle had an M-16 with a 40mm grenade launcher attached. The grenade launcher had a canister round chambered, making it a heavy-duty shotgun. Jess Tolison, on the right flank of the ambush, carried the same load as Doyle. Each man with an M-16 carried 230 rounds of ammo. Our "bullet launchers" could put out a lot of rounds in a few seconds, and that's all it would take. Each of us also carried concussion and fragmentation grenades. Satch, in the river with our mini-battleship, could move to the mouth of the canal and make anyone giving us a hard time wish he hadn't been there that night. The .50-caliber machine guns on the boat could cut a man in half with two rounds and would easily penetrate the nipa palm. The M-60 machine guns could clean up the rest. The recoilless rifles and naval mortars could lay down a dense cover fire that only a deranged person would attempt to move through. And if all that wasn't enough, Satch would call for PBRs on patrol in the river to add their .50-caliber and 7.62mm M-60 machine guns to the fray. Satch could also scramble the Seawolf light helo fire team on call back in Binh Thuy and they'd come running with their 7.62mm miniguns and 3.2 rockets blazing. You get the idea. I wasn't afraid to take on a battalion of VC with all that firepower on hand. We'd start it, and my friends would finish it.

We'd reached the ambush site at 2130. I planned to stay there until just before first light, unless we got a hit first. Ambushing was like rolling dice: you picked a spot and hoped your numbers came up. As ambush sites went, we were in a fairly good one. The area was under VC control, and they moved along the canal system at night with impunity. The primary purpose of our routine ambushes, apart from killing as many of the enemy as we could, was to remove some of that "impunity." We wanted not only to take the night away from the VC, but to make them afraid to move their men and supplies. We were few in number—only two SEAL platoons operating in the lower Mekong Delta, a vast area that covered a large part of South Vietnam. (The three SEAL platoons at Nha Be weren't considered part of our force because they had to stay close to the shipping channels going to Saigon.) But already we thought we were making our presence felt. The word seemed to be getting out among the VC; it seemed that some canals upriver near Binh Thuy, where we'd been honing our skills, were no longer used as much as they had been. To get hits, we had to travel farther and farther away from Binh Thuy. Tonight we were about forty miles downriver from our base.

Ambushing takes patience: you have to remain motionless for long periods of time. That night my patience was tested. As I sat in the mud, waiting for action, I began to feel movements in my crotch. We wore camouflage uniforms and jungle boots. Instead of "blousing" our trousers in our boots in standard military style, we left the bottoms outside to allow water to drain. Of course, while water ran out, critters could crawl in. What kind of visitor did I have? I hadn't felt anything climb up, so it probably wasn't a roach. Now that the tide had started coming back in, our feet were almost in the water, but sea snakes normally weren't a problem. Up the river toward Binh Thuy we had a problem with leeches, but not down here, where salt water predominated. Looking slowly down, taking care not to bump my rifle against anything, I saw a slight bulge in the earth just below my thighs. An anthill!

"Shit," I thought, "fire ants." Fire ants lived in nipa palms as well as in the ground. On an earlier patrol through an area covered with that damn plant, some fire ants had dropped out of the leaves and down my neck. It took me ten minutes to get rid of them. I'd had to strip completely, rub them off my body, shake out my cammies, and cover myself with insect repellent. I couldn't do all that now.

They must have infiltrated between the buttons of my fly. Sneaky little bastards. I felt a sharp pain on one of my testicles. It's impossible to adequately describe a fire ant bite; the closest I can come is to say it's like being stung by a wasp. There's a big difference, though: normally a wasp stings just once. Fire ants are never found alone, and they chew until they're full. I slowly reached into the left chest pocket of my cammy jacket and felt for the plastic bottle of repellent. We usually didn't use mosquito repellent in ambush, because the VC could smell it. Instead we used unscented camouflage "face paint," which supposedly repelled mosquitoes, and wore aviator gloves to cover our hands. Also, as long as you were moving, mosquitoes weren't a big problem. Once we'd reached our ambush site we pulled mosquito nets over our cammy hats and gutted it out. But fire ants were a different story. If I didn't act fast, I'd embarrass myself in front of my men. There was no such thing as gutting out fire ant bites.

As more critters started feasting, I opened the bottle, unbuttoned my fly, and squirted repellent into my groin. It had an instant effect: the fire ants hauled ass. Then the secondary effect took over. The repellent was giving me first-degree burns, much the same as gasoline might cause. It was a small price to pay, and the heat felt good.

As I went through these subtle gyrations, Bump on my left and Doc on my right looked on. "Fire ants," I whispered. They nodded and grinned. No pity. I gave each of them my sternest look, and then I found myself grinning, too.

All this took only about five minutes, but it seemed longer. Above the background noise I now heard something else—a low roar, much like a strong wind. I looked down at my feet and found that they were now immersed. The tide was coming in—and fast. The Mekong Delta has a greater tide range than most places at its latitude. The reasons for this are complex, but mostly have to do with the shallow depth of the South China Sea off the Vietnamese coast. Also, when the tide came back in, it had to fight the natural flow of the Bassac. The two forces meeting made noise: the low roar I was hearing. The full moon tonight heightened the effect, because full moons create higher and lower tides.

As the tide roared in, I began to think maybe we weren't in the best place. When the water reached my waist, I looked around. The men were squirming. It was now around 2300, and we hadn't heard any enemy activity. But the VC liked to wait until after midnight to move. Also, the rising tide would help them float larger loads.

By now the moon was up, and I could see across the canal almost as clearly as if it had been high noon. In the shadows we were nearly invisible. Anyone moving on the canal would be in the spotlight. But the incoming tide created another problem.

I squeezed Bump and Doc McCarty and motioned upward, then started slowly to get up. Pressing against the nipa palm, I got my feet under me and pushed. We'd been in position for nearly two hours, so I was stiff and my legs had gone to sleep. They tingled in protest. All of us had taped the metal buckles on our gear to keep them from rattling, and as we rose to full standing positions, we made no more noise than ghosts.

Still the water rose. By midnight it had reached my chest, and I was struggling to keep my M-16 dry. A plastic muzzle cap kept mud and dirt out of the barrel, but it wouldn't keep out the rising water. Even though the weapons worked fine after immersion, we kept them dry as much as possible.

Our position was becoming untenable: with the water at our chests, we'd be shooting up at any sampan we saw, and even for us SEALs "the high ground" was the byword.

I turned to Bump. "We're getting out of here."

"I was wondering when you were going to say that."

I moved down the line of men to Jess. "Wasn't it higher back by the river?"

"I think so," he replied.

"We're going to move back there."

I turned and motioned. The rest of the men started walking, Jess taking the point as we made our way back to the mouth of the canal. In the chest-high water, moving around was easier.

When the patrol had passed me, I fell in behind Doc McCarty. We all used the nipa palm stalks for stability. The bank was steep and the mud beneath the water very slippery. We'd almost reached the river when Fred lost his footing and started down. Grabbing the PRC-25 on his back as he slipped beneath the water, I jerked him up and turned him around, to see a grin on his face. I almost laughed. Behind me, Bump chuckled. We all learned long ago that when things got tough, you can lose just about anything except your sense of humor and get by.

Fred took hold of a nipa palm and started forward again. I released my stalk to follow him—and promptly disappeared underwater. I had on my life jacket, as we all did, but I tried to kick my way back to the surface. No dice. Sinking, I thought fast. If I pulled the toggle to inflate the life jacket everyone would laugh at me when I popped back up. Not an option. Finally, I figured if I held my M-16 straight up, the tip of the barrel would be above the surface. Someone would grab it and pull me up. When my feet hit the bottom of the canal, I poked up my rifle. Nothing happened.

I waited for what seemed like several minutes. I was just about to swallow my pride and pull the toggle when there was a tug on my M-16 and I started up. Good thing—I was nearly out of oxygen.

I broke the surface, looking right into Jess's eyes. He'd come back to ask me something just as I went under. I grinned at him. "Took you long enough."

"Next time, pull your life jacket," he replied with a big smile on his face.

Looking around, I saw the moon reflecting off five sets of teeth. They all loved it when they got one up on their officer.

"Looks like we have some high ground at the river," Jess said more seriously.

"Good. You and Doyle set up facing the river. The rest of us'll face the canal."

As we settled in again, I looked around. A light wind blew on the river, and I was getting a little chilled in my wet clothes. The rest of the troops were probably cold, too. We needed some action to warm us up. I could see a long way under the full moon. If anything came along, we once again had the high ground and would wreak havoc.

Around 0200 I heard the chugging of an outboard engine—the "one-lunger" the Vietnamese used—somewhere up the canal. All of us came to full alert, like hounds who'd caught the scent. The engine RPM went up, and so did my adrenaline. I listened as the sound got closer. Seemed to me it was about a hundred meters back up the canal when the engine idled briefly and then shut off.

I heard muffled *snicks* as each man eased his weapon selector switch off "safe." I didn't have to give any orders. They all knew what to do. None of them would open fire until I gave the signal. Normally, I would fire a handheld illumination flare in the air over the target, and then the troops would cut down. Tonight we didn't need a flare.

I stared back up the canal. Bump squeezed my arm and pointed.

Looking across the canal, I saw a sampan come into view, hugging the other canal bank. The canal was about twenty meters wide at the river mouth. The sampan was still more than fifty meters away, and I strained my eyes to see the occupants. Finally, I saw one man in the rear, paddling quietly. The other man stood in the bow holding a rifle. Definitely not fishermen getting an early start.

The sampan neared the river mouth. When the bow edged out past the other bank, the critical moment had come. If they turned back, I'd let them go, figuring they were scouts for a larger force about to cross the river. I wanted them to give the all-clear so we could get the main group.

The paddler held the sampan in position as the other man looked up and down the river. I held my breath, my M-16 aimed toward the boat. My heart slowed and the world seemed to grow quiet. All the night sounds were blocked from my brain as I concentrated on the scene before me. I didn't have to look around to know the men were equally focused. I felt no fear, just anticipation, as I waited for them to make their decision—a matter of life or death for them.

Suddenly, the man with the weapon turned toward the paddler and said something. The paddler fired up the engine, shattering the silence. To me, the engine sounded as loud as a C-130 on takeoff. I felt another adrenaline rush. I had to make a split-second decision. If I let the sampan get too far out in the river, we'd miss our chance for a kill. But I had to be sure they weren't going to turn around. I'd just about figured they weren't, but—

The bow of the sampan lifted as the engine accelerated.

I squeezed the trigger on my M-16. The noise of the sampan was drowned out by our horrendous fire; our muzzle flashes lit up the night in front of us. Tracers hit the water near the sampan and ricocheted into the air across the canal. Despite the magnificent light show, I was completely focused on the target. I fired single action, keeping my sights on the man running the engine. My first tracer slammed into him and I swung my rifle forward, just in time to see the man in the bow fly out of the sampan. Our tracers seemed to lift him straight up. I turned back to the rear man, but he had also disappeared.

"Cease fire!" I yelled.

At once it got quiet again. Maybe six seconds had passed. That was the nature of an ambush: hours of boredom followed by seconds of excitement.

Bump and Pierre blew some air into their life jackets (that was SOP; using the toggle to inflate it was an emergency maneuver) and started to slide into the water to go check out the kill zone—that is, the sampan.

"Wait," I said, wanting to be sure there wasn't a large force back up the canal, coming our way to see about all the shooting.

I listened for about thirty seconds, but heard nothing.

"Boss, the sampan is sinking," Jess whispered.

The sampan disappeared below the surface of the water. I reached over to Fred and turned on the radio he wore. "Call for extraction."

I knew Satch had seen the action, but he wouldn't come our way until I called him. Sometimes we held our position in case the VC sent anyone to investigate. Then we got to kill again—sort of a two-for-the-price-of-one deal. Still, my instincts told me we weren't going to see a reaction force. And with the full moon I didn't want to wait around too long. If a large force did come down the canal firing, we were in a bad position. We had no cover and we were standing waist-deep in water. Leaving was the prudent thing to do.

I heard Fred whisper, "Extraction, extraction." A few seconds later he turned to me. "They're on their way."

Satch knew to pick us up at the canal mouth. I looked out into the river and saw the bow wake of the STAB. It was cruising toward us at half-speed. If I'd called for an emergency extraction, the boat would have been at full plane on top of the water.

When I figured the boat was about 200 meters out, I pointed my red-lens flashlight at it and gave three quick flashes. The boat turned directly toward us and slowed. As it idled into our site, I grabbed the gunwale and held it as Bump pulled himself aboard and the rest of the men followed. Once Jess had backed out of his covering position and climbed in, I passed my M-16 to him and pulled up. Hands grabbed my H-harness webbing and hauled me over the railing as the boat backed away from the riverbank.

Crouched in the boat, my weapon pointed toward shore, I looked out toward the river. The LCPL was loitering about a hundred meters out, guns trained on the canal to cover our withdrawal. The STAB turned and the coxswain pushed the two throttles completely forward. The boat hesitated for a split second, then took off. Without the added weight of the ceramic armor ringing the inside of the gunwales, it would have leaped nearly out of the water. Pierre and Bump manned the two pintle-mounted M-60 machine guns on the port and starboard railings as we hurtled forward. When the coxswain throttled back and came starboard of the LCPL, I saw that Satch had all his weapons manned and ready to fire. He looked disappointed at having nothing to shoot at.

I jumped aboard the LCPL. "Got two," I told him.

"I'll kack up a message to the TOC and let them know the results," he replied.

"Okay. Tell them we'll be back in about two hours."

"I'm going to hang around to see if anything else comes out of the canal."

"Don't think you're going to see anything," I said. "Just make sure you clear the area before light."

I didn't want to show the VC in the area what our LCPL looked like. So far we'd been trying to keep them from putting us together with that boat. Outwardly, it looked just like one of the old riverboats the French had used in the fifties and then turned over to the Vietnamese. I wanted the VC to think our LCPL was just another boat belonging to the South Vietnamese River Assault Groups.

I jumped back into the STAB. "Home, James," I said to the coxswain.

As we cruised up the river, the men slept on the deck, all except Jess and me.

"What d'you think?"

"Not bad," he said. "I figured we'd get more, but two ain't bad."

"When I saw the bow lift on that sampan, I knew they were headed across. I figured two were better than none."

He nodded. "Yeah, the VC'll probably think twice before they use that canal again."

We'd taken the night away from two VC, but the psychological gain of our mission far outweighed any material gain. Two dead VC wouldn't be missed by anyone but their families and friends. But the fact they'd been killed doing something that had probably been routine for years would affect the morale of all their VC buddies.

7

ATTACK IN BROAD DAYLIGHT: BASSAC MISSION

Near the end of April 1967 we learned that the National Police in Can Tho, just down the river from Binh Thuy, had picked up a farmer who told them there would be a high-level VC meeting in a village down the Bassac that afternoon.

Normally I would have been very suspicious of anything coming out of the National Police, but the CTF-116 TOC watch commander told me one of the river patrols had searched a sampan on the Bassac last night and interrogated the owner, who'd told them that "something big" was going to happen the next day in about the same place the National Police informer had fingered. To sweeten the pot, the IV Corps naval intelligence liaison officer who worked routinely with the National Police told me eight to ten guerrillas, including the VC district chief, would be at the meeting. The fact that they were holding the meeting right on the river during the day didn't surprise me: they were used to operating with impunity. Going after a district-level VC cadre was a good chance to do something worthwhile for the war effort. I decided to go with the information.

The suspect village, it turned out, was in two different places! Really the "villages" were small clusters of the Vietnamese mud-and-thatch houses we affectionately called hootches. We decided that Larry Bailey's squad would go to one area, mine to the other. Lieutenant Jake Rhinebolt, our detachment officer-in-charge, elected to go with us, as he often did. I considered Jake a member of my squad, and I liked having him along. He was a hunter and one hell of an operator. Even though he was senior to me, he had made it clear from the start that I ran the missions.

This had to be a daylight operation, which wasn't completely to my liking; so I decided we'd insert by PBR instead of using our smaller boats. I figured that would give us a little edge; by now, I was sure, our STABs were familiar to the VC, and the PBRs could provide us good fire support.

The plan was simple. We'd take one of the two boats in a routine PBR river patrol and beach it in front of the target. After doing our thing, we'd get back on the PBR and get the hell out of there before any large force of VC in the area had time to react. We didn't know exactly in which hootch the meeting was to be held, so I planned to hit fast in hopes of spooking the VC. Quick in, quick out.

I made last-minute arrangements with the CTF-116 TOC, briefed the two PBR crews assigned for the mission, and briefed my men. By this point in our tour, our squad briefings were *really* brief. We'd worked together long enough for everyone to know what he and everyone else should do in any given situation. Everyone was hot to go—daylight operations didn't bother them—and I fed off their enthusiasm.

We got our gear together and headed downriver to the villages, about five miles south of Can Tho. I remember thinking that the weather was too perfect, with no clouds and almost no wind. The usually choppy Bassac looked like a lake. I'd rather it had been raining, but this was the dry season. We arrived off the village about three, and I started looking through binoculars for the hootches described by the informant. Things looked pretty quiet on shore, though I did find what appeared to be the target area. I hadn't expected a sign saying "Meeting This Way," but I *had* hoped to spot sentries. There was nothing. I figured we were either early or late.

I was wondering, as I had earlier, whether this was a setup, so I told the PBR patrol commander to position the other boat on our right flank, because that would be the best firing position for supporting us. I also told him to close the distance to the shore at high speed, and as soon as the boat touched land we'd be off. He was then to back out, giving us fire cover to our left flank. I gave the guys a final quick check, and Jess offered me the thumbs-up. Off we went.

The PBR was a highly maneuverable boat because of its water-jet propulsion system; at top speed it could do a 180-degree turn in its own length. We closed to the shore rapidly, my men and I riding in the bow, left and right of the forward dual .50-caliber machine gun. About ten yards from the beach, the coxswain went from full ahead to full astern by reversing the water jets. We jumped forward just as the PBR's bow hit the riverbank. It was like being shot out of the end of a banana peel, but we were off the boat in seconds.

The boat continued backing out into the river, keeping its machine guns trained on our left flank. Out of the corner of my eye I could see the other PBR in position about a hundred meters to our right. We moved about ten meters in and set up a quick perimeter. This was the critical time. I expected the worst, but after about a minute ashore I felt we were secure and we'd better start moving.

We were just to the right of the hootch that was our prime target. Jess Tolison and I ran through the door. It was a good-sized hootch, with a main room and a bamboo partition at the rear. As we went through the open door, Jess on the left, me on the right, I caught movement just in front of me. It was an old mama-san holding a baby. I saw Jess grab a young woman. Both were in shock. I guess they never expected two wild-eyed guys in full camouflage war paint to be joining them for tea. Apparently, the noise we made on insertion hadn't alarmed them: they were laying out about five places on a floor mat. Bingo! Maybe we were going to get lucky.

Jess had served a tour in Da Nang in 1962 training Vietnamese SEALs, so he spoke a little Vietnamese. He asked the young woman when the VC would be there and she was so astonished she blurted, "In a few minutes." But she was talking at a good clip, so it took Jess a while to realize what she'd said. The old woman was jabbering also and between the two of them anyone in sight would have known something was wrong. They were really scared.

At that moment I heard Pierre Birtz's Stoner machine gun open up. Jess and I bolted out of the hootch and saw three VC with weapons running away through the tree line toward rice paddies a hundred meters off the river. Pierre yelled that he had seen five VC, and he thought he'd hit one.

Jess, Bill Garnett, Charlie Bump, Fred McCarty, and I went after them. I told Pierre and Jake to move to the edge of the rice paddy to cover us. We neared the edge of the tree line, and one of the guys shot a VC in the head. We charged forward. As we went past the fallen VC, I yelled at Fred, "Patch the guy up—I want to talk to him when I get back!"

As we broke out into the rice paddy, I quickly scanned the area. To our right about fifty meters away, another line of trees ran inland, perpendicular to the one from which we'd emerged. Three VC ran down along the tree line to our right and disappeared into the trees fifty meters in front of us. We fired at them and started moving forward across the open rice paddy. As we raced across the open space, my pucker factor started going up. Only our aggressiveness and speed would keep the VC from stopping just inside the tree line and firing on us. Finally, we reached the trees. There was another hootch complex ten meters away. No sign of the VC. Suddenly Jess yelled and we hit the ground. Just in front of us was the firing slit of a bunker. I expected to come under fire, but there was only silence. More bunkers were set among the hootches. It was a defensive perimeter, and we were right in the kill zone. We peered through the dense foliage, expecting to come under attack at any second; a few pigs wandered among the hootches but there was no sign of human life. The villagers, VC or not—but probably VC—were no doubt lying low in the bunkers, waiting for us to make a move. Bill and Charlie, weapons at the ready, were at my right; Jess was at my left elbow, his M-16 glued into his right shoulder, ready to fire. I figured if there was a fight, we'd give better than we got. Still, all was quiet—too quiet.

I was about to advance on the bunker complex, but Jess pointed out that we were in a bad position. First of all, we didn't know what was in front of us. Second, we were beyond the PBR's fire-support fan. I always paid attention to Jess. He was as aggressive as any man I'd ever seen, but he also had great operational savvy, and when he got cautious I got cautious. I said, "Let's make it."

Cautiously, we crawled backward to the edge of the tree line, then got to our feet and hurried toward the river, keeping as much foliage as possible between us and the hootch complex. Bill Garnett walked backward, providing rear security. Charlie Bump was in his usual position on the point. Unopposed, we moved back down the tree line to where I'd left Fred. He was hunched over the VC, who had a triangle bandage wrapped around his head. Only problem was, most of his brains were about two feet from his head. Fred looked up, and I could see he was really pissed. "Thanks a lot, boss," he yelled, "for leaving me alone here in the open while you assholes chased VC!"

"Pierre and Jake had you covered from the tree line," I said.

I could see Fred wasn't buying this, but he didn't argue. "I just about got the guy patched up," he replied instead.

"Yep, I can see that, Fred."

Fred got pissed again because I had so little confidence in his medical abilities. I told Fred he was the best I'd ever seen, but if that guy came back to life he probably wouldn't be able to talk without his brain. As Fred and I enjoyed our rice paddy repartee, Jess made another astute observation:

"Hey, boss, we're hanging out here. We need to haul ass."

"Roger that, Jess. Let's go find Pierre and Jake."

"Fred," Jess said, "you done good. Now get your shit together—we're leaving."

We moved back to the tree line along the river. All of this had taken no more than fifteen minutes.

We picked up the weapon our brain-dead VC had dropped and moved to the hootch where the two women and the baby were hunkering down on the floor. The women started begging us not to kill them. Jess told them we had no intention of doing that and to calm down. He was able to determine that we had indeed broken up a meeting. Apparently the young woman's husband was in the group we had jumped.

I called the PBR commander, who'd been wondering what was going on, and told him to come pick us up. We extracted without incident.

The National Police later told us that the older woman's husband was the local guerrilla leader. He had been waiting in the tree line we charged. I figured he was in one of the bunkers, watching us as we waited for the firing to start.

Though we didn't get what we came for, all in all it was a good operation. It was the first time we'd used the National Police intelligence system. On balance, the information they gave us was accurate. Clearly, some sort of meeting had been scheduled, and we got there just in time to spoil the party.

8

SNEAK AND PEEK: LONG TUAN SECRET ZONE

I could do ambush missions without fear of killing non-VC in any of the three "Secret Zones," which lay along the coast of the South China Sea on each side of the Bassac River. The Long Tuan, Vinh Long, and Ba Xuyen Secret Zones were bad areas, designated free-fire zones. They were transit corridors for VC units moving north into the Saigon region and were also used to store food, weapons, and equipment. Because all three areas were mostly thick mangrove swamp, the only way to get around easily was by sampan. The enemy operated freely because no U.S. or Vietnamese forces ever went there.

One day I paid a call to the subsector adviser responsible for the Long Tuan Secret Zone. I had requested and gotten one of the few U.S. Army "slick" helicopters at IV Corps headquarters. When I told the pilot where we were going, he looked at me like I was nuts. We took off from Can Tho Air Field and headed for the mouth of the Bassac.

The subsector headquarters lay west of the Long Tuan Secret Zone, just outside the mangrove swamps. Once we were airborne, we raised the command post on the radio and got landing instructions: the pilot had not been there any more than I had. At IV Corps headquarters I'd been told that the command post came under artillery, mortar, and rocket fire every night. One of the advisers had been killed by a sniper a week ago when he poked his head out of the command bunker. Sounded just like the kind of place I wanted to operate.

As we approached the area, all I could see was mangrove swamp, stretching for miles to the South China Sea. At first we couldn't even find the landing zone (LZ), so the subsector command post gave us a vector to follow. They said we'd soon see the small town of Long Tuan. Two minutes past that we'd see a wind sock—that would be the LZ. We finally located the wind sock and the LZ. We were flying at 1,500 feet—too high for my liking, but that altitude was SOP for Army helos in the delta then. Following our landing instructions, the pilot auto-rotated straight down to the LZ.

The skids touched down, and Jess and I jumped out. We hadn't touched the ground before the helo was airborne again, screaming toward the Bassac River. The instant he cleared the edge of the open area, he climbed as fast as he could and was gone. (I later learned from a contact on the IV Corps staff that he called back to the IV Corps command center and tried to get out of picking us up. The watch officer told him not to come back without us.)

Meanwhile Jess and I were zigzagging across the LZ, following the sergeant who had met us to the command bunker. Sniper rounds cracked over our heads from the nearby tree line. I dove into the bunker and met the acting adviser, an Army captain in battle dress minus his helmet. We shook hands all around, and he offered coffee. Being good Navy men, Jess and I accepted.

The captain, who'd been told only to expect two Americans who wanted to talk to him about operating in the Secret Zone, was looking at us the same way the helo pilot had. I explained that we were SEALs and asked that the captain and his sergeant keep that piece of news to themselves—the fact that SEALs were operating in the delta was classified Top Secret at that time. I explained that we'd been operating upriver and weren't getting the results I wanted. I'd heard that his area was a target-rich environment, and we wanted to give it a shot.

He laughed. "Great, I haven't been able to get any force to operate in the Zone. You guys can have all you want. How many men you plan to go with?"

I said, "You're looking at a third of them."

The captain started laughing again. "No, really, how many men are you going to take in?"

"Six."

He just looked at me strangely, and I said, "That's right—six." I wasn't going to explain our modus operandi because he didn't have a need to know.

"Okay, let me give you what I know about the area."

His brief was quick because he didn't know much about anything beyond the perimeter of his barbed-wire-enclosed command bunker complex. He explained that the Americans never left except to fly out for a break once a month. He also told me about the adviser who'd just been killed. The sniper who'd fired at us as we were leaving the helo had a reputation as a poor shot, so the advisers had gotten lazy about moving from bunker to bunker. The major had been shot because instead of running, he was walking.

The captain finished his rundown by saying, "We get shot at every time we stick our heads out of the bunker. Since the major bought it, we don't go out much."

This situation was familiar to Army and Marine troops operating in the North, but it was not the norm in the delta at that time. He said there just weren't any friendlies around. I asked about his VN counterparts.

The captain chuckled and said, "They've made their accommodations with the VC."

The VC could have attacked and captured the command post any time they wished. But because they could obtain hard-to-get American consumer items from the Vietnamese, they left the command post alone. "All the local VC are smoking Camels," he explained. "They don't want to screw up a good deal."

The captain showed me his "rumor board," on which he had plotted such things as munitions factories, supply points, and base-camp areas.

He had no idea how accurate the information was, and he only kept the map for something to do.

"My VN counterpart puts H & I [harassment and interdiction] fire into the Zone every night with his artillery, but he's always careful not to hit anything. I figure my info is right if I can't get him to shoot at it."

He was painting an interesting picture. It really was a target-rich environment—Jess was drooling.

"I'm gonna take my guys in and have a look," I said. "Don't say anything to your counterpart about us."

"Have at it, but don't send me any message traffic. In fact, don't even use the radio to tell me where you're going."

I understood. The VNs might learn about the operation. In those days there were no secure voice radios in the delta.

"You guys are clear to operate at any time and any place in the Zone. Shoot anyone you see. They're all bad guys in there."

I couldn't ask for better rules of engagement. "I'll take my chances on the H & I fire," I replied.

"You won't have a problem."

"Can you give some artillery support if we get in some shit?"

"Better not count on it."

When the helo checked in on the radio, we stood by the bunker entrance. As he started down we shook hands all around; they wished us good luck, and Jess and I headed for the LZ. The sergeant and the captain stayed in the bunker, and the sniper fired a good-bye as we jumped on the helo and took off.

"Jess," I said, "this is the place we've been looking for."

"You got it, boss," he agreed. "But we'd better take it easy at first."

Back at Binh Thuy, Jess and I met with Satch Baumgart to start planning for the Long Tuan. Our biggest problem was not being able to expect fire support if we got in serious trouble. We could use Army helicopter gunships, but they wouldn't have much staying time—their nearest refueling point was Ba Xuyen airfield, about thirty minutes away from the middle of the Long Tuan. Nor would our boats be of much help: if they came up any of the large canals they'd be sitting ducks. Since we would be the first force in anyone's memory to operate in the Zone, we'd have surprise on our side, but we'd have to be careful, as Jess had said. We'd just write the book one page at a time.

Our other problem was getting there. Helos were out of the question; I knew I couldn't get any slicks to insert us at night, and daylight helo insertions would give us away to any bad guys in the area. We'd have to use our boats to insert, then patrol on foot to where we wanted to go.

On the way back Jess and I had talked about what kind of operations to do. We settled on ambush patrols, which would allow us to reconnoiter an area before a hit. I figured we'd start with two-day operations—a limit set by how much water we could carry. (We couldn't get more in the Zone.) We'd insert early in the morning, around 0400, patrol the mangroves during the day, and lay up in ambush at night on one of the interior canals. If we got a hit, we'd assess the situation and probably get out. If we didn't get a hit, we'd sleep the next morning, patrol to another canal in the afternoon, and repeat the process.

Satch looked at the map and charts of the area and said the LCPL couldn't operate at the mouth of the Bassac because the seas were too high for the boat's low freeboard. I always paid a lot of attention to what Satch said: it was his second tour, and he was one hell of an officer. Satch said the STAB, our twenty-two-foot trimaran, would be okay but it was fuel limited and because it burned gasoline, not diesel, getting fuel from the nearby Junk Force base was out of the question. Satch figured the best thing was to use two PBRs to get us into the area, leaving Binh Thuy late in the afternoon so as to arrive off the Secret Zone about 0200. The STAB could load extra fuel bladders and transit at night, on its own.

For our first operation, a simple one, we'd go someplace accessible from the Bassac River. Jess threw a dart at the map and we started planning. Canals ran all over the Zone. We picked two that were about a kilometer in from the river and ran parallel to the South China Sea. To get there, we'd insert about a mile upriver and walk the rest of the way. We knew moving in the Secret Zone would not be easy, so we planned to go light, with no machine guns and minimal hand grenades. The grenades would be next to useless because in the thick mangroves we couldn't throw them far enough to get us out of the kill radius. Besides, hand grenades don't have much effect when they detonate in the water. Everyone was enthusiastic about going to the Zone. It would be the first time U.S. eyes would be on the ground there, and it would really bother the VC to have someone shooting at them in one of their safest areas.

The IV Corps intelligence officer, an Army colonel, gave me what he had on the area. It was basically what I'd seen on the subsector rumor board, but he did think there was a weapons factory in the area through which we had to patrol to get to the canals. It gave us something to look for.

About 1400, we left Binh Thuy on two PBRs headed downriver. Satch came along to run things on the water. The trip was uneventful and the STAB showed up about midnight. Because the thick mangroves would probably cut down the range of our radio transmissions, Satch wanted to keep the PBRs closer to shore than we had originally planned. I agreed; we were playing it safe until I had a feel for the area. We boarded the STAB and slowly headed for shore. I wanted to insert at low tide so we could walk up a small canal for a couple of hundred meters before striking out cross-country.

I hadn't considered one factor carefully enough: the mud. The charts showed a sandy bottom well inside the Bassac. When Jess and I flew to Long Tuan the tide had been in, and although I had noticed mud, I thought it would be confined to areas near the riverbank. The squad was well acquainted with delta mud, but nothing prepared us for what we found here.

With the PBR radar, Satch vectored us to a point just inside the canal I wanted. We were about a kilometer from the shore when the boat grounded out. Mud.

"No problem. We'll walk from here," I told the coxswain. I climbed over the gunwale and promptly sank to my waist in the mud. Light though we were, we all sank in.

The next three hours were like nothing I'd ever experienced. All the trips I'd made through the mudflats at Little Creek during UDT Basic Training—they couldn't compare. This was like that nightmare in which you're trying to escape some unseen threat but you find yourself unable to move your feet. To make matters worse, we had to be quiet because there were small, inhabited sampans sprinkled around us like little islands in a sea. We had to assume they had come from inside the Zone and wouldn't be friendly.

Charlie Bump, being the lightest of us, was having the easiest time. I told him to move at his own speed and cover us as we neared the mangroves. The rest of us slogged on, until we finally made it to the canal at first light. Once we got into the mangroves, Bump found a spot of dry land and we stopped. Each of us had consumed one of the three canteens he was carrying. Jess and I talked, and I decided we'd come out that night whether we made a hit or not.

I called Satch on the radio and gave him the change. He checked the tide tables and said we had to be at the mudflats by 2300 if the STAB was to float. At that hour it could get a lot closer, so we wouldn't have to walk as far.

Since it was now daylight, I decided not to walk down the canal. Instead, we struck off through the mangroves, following a compass course that would take us near the purported weapons factory. I figured if there was one, we'd hear mechanical noise from some distance.

We found the mangrove swamps weren't all water—we crossed many dry areas—but I had underestimated the thickness of the foliage. It was worse than the Rung Sat. We had to contend not only with the thick brush but also with fire ants, which dropped on us out of the trees when they sensed our warm bodies. The heat and humidity were incredible. There was no breeze, and we were soon sweating like racehorses. We were also making a lot of noise, but I wasn't worried about that—I figured the VC were too smart to do what we were doing. They'd be in sampans on the canals.

About 1400 we got near where the factory was supposed to be, and

I called break. We established our usual perimeter, then sat down and listened. Both Jess and I heard voices, and all of us heard metal clanking. The noises seemed to be coming from about ten o'clock on our line of march. I couldn't believe we were going to get lucky.

We formed up and started moving in that direction, very slowly to stay as quiet as possible. It was impossible to move silently; a Seminole Indian couldn't have moved silently through that terrain. After half an hour of walking the noises didn't seem to be any closer, and they seemed to now be coming from our 1300. I stopped the patrol in an "open area" of eight-inch elephant grass. Jess and I looked at the map and saw we should soon be at the first canal. The maps were so inaccurate that I didn't put much faith in them, but they were all we had.

We pushed on. About 1500, we reached a canal, but it didn't look large enough to be the one I wanted. We stopped, and again we heard the same noises, this time down the canal to our right. I decided that someone was in a sampan doing something, but probably nothing to do with weapons.

We were all beat, and this canal would do as well as the next, so we got in ambush formation along it, pulled our mosquito nets down over our faces, and waited. If something came by, I wasn't going to wait until nightfall to shoot; I figured no one was going to chase us through this terrain. I gave the word for one member of each buddy pair to get some sleep. My buddy, Pierre, told me to go first because he wasn't sleepy. No problem.

Some time later, I was awakened by Pierre shaking my shoulder. I was alert instantly, listening. He pointed to our right, where I heard the same noises as before, only closer. The others came awake and I told them to get ready. We waited and waited. The noises—voices and clanking—got closer. We couldn't see more than twenty meters down the canal, so all we could do was listen. Suddenly, just as I thought they were coming close enough for us to see whom they belonged to, the voices seemed to be coming from right in front of us. I figured they must have been on another canal, one that intersected ours. We couldn't shift without making a lot of noise, so we sat tight, listening, as the sounds faded.

The tide was in far enough for us to get in the canal and move. About

1700 I decided it was time. We partially inflated our life jackets and slipped into the water. Bump and I went first. I wanted to see the other canal, which had to be only a few meters to our right. We pulled ourselves along the bank. About fifty meters down we did indeed see a canal, about thirty meters wide, leading northwest into the interior. This had to be the canal that led to the Bassac, I thought, the one I had originally planned to patrol.

We crawled carefully out of the water and took our standard formation for a canal ambush, in a line parallel to the canal. I didn't use rear security—we were all rear security. No one was going to sneak up on us in that terrain anyway.

It got darker and darker. We hadn't heard anything since we had set up. I had been trying to sort out our location, and as near as I could figure we were about a kilometer up the canal from the river. If I was right, getting back to the river was going to be easy.

I passed the word down the line that we'd pull out about 2230. It was now 1830. There was no moon and it was pitch black. My night vision had kicked in, but I could barely see the other side of the canal. I wasn't carrying a night-vision device; I had found them to be useless in mangroves, so it was weight I didn't need.

About 2100, I heard the distinctive sound of a sampan engine starting, up the canal to our left. We all came alert. Then we heard several more engines start up. The noise of a "one-lunger," a sampan engine, was unmistakable. We were going to have some business. Wait . . . listen . . .

Down Doppler, down adrenaline. I couldn't believe it. They were going the other way. The engine noise receded and then disappeared. Jess sent word down that maybe they were going to pick up supplies and come back our way. Maybe. Jess was such an optimist.

I waited until 2130 and heard nothing. I tried to reach Satch on the radio, but we must have been out of range. The mangrove terrain absorbed the line-of-sight signal the radios emitted. If we didn't show up for extraction, Satch would call out the cavalry and start looking. I didn't want that; up to now, no one knew we were there, so we could come back. I gave the word and we got in the water and started pulling ourselves down the canal.

We were being really quiet in the water, but after about a hundred meters Bump froze. I eased up to see what was the matter. He pointed to our right front: A bunker complex and hootches. A base camp. There were no lights in the hootches. No one was home.

We carefully approached the base camp. I'd not yet seen anything like it. The hootches had four-tier bunks in them, and the complex could have accommodated about a company-sized unit. Plus, the bunkers were formidable. That I couldn't understand. Nobody bothered these guys in here. I guess, like our military, they had standards that applied everywhere. I laughed to myself as I imagined some VC operator arguing with his staff engineer about the building of needless defenses. We spent about twenty minutes taking a good look around, then slipped back into the canal and headed out again, reaching the river at about 2215—not bad.

I signaled with a red-lens flashlight and got a return signal from out on the water. Back on the PBR, Satch said he'd been running radio checks since dark but never heard us. Lesson learned: range was shorter than we'd figured.

We were all exhausted, but not too disappointed. We'd penetrated the Long Tuan, learned a lot about the area, and lived to talk about it. We'd be back. As it turned out, though, the minimal fire support we could count on kept me from operating too aggressively. And no other force in the delta was much interested in running operations in the region, so no one was going to react to any intelligence we brought out.

9

A CLOSE CALL: TAN DINH ISLAND

By early June 1967 I was getting antsy for a big operation. It was near the end of my tour, only three weeks before we could go back to Little Creek.

My dream at the time was to draw a VC platoon or company-sized element in the open and, with my five men, shoot the shit out of them. I was so confident of our firepower and the ability of my men that the difference in numbers was not a factor. Plus, we had plenty of help on call. So when I received word through the river patrol force intelligence officer that the VC were about to make a large crossing in the vicinity of Cu Lao Tanh Dinh, an island complex in the Bassac about ten miles downriver from Can Tho, I seized the opportunity.

The CTF-116 deputy commander suggested that we go on the main island as soon as possible and destroy as many as we could of the heavily fortified bunkers that fronted on the Bassac. When the VC made a large crossing in that area, as they routinely did, the only real burr in their saddles had been the PBRs, which attempted to interdict the sampans as they crossed the 2,000 meters of open water. So the last time they had made a large crossing, the VC had manned their bunkers with heavy machine guns and rocket-propelled grenades and kept the boats at bay. When they hunkered down in those bunkers, the only way to disturb them was with ground forces, and there weren't any U.S. forces in the delta at that time. The Vietnamese would have no part of the hand-to-hand fighting needed to dislodge the VC. Even air strikes had little effect, because the bunkers were so well built.

I decided we should take out those bunkers. When large forces weren't in the area, the VC kept only a platoon-sized force spread over the entire two-mile length of the island. I got in a helo and went to the subsector headquarters to talk with the U.S. Army advisers. Their intelligence also suggested there would be a major crossing soon; most tellingly, the Vietnamese had reduced considerably the number of daytime patrols on that side of the river, and the senior officers had found compelling reasons to go to Saigon within the last two days.

The senior U.S. adviser was getting nervous because, given the reaction of the Vietnamese officers, he thought the VC might take a shot at his headquarters this time. He was really glad to hear we were coming; he figured we could cause enough problems for the VC that they might leave him alone. I shouldn't give the impression that the two Army men were "shy." On the contrary, they were brave men, but they were the only two Americans within twenty miles of the river.

I decided we'd insert just before first light and do our business early in the morning. We needed to bring a lot of explosives, much more than the six of us could carry. (Though Jess had already gone back to the States to be promoted, we now had Quan, a Vietnamese SEAL, attached to our squad.) I felt the best thing to do was to put all the demolitions on our armored LCPL and run our Boston Whaler back and forth as we needed. Because I didn't expect any real resistance, I figured we could shuttle without worry. Also, we'd be right on the river during the whole operation; we could always swim out to the boat if we got into more shit than we could handle.

I went over the plan with the troops and Satch Baumgart. As my boat officer, Satch played a major role in all our operations, but this time he would have even more responsibility. And, sitting on the LCPL in the middle of the river, he'd be a very visible target. Satch said he had no problem with plunking himself down offshore on a 1,500-pound bomb with a bull's-eye painted on the side. He wasn't much smarter than I was.

We left the base at 0100 on June 7 for our four-hour transit to the launch point. The river was quiet that night. We passed two PBR patrols, which reported no action, but the tactical operations center back at the base radioed us that a large VC force had been reported moving about ten miles inland on the south side of the river, just about opposite where we were headed.

We were going at the right time. The VC would probably take until the next night to reach the Bassac, since they normally moved only after dark so as to avoid air strikes while they were in the open. As for the actual crossing, their advance element might go the same night, but the rest of the force would likely wait till the next. A VC advance force was usually a company-sized unit; they'd man the bunkers and cover the main force as it crossed. I figured we would have the place virtually to ourselves, and if we did a good job on the bunkers, the advance force wouldn't have a chance to repair them in time for the main body's crossing. CTF-116 was planning a ten-boat PBR operation supported by Army and Navy Seawolf helo fire teams. If the VC didn't have the bunkers, they'd take a beating.

We reached our launch point, loaded the Whaler, and headed for shore. When the Whaler nudged the riverbank we quickly hopped over the bow and, in keeping with our SOP, moved inland about ten meters and set up a defensive perimeter. The boat quietly backed out into the river. I listened intently for sounds that would signal VC in the area. I heard the normal night sounds: frogs croaking, the river swishing by as the tide changed, and night insects chirping. After we'd sat in our perimeter for about twenty minutes, I was satisfied all was normal. We started patrolling along the south side of the island. Charlie Bump was on the point as usual, and I was behind him. Fred McCarty was next with the radio. Our Vietnamese SEAL, Quan, was behind him, followed by Pierre Birtz. Bill Garnett, my second in command, was rear security, the position Jess normally occupied. We were all carrying M-16s, and Pierre had a grenade launcher on his. (This rig was later developed into the MK-148 system.)

We each carried one twenty-pound pack of C-4 plastic explosives. All of us had fragmentation grenades, and because we were going to be dealing with bunkers we carried more concussion grenades than usual. We were weighed down much more than normal, but the terrain was benign, and I figured we'd lighten the load as we got to the bunker complex.

We moved cautiously, listening for human sounds—a cough, say, that would suggest someone was getting up and clearing his throat before going outside to relieve himself. We also looked for the glow of the candles Vietnamese left burning inside their hootches all night. Our targets, offensive bunkers, were located inside hootches for camouflage and concealment.

All who served on the ground in Vietnam know that virtually every hootch, friendly or enemy, had a bunker. Our air guys had a habit of putting strikes into tree lines whether or not there were any enemy present, so the bunkers were the only way for people to avoid the bombs and rockets. *Defensive* bunkers were under every hootch I ever saw. What we were looking for was different. Offensive bunkers had well-built firing slits, from which a gunner could shoot with impunity. They were giving the PBRs fits.

There were hootches all along the river. Some were homes, but others were there only to camouflage an offensive bunker. We patrolled for about thirty minutes, passing two homes occupied only by women and children, before we found the first offensive bunker. It was deep and fronted right on the river. We could see the firing slits from the riverside as we circled the hootch. Offensive bunkers were well cared for, covered with live brush to make them virtually invisible from the river. And usually where there was one there were more.

Bump found two women and a baby in the hootch. We took them outside under protest. Because they made such a fuss, I figured there just might be men in the bunker. I positioned the troops in a security perimeter, and Bill lobbed a concussion grenade into the bunker. No result. We put in a Hagensen pack containing twenty pounds of C-4 explosives and blew it, then moved off, leaving the women and children there.

We found the next bunker fifty meters from the first. This one was not under a hootch and it was enormous. It went down about ten feet, well below the level of the water. The firing positions commanded an excellent view: through the slits I could see our LCPL just offshore as it followed us down the island. Outside, the bunker rose about six feet above the ground. The ceiling was supported and reinforced by large palm trunks, and the roof was three feet of baked mud, hard as concrete. We put two packs in this one and fired. The bunker collapsed.

The third bunker, smaller than the second but just as well built, was hidden in a hootch about twenty-five meters downriver. I put three packs on the bunker, fired, and watched the hootch fly about a hundred feet in the air. A large hole appeared where the bunker had been. I had used the SEAL formula for precise, surgical demolition work. If twenty pounds will do the job, use forty to be sure. In this case I used sixty.

Just before the boat came in with our resupply of demolitions, Charlie Bump came to me and said, "Hey, boss, look at this."

He pulled up his fatigues. His legs were swollen to almost twice their normal size.

"Fred, come here," I called.

Fred took one look at Charlie and said, "Must be an allergic reaction to some shit in the ditches we've been wading through."

I sent Charlie out to the LCPL and took over the point.

We traveled about a hundred meters before we encountered another hootch. This one had only a defensive bunker. There were three women and two children inside. One of the babies had a terrible eye infection, so Fred broke out his medical bag and applied antibiotic cream. He gave the mother the rest of the tube and showed her how to use it.

I noticed that the women were "nervous as whores in church"—even more nervous than I would have expected. So as we moved off, I told the troops to be even more alert. We were setting a very clear pattern, moving down the river and blowing bunkers—and we weren't, obviously, being quiet about it. Still, I wasn't too worried. We had Satch out in the river watching in front of us, and he hadn't reported seeing anything.

Suddenly, something caught my eye, and I stopped the patrol. Crouching down to get a better look, I saw that to the left of the trail some grass, pressed down by someone's foot, was straightening into its normal upright position. It was the movement that had caught my attention. Looking in the direction the pressed-down stalks pointed, I saw an overgrown trail leading directly away from the river. Someone had just walked inland, probably after checking us out. I decided to follow the trail.

"Heads up," I whispered to Fred just behind me. "Pass it back." I waited until I could see everyone had the word.

We patrolled very slowly down the overgrown trail. The grass under the footprints started getting flatter and flatter. About fifty meters down the trail I stopped. Something didn't seem right. Our standard procedure when stopped was for everyone to get low and watch in alternate directions; the point concentrated ahead, while the last man watched the rear.

As soon as I squatted down, I saw movement about five meters in front of me. It was an AK-47 assault rifle, followed quickly by a helmeted head looking in our direction. The man wasn't walking, just standing and looking.

I remember thinking, "Oh, shit, we got problems," as I rose quickly and shot him on full automatic. I had fired about four rounds when my left hand flew off the heat jacket and I felt an awful pain in my wrist. I thought my weapon had exploded.

In the next split second I realized that I'd been shot and that we were in a hell of a fight. We were taking heavy fire from our right flank and our front. I sensed we had just about been ambushed. Incredibly, it looked as if I was the only one who had been hit. The guys were returning fire, but we needed to get out of there.

I yelled, "Leap-frog back to the river! Move it!"

We took off, firing on the run. The river seemed to be a mile away instead of sixty meters. The leapfrog tactic works well, but it's designed for more than five people. With three moving and two shooting, we fought our way back to the river, rounds slapping the ground all around us. We broke free of the trap within seconds, but it seemed to take forever.

We set up behind the berm at the river's edge and kept returning fire to our right and front. Now my left wrist really started throbbing, and for the first time I took a look at it. Shouldn't have done that. All I saw at first was a bloody stump where my hand had once been. When I looked again I realized that the entire top of my left hand appeared to be missing. Fred was on me like a tramp on a muffin, jabbing two morphine syrettes into my leg. We had to get out of there. VC rounds were hitting the berm all around us.

Satch knew we were in trouble before I called him—the heavy fire going over our heads was also cracking over his. But he couldn't do anything until he knew exactly where we were. That problem was solved when we reached the river.

I told Satch to get some air support in (he'd already called the TOC), and tried to position the rest of us to get maximum firepower where it was needed. My troops told me later I gave Fred trouble because I wouldn't stay put. I kept moving around, shooting and giving orders. I don't remember that. I also don't remember how long we were on the riverbank. I do know my hand hurt like hell.

We were in trouble, but we did have the river at our backs, and our LCPL was putting out horrendous fire to our right flank. (Charlie Bump had taken over the .50-caliber machine gun.) So my original concern about being overrun was groundless.

The LCPL's firepower soon suppressed the enemy fire long enough for our Boston Whaler to come in and get us. Satch had already called for a medical evacuation (MEDEVAC) helo from the Air Force base at Binh Thuy; it would pick me up at the sector headquarters, just up the river. Fred and one of Satch's guys jumped into the Whaler with me, and we headed that way.

At the sector headquarters, we learned the MEDEVAC helo was inbound. Fred had managed to get my wrist bandaged somehow, and since I hadn't gone into shock I opted to walk the 200 or so meters to the LZ rather than be carried on a stretcher. The morphine really must have taken effect.

We got to the LZ just as the bird landed. In thirty minutes, Fred and I were in the dispensary at the Binh Thuy Air Force Base. Larry Bailey met us there. As I sat on the examining table with my left wrist hanging loose, I told Larry I would probably have to become a fag if the doctors couldn't fix it. SEAL humor. By that time I'd had four morphine syrettes, two from Fred and two more from the medic on the helo. I think medics like to give morphine shots—they probably make the patient easier to handle. The doctor put me on a C-123 leaving for Saigon.

Two hours later, I was admitted to the Third Field Evacuation hospital, a grungy, filthy SEAL still in his cammies and war paint—an oddity, because they usually got only Army personnel who had been well scrubbed at field dispensaries. They took me to an operating room and started working.

The doctor gave me a radial block, which completely numbed my left arm. It was pretty impressive: he put a needle in my left armpit and said, "You should feel a tingle in your left thumb as I put in the needle." Yes indeed, my left thumb started tingling. I remember thinking, "This guy's good."

Once they'd completely numbed the arm, they went to work, scrubbing the hell out of the wound and talking all the time, as I lay there and watched. The bullet had entered the underside of my left wrist, shattering when it hit my bones; the exit wound opened up the entire top of my left hand. In passing, the bullet had destroyed my SEAL Team–issue Rolex watch, most of which ended up in my wrist along with the bullet fragments.

The doctor asked if I knew what kind of weapon had shot me. I didn't, but from the amount of damage done by the round he figured it was probably an AK-47. He also reconstructed the path of the bullet. From behind and to my right, its trajectory was from about four o'clock to nine o'clock. He told me I was lucky (I'd already figured that out for myself). They worked on me for about an hour, and then the doctor said he wasn't going to do any more because I would need a hand specialist—and, he said, I stunk so he couldn't stand me any longer. I like a doctor with a sense of humor. Later, on the ward, he brought me a plastic bag full of metal and glass—the remains of my Rolex, plus bullet shrapnel. He hadn't gotten all the shrapnel out; some of the fragments, he said, might work their way to the surface of my skin and I could just pull them out. The rest I'd probably carry in my wrist for the rest of my life. (I do, and it sets off airport metal detectors.)

Next a nurse came in to ask if I'd urinated yet. I told her I hadn't had the urge—and besides, I whined, my wrist was hurting so bad I couldn't get out of bed. This crusty old major, who looked as if she could go bear hunting with a switch, told me if I hadn't pissed in twenty minutes she'd put a catheter in me and drain my bladder. I came off the bed like a Polaris missile. She was laughing as I staggered to the head. (But she turned out to be a kind person. Later that night, when the pain in my wrist got worse, she gave me a morphine shot stronger than the pills the doctor had prescribed.)

The next day my old commanding officer, Lieutenant Commander Dave Schaible, visited me. In his new position on an amphibious ready group staff off the coast of Vietnam, Dave had seen the after-action report that said I'd been shot. So he'd hitched a ride on a helo to Saigon to harass me about trying to catch bullets.

While he was there, Fred McCarty came in. The platoon had been told to stand down for a few days, and as my corpsman, he figured he ought to come to Saigon to see how I was doing. He told me that our LCPL, every PBR in the western Bassac, and most of the local air assets spent the rest of the day battling the VC on the island. Though they never completely suppressed the VC fire, they probably screwed up or delayed the big crossing.

Intelligence figured the advance party of a regiment-sized force had reached the island the night we arrived. When we started blowing bunkers, they sent out a group to set up an L-shaped ambush, with the long side along the river just past where I turned us inland. The tracks I led us down were on the short side, so we'd surprised them. If we hadn't turned off the main trail when we did, chances are none of us would have survived.

Fred also reconstructed our fight. Apparently the VC force never saw us until I opened fire. I had been shot over my left shoulder, from about ten feet away (that VC was a terrible marksman); our Vietnamese SEAL, Quan, immediately greased the guy. If I'd been standing upright, I would have been shot in the back. No one else had even been scratched: our initial volume of fire had made them lie low long enough for us to leapfrog back to the river. In retrospect, our fire discipline and tactics had gotten us out.

10

PATCH ME UP AND SEND ME BACK

I left Saigon on a C-141 MEDEVAC flight on June 10, 1967. When I got on, I realized how lucky I was. There were men going back to the States with no arms, no legs, no arms *or* legs. One of the saddest was a young sergeant who had been a tank commander in III Corps. He had seen a lot of combat and now had suffered his third wound, which, under the Army policy in effect in those days, meant an automatic return to the States and no more war. He looked fine, so I asked where he had been wounded. Seems his tank hit a mine. He was blown out of the top hatch unharmed, but he landed feet first in a punji pit. One of the upright, razor-sharp stakes had gone into his groin, severing the muscles and nerves at the base of his penis. The kid had been married two days before coming to Vietnam, and he'd had no R & R since. He'd spent two nights with his new wife. Doctors in Saigon told him he would probably never be able to use his penis except to piss. Yeah, I felt very lucky.

When my second-leg flight pulled up to the terminal in Norfolk, a couple of guys from the Team were standing on the tarmac near another plane. They turned out to be members of the platoon replacing mine at Binh Thuy, so we talked for a while. I gave them a quick-and-dirty about how I got wounded, and some words to live by when they started operating. As they stared at my bandaged left hand, I could tell they were wondering if they'd get dinged too—or worse. I was the second member of SEAL Team Two to get wounded, and the first man had also been shot in the hand. We were just the first of many. In the first two years the command had platoons in Vietnam, we had a 95 percent casualty rate—but only seven guys killed.

Naval Hospital Portsmouth was a good hospital, but I hated hospitals (still do), and all I wanted to do was get out and get back to work. The doctors had other ideas. (Coincidentally, one of the doctors treating my wrist was the same fellow who'd delivered my daughter in February. I never did figure out whether Becky had been attended by an "orthopod" or I had been treated by an obstetrician.) At any rate, they told me the damage to my wrist and hand was worse than they had first thought. All the bones in my wrist had been broken, the tendons leading from my fingers had been severed, and all the skin had been torn off the top of the hand. There was also extensive nerve damage, which they said might not heal (it hasn't). I needed at least two operations to patch things up, and they said I might be in the hospital six months.

I had other ideas. My first priority was to get out of the hospital to spend time with my wife, son, and daughter, whom I had not yet seen.

The doctors operated on my wrist the first day, checking the work that had been done in Saigon and resetting the bones. Even in a cast, my wrist still hurt like hell. I'd taken myself off pain relievers stronger than aspirin after I found myself levitating three feet off the bed after taking a codeine pill in the hospital in Saigon. Aspirin was all I was taking in Portsmouth.

Becky had been to visit me every day and stayed well past normal visiting hours. On my third day there, I called and told her I was leaving for the weekend and to bring me some clothes. When she arrived, I told the duty nurse I was going to the cafeteria. I left the ward, found the nearest head, went in, changed into the clothes Becky had brought, put my hospital pajamas and robe in Becky's handbag, and left.

Sunday evening the phone rang. It was the nurse on my ward, letting me know I'd better be back by Tuesday because that's when my doctor was due. She must have noticed the look in my eye when I told her I was going to the cafeteria—most likely I wasn't the first to pull that maneuver. At any rate, she covered for me, and I made sure I was back early Tuesday morning to cover for her.

That week I had another operation, in which the surgeons sewed the tendons of my middle two fingers to those of the forefinger and little finger. This gave me two tendons to control all the fingers on my left hand. They also shortened the tendons so I'd have better control of my fingers. In addition, they fused the bones in my left wrist, which gave me about 30 degrees of upward motion but none downward—the best they could do to allow me maximum strength in the joint. Then the doctor assigned me to therapy. I lasted for two sessions, then convinced the therapist I could do the work by myself. I promised to come back once a week so she could check my progress.

All I really wanted to do was get back to the Team and get to work. I had the use of only one arm, but I figured I could train the platoons going over. Only a few of us had seen any fighting, and there are no better trainers than those who have been in combat. So I returned to work full-time.

My doctor, who didn't happen to know I was back at work, was considering me for medical retirement. At my next visit he gave me what he thought was the good news. I told him I didn't want out—an attitude the medical folks weren't used to. I was the first SEAL officer they had treated for combat wounds; all the others—mostly Marines—wanted out as soon as possible. I let him know that not only would I fight any medical discharge, I wanted out of the hospital right away so I could get back to the Team "officially." He said he'd do what he could about the medical board, but until they made a decision, I would be assigned to the hospital. Unofficially, I could return to the Team—for paperwork only. I promised.

I convinced Bill Early to put me in charge of predeployment training. Over the next six months I also took whatever officer jobs needed doing—executive officer, operations officer, you name it. All the healthy officers except Bill were either in Vietnam or getting ready to go. Bill wanted to go as the OIC of our three-platoon detachment, but we convinced him he was more important to the Team in Little Creek, making sure the money continued to flow.

In May 1968, SEAL Team Two had a change of command. The new CO, Ted Lyon, had spent a year in Da Nang on a staff that controlled PT boat operations. But he was completely different from Bill Early. Bill was an "operator," and he worked twenty hours a day.

All of us in Little Creek were putting in long hours and loving it because the work was paying off. Bill had gotten us to Vietnam and made sure we had the best equipment and training. Our platoons were doing great, and it wasn't by chance—we worked very hard preparing them for combat. We had focused, realistic predeployment training that occasionally got people hurt but saved lives once the platoons got in-country.

When Ted took over, there seemed to be a shift in command emphasis. Ted seemed to be more of a staff officer. I didn't have the same confidence in him—not that that's unusual when a new boss comes on the job. One morning just after he took over, Ted gathered all the officers to give us his guidance. We all sat in his office in our UDT swim trunks and blue-and-gold shirts, the standard dress around the Team area. He was wearing his tropical white uniform.

Ted planned first and foremost to make us all good little naval officers—not that most of us didn't need some polishing. He told us he expected each of us to pay calls on him and his wife, Judy. Paying calls is an old Navy custom, and it does serve a useful function when there is a new CO. Ted and Judy were great people and everyone liked them. But in that command at that time, requiring us to call on them sent the wrong signal, at least to me. He also said he expected all of us to drop calling cards in the tray as we came through the door. And, "oh, by the way," we'd better have our own swords. At first I thought he meant we had to pay the call in full dress uniform.

These were the wrong first things to say to a group of combat veterans and soon-to-be combat veterans. They implied that social life had precedence over training and operating. Being a young "gunslinger," I didn't much care for Ted's priorities. I had to figure out how to get myself back to Vietnam.

A serendipitous opportunity arose. Someone had to relieve Jake Rhinebolt, already in his second tour as Detachment Alpha officer-in-charge. It had to be a lieutenant senior to the three platoon commanders. Dick Anderson, the 9th Platoon commander in Vinh Long, fit the bill, and I was the only officer with combat experience available to replace Dick. I jumped at the chance, and got out of Dodge in mid-May, eager to be back in action.

PART 3

Fire Two: Second Vietnam Tour

It was not a good year for the U.S. war effort in Vietnam. The Tet Offensive at the end of January 1968 showed that the Communists could penetrate everywhere in the country if they were willing to accept horrendous casualties. Throughout the Mekong Delta, Vietcong forces seized key Vietnamese government strongholds. In a few days of fierce fighting, U.S. forces dealt them enormous defeats throughout South Vietnam. But the Communists won a strategic victory. The American public was shocked by the ferocity of their attacks, which went to the heart of Saigon. Pressure mounted for us to get out of the war. In late March, President Johnson announced bombing restrictions in North Vietnam. By mid-May, U.S. and North Vietnamese delegates held their first peace talks in Paris.

After Tet, North Vietnamese regular units began appearing in the Mekong Delta, since Tet had virtually destroyed most of the Vietcong main force units. SEALs were mostly unaffected. We figured we'd just have more to shoot at as the NVA infiltrated our hunting grounds. The NVA did, though, bring more sophisticated weaponry than their southern cousins had been allowed to have. Otherwise, things were much as they had been when I left in June 1967.

11

FIRST MISSION: CHECKING OUT ALL THE PARTS

May 15, 1968

The moment I stepped off the plane at Tan Son Nhut airport in Saigon, I knew I was back in the war zone. Vietnam was as hot and humid as I'd remembered. Bill Early, who was now the SEAL officer on the Naval Forces Vietnam staff, greeted me. It was good to see him. He told me he had some briefings lined up for me the next morning to bring me up-to-date on the tactical situation in the Mekong Delta. I told him I didn't need any staff briefings. All I needed was to get right down to the delta. Bill relented, and that afternoon I got on another airplane for Vinh Long.

Lieutenant Junior Grade Dave Purselle, my new assistant, met me as I stepped off the plane. A large guy—six feet four inches tall and 210 pounds—he'd played college football, was covered with hair everywhere but on the top of his head, and was one of the strongest men I've ever met. After a few beers he could become dangerous. We left immediately for the villa where the platoon lived. It was a good way from the river, and I asked Dave if that created any problems. He said no because the platoon wasn't operating that much anyway.

Even before leaving Little Creek I had been well aware of this platoon's frustration. In-country three months, they'd seen little action and had had no real successes. I'd sent word ahead that I wanted some missions ready when I got there. I planned to get the guys in the field as soon as possible to see what I had. Though I had put them through predeployment training, that wasn't the same as fighting with them. On the way to the villa, Dave told me he had set up an operation for the next night.

When we got to the villa, I saw one reason they hadn't spent much time in the field. The place was a palace compared with what we'd had in Binh Thuy. That night, in a club attached to the villa, they held a going-away party for Dick Anderson. They had a blast drinking his good-bye. I stayed in the background—it was Dick's party—but I spent a lot of time talking to the guys.

One of them was Chuck Newell, the leading petty officer. He'd been one of my instructors in UDT/SEAL basic training and had later served with me in UDT-22, so we were old friends. "What the hell are you doing back over here so soon?"

"My job."

"You're already a hero. You got the Silver Star and a Purple Heart on the same op and a Bronze Star for all the other shit you did."

"I'm no hero. I just want to get back in action because that's what I like. I'm lucky enough to be getting paid for it."

This conversation told me the platoon was apprehensive about me: they knew about my first tour and knew that I wasn't going to let them sit around in the villa drinking beer. Getting in the field as soon as possible was definitely the best thing to do.

The next day, Dave Purselle gave me a brief on the operation for that night. Did I want him to run it, so I could see what they were doing without worrying about command functions? I told him no. I really wanted to see how the platoon would act under fire. Also, I wanted to see how *I'd* act under fire for the first time since I'd been shot. I wasn't really concerned, but I knew the platoon was worried about me because my left hand was still in a "mobility device" to help it recover from the wound.

The mission was simple. We were going to search a suspected VC hootch area and set an ambush on a canal that was supposedly getting heavy VC use. The place seemed like one I'd have picked for a platoon's first operation in-country, just off the main river on a narrow canal with good cover. To me this spoke volumes about the platoon's experience and confidence.

We inserted by boat, patrolled to the hootch area, where we found nothing, and moved on to the ambush site. After two hours there I began to think it was a bust. I could see torches moving about on the other side of the canal—but, as I explained to the guys, farmers out in the rice paddies were trying to jacklight frogs. The torches were not a sign of sinister doings by the VC. I decided to call it a night for the ambush and do some "practice patrolling" inland.

As we set off, we heard a sampan somewhere back up the canal, coming toward us. I moved the platoon back into the ambush position but told them not to fire until I did; I didn't want to kill some fisherman breaking curfew, even though we were in a free-fire zone.

As the sampan approached the river, I could see two people with weapons, hunkered down. I cut loose with my M-16. The two VC disintegrated under withering fire from the platoon—twelve SEALs on full automatic are a fearsome sight. We did such a good job that we sank the sampan before I could get them to cease fire. Two of my men jumped into the canal in an attempt to retrieve whatever they could, but there was nothing left to retrieve. We found punji stakes floating where the sampan had been, so I surmised the two VC had been on their way to build punji pits for unsuspecting American boys.

We had partly accomplished my objectives for the night. We hadn't been shot at, but at least we had done some killing and I had seen the platoon in action. More important, they had seen themselves in action. I later learned it was the first time they had killed anyone, and they were happy as hell to have had the chance. All in all, it was an okay night. I had seen some "procedural" things I didn't like, but those would be easy to correct. What I did like was the way these men reacted to the hit—they had been aggressive, and they seemed to like it. I felt much better. My hand hadn't bothered me, and it was great to be leading a group of SEALs in combat again.

* * *

One of the reasons the platoon had seen little action was that Vinh Long was not a target-rich environment. As it turned out, Dick Marcinko's platoon was about to leave Binh Thuy to be replaced by a SEAL One platoon. Hearing of this, I started politicking with Bill Early in Saigon. He convinced higher headquarters that U.S. interests in Vietnam would be best served if I were to move my platoon to Binh Thuy instead. I knew the Binh Thuy area, and I also knew it encompassed more turf than Vinh Long. It included all the area described by the Bassac River, the South China Sea, the Gulf of Thailand, and the Cambodian border. In other words, it was huge. And it contained a lot of bad guys.

On June 6, 1968, we arrived in Binh Thuy. The move was uneventful and the turnover with Dick's platoon was equally so. They'd had some great operations, particularly during the Tet Offensive, when they had been very active in Chau Doc. It turned out that the platoon had been a lot more active than Dick. When his assistant showed me a compilation of their operations, I was surprised to see that Dick had been on only about a tenth of them. I asked and his assistant confirmed it. Seems Dick spent a lot of time coordinating and setting up operations that others in his platoon ran. He was ahead of his time, commanding from the rear. I later found out that Dick, having lost one of his men, had been deeply affected by the violence of the operations in Chau Doc. Apparently, he led only a few operations after Tet, for one of which he was awarded the Silver Star.

Dick admitted to me later, over a few beers, that he had written his own award recommendation for the Silver Star. I'm sure he deserved it. The recommendation had to be approved by higher authority, and at least two witnesses had to testify to his actions. Still, I didn't like this business of starting the recommendation yourself. True, some of the officers on the CTF-116 staff were doing the same thing. But in SEAL Team Two, you didn't write up your own awards for heroism. Dick was more politically astute than the rest of us SEAL Two officers. He knew that down the road the number of medals collected during Vietnam would pay dividends for promotion. The rest of us weren't thinking about our careers, just trying to do the job at hand. At that time I had no concern about getting promoted—hell, I was doing exactly what I wanted to do.

Some things had changed in Vietnam since my first tour. Making the rounds of the subsectors, I learned that as a result of the Tet Offensive, North Vietnamese Army (NVA) units were operating south of the Bassac River. There seemed to be more bad guys than when I'd left, and they were more aggressive. I also noticed that their activity had moved farther away from the main river. Except for crossings, large units were seldom seen near the Bassac. We'd have to go farther inland to get to the areas they considered safe. Except for the fact we didn't target innocent civilians, we did in fact employ "terrorist" tactics on the VC and NVA—we terrorized them in their safe havens.

I also found out that the VC and the NVA knew who SEALs were now—because we were making their lives difficult. When I got to Binh Thuy I heard a rumor that the VC high command (COSVN) had put a price on the heads of what they called "the men with green faces." I was flattered. This was a sure sign we were hurting them. I went to the IV Corps NILO to see if there was any truth to the rumor. He was surprised I hadn't heard. He said the COSVN was offering the equivalent of $10,000 for any SEAL officer captured. The bounty went down to about $8,000 for a captured enlisted man, and any SEAL was worth about $5,000 dead. Was this true? Who knows? No SEAL was ever captured, and we brought all of our dead back with us.

The bounty talk changed how we went on liberty, but not much else. Can Tho, the largest city in the Mekong Delta, was a good place to go for a decent meal. I just made sure we didn't set any patterns. No insignia marked the jungle green fatigues we wore when not in the field. I didn't allow the troops to wear cammies except on operations. Out of cammies, we blended well with the rest of the Navy guys. Usually we wore civilian clothes to Can Tho. And though an edict had come out forbidding U.S. military personnel from carrying concealed weapons, I carried a concealed .38-caliber revolver in a shoulder harness whenever I left the base. I ordered the troops to do the same every time they went off base in civilian clothes. The ban on concealed weapons was a stupid regulation, probably started by some Saigon bureaucrat. It made no sense in a war zone.

Also new since my first tour was the full establishment of the Provincial Reconnaissance Units (PRUs). The "Phoenix" program, established to attack the Viet Cong infrastructure and just getting started when I had left in June 1967, was now pushing ahead and achieving great success in the Mekong Delta. The action arm of the program, the PRUs, were being "advised" by SEAL enlisted. Each province in the delta had its own PRU, and with the exception of the one at Chau Doc, they were advised by SEALs. Most SEAL platoon commanders worked closely with PRUs in their operation areas—I was no dummy, I did too. The PRUs were for the most part former VC who had decided life was better on the other side. They knew what was happening in their area, and they always had more information than they could act on, so we often did operations they couldn't.

Because PRU advisers got lonely, being the only Americans in their units, I allowed each of my guys to go to a province for two weeks to work with the PRUs. It was all done unofficially, but it was good for us and the PRUs. Our guys came back with a wealth of information, and the PRU adviser had company. Another bennie for the PRUs was that we had priority access to the Navy helicopter gunships (Seawolves) attached to CTF-116. When we called, they came fast and they were effective. When we operated in squad-sized strength with the PRUs they had that access as well, and it enabled them to take more risks.

However, because there were so many more NVA troops in the delta, I began to run a lot of platoon-sized operations. Not that we often had a full platoon—but ten shooters were better than six. We needed firepower. The enemy's situation had changed, but our self-proclaimed mission remained the same: to kill VC and disrupt their operations wherever and whenever we could. My old operating area was a more target-rich environment than it had been a year before. It was time to kick ass again.

12

ATTACK AT DAWN: DUNG ISLAND

Not long after we relocated to Binh Thuy, the action picked up. I found out through one of our intelligence networks that the VC leadership in Ba Xuyen Province was planning a high-level meeting on Cu Lao Dung, an island near the mouth of the Bassac River. The VC cadres ran the show. They "recruited" people for their main force units by terrorizing the Vietnamese villagers, threatening to kill relatives unless the people joined. And to establish "credibility," they often carried out their threats. Getting rid of the VC cadres was the key to success in the delta.

I contacted the Seawolf detachment at Binh Thuy, and we set up a reconnaissance flight. Seawolves normally patrolled all up and down the Bassac supporting the PBRs, so the flight over my prospective OPAREA wouldn't sound any VC alarms.

We left Binh Thuy in two helos (the normal flight configuration) in midafternoon so I could see the area in daylight and after dark. Flying down the Bassac, I was again struck by the raw beauty of the river and the surrounding delta. The Bassac was like a freeway to the Vietnamese. There were precious few good roads in the Mekong Delta, and most of the people couldn't afford cars or trucks anyway, so they used the river and canal systems. Dung Island was at the mouth of the Bassac, about eighty miles from Binh Thuy. The trip took about an hour and a half flying low and slow.

Dung Island, really a close group of three islands separated by canals, was a notorious VC stronghold, strategically situated between the Long Tuan Secret Zone to the north and the Ba Xuyen Secret Zone to the south. Dung Island was on the route the NVA forces took as they infiltrated out of the U Minh Forest, across the Mekong Delta, to the region around Saigon. It was, in effect, an extension of the famous Ho Chi Minh Trail.

As we neared the island complex, I began recognizing landmarks from previous visits during my first tour. Just after we relocated to Binh Thuy, we destroyed a rice processing plant and captured an eighty-foot junk, which we turned over to the local Vietnamese River Assault Group to use against the VC. In fact, our target this time was not far from the rice factory, which I'm sure the VC restored a few days after we did our damage. That was the nature of the war.

I told the pilot to fly along the south side of Dung Island, looking for evidence of a large VC presence. As at all crossing points on the river, the VC kept only a small group of caretaker soldiers on the island to maintain the hootches and bunkers that would serve as rest areas for the NVA moving north. As we flew, some ambitious VC shooter decided to take a few potshots at us with his rifle. We ignored him. The VC kept .51-caliber antiaircraft guns on the island, and he could have been baiting us.

As we turned north, just before reaching the easternmost part of the island, our prospective operating area started to come into view. Dung Island was densely wooded, with far fewer paddies than most areas in the delta and some of the densest canopy outside the mangrove swamps. On the rice mill operation, we had inserted in an area that, from the air, looked devoid of people. Ten meters off the river we had encountered a cement sidewalk leading through a hamlet that was completely invisible from 1,200 feet up. Near the sidewalk we saw two "hootches" that were two stories high and would have looked perfectly natural in southern California. It was a very interesting area, and I was looking forward to getting back.

As we flew over the target area, I noticed some large hootches—

possibly a rest area, if the size of the complex was a clue. It was tucked between two large canals. Our best bet would be to insert to the northwest, patrol until we reached one of the lesser canals running toward the hootch complex, and take the canal the rest of the way to the target. We'd have to cross three large, open areas, but I wasn't too worried since we would be moving at night.

We flew over the area only once, so as not to attract attention. The reconnaissance was also helpful to the Seawolf crews, whom I'd use on the operation. As we broke away from the island, another VC gunner started shooting at us, this one with an automatic weapon. I let the birds attack him, because to ignore fire from an automatic would have been abnormal behavior for a Seawolf patrol. They made a couple of passes, shooting up the trees. Then we headed southeast to the subsector headquarters to clear our operation. As usual, the advisers said, "Have at it and good luck." After refueling at Soc Trang airfield, we headed home.

As we flew over one of the VC-controlled islands in the Bassac on our way back to Binh Thuy, the helo suddenly lost RPM. An "unpowered" helicopter has the glide path of a rock. Fortunately, having the wings overhead allows the pilot to "autorotate." This is an emergency procedure for landing a helo when the engine quits. To do it right, the pilot needs as much altitude as possible. We were at about 200 feet—way too low. The pilot jerked back on the collective (a control lever) to give the blades as much lift as possible, and we started up. The problem is, when you pull collective without power, the blades tend to slow down considerably. We got to about 800 feet and, just before we stalled, he killed the collective. We started falling fast, but the blades, free to spin, began to turn. That was the trick: you got the blades turning fast, so that when you pulled collective again, at about fifty feet, you could generate enough lift to bring the bird to its minimum rate of descent just as it hit the ground. This was not a challenge for a Seawolf pilot if he started the process at 1,200 feet. But with only 800 feet we hit the ground with a distinct thud. My seat collapsed and one of the gunners was thrown partly out of the bird. The other helo kept circling overhead, providing eyes and cover.

I was out of the bird as soon as it hit. We set up security while the crew chief tried to sort out the problem. All was quiet.

The second important trick in auto-rotating is to find a dry, level place to land. Again, not hard to do when you start at 1,200 feet in daylight. If we had landed in a flooded rice paddy we would have had a hard time breaking the suction to fly out, but somehow our pilot had managed to find a nice dry spot in the dark from 200 feet. As it was, the Gormly luck held (I'd been through this before, on my first tour), the crew fixed the problem, and we lifted off smartly about ten minutes later.

The next morning, I held a briefing for the troops. We all massaged the plan, making some good changes based on recommendations from the troops. Given the expected number of VC and the area where we were going, I opted to take the entire platoon, minus two guys I'd sent off to work with one of the PRUs. In all, there would be ten of us, plus a National Policeman who knew the area. I told them to be ready to leave by nine the following morning.

The next day we boarded our slow but heavily armored LCPL and headed downriver. Long boat rides were a pain, but I wanted the troops to be well rested. There's no sleep like the sleep you get on a boat moving slowly downstream. Just after dark, about five miles northwest of Dung Island, we rendezvoused with our Light SEAL Support Craft (LSSC). (LSSCs had replaced STABs as our primary insertion boats soon after we got to Binh Thuy.) The LSSC had traveled independently from Binh Thuy, picking up our policeman on the way. I had already contacted the PBRs patrolling in the area; they came alongside to get briefed, so they'd know where we were and what to do if we got into more shit than we could handle. The Seawolf fire team, which had already relocated to Soc Trang Airfield, would go on alert when I radioed them we were about to land. All forces were in place, We were ready to go kick ass.

With the sky cloudy and the moon in its fourth quarter, the night was dark—almost perfect for operating. We made our last-minute preparations and boarded the LSSC. Soon Dung Island came up on the boat radar, and I could see the canal mouth I had picked as a reference point. I wanted to insert at a spot northwest of a large canal that marked the northern boundary of our target. To extract us, the LSSC would come to the other end of the canal. Unless I really needed them, I didn't want to bring the LCPL or the PBRs into the canal. Though it was big enough for them to navigate, it was not big enough to allow the boats to stay out of range if we were taking fire from heavy weapons. Also, the canal was off-limits for the PBRs at that time (too dangerous), though I knew if we needed them, they'd be in there in a flash.

The LSSC eased into the insertion point about 0200. I looked through my night-vision device, but because the foliage was so thick I couldn't see much. There seemed to be no hootches in the area, and it was quiet. The boat nosed into the brush overhanging the riverbank, and we slipped silently off the bow two by two.

Insertions always got our adrenaline pumping. No matter how quiet it seemed, we all expected to get hit as soon as we stepped off the boat. As I've said, our SOP once we were off the boat was to get inland about ten meters, set up a semicircular perimeter facing away from the river, and wait while the boat backed out as quietly as possible. At about that point, your adrenaline starts to wear off, and most people have an overwhelming urge to "clear bilges." I factored that into the patrol plan: as we sat in the perimeter, those who heard the call of nature dropped their cammie pants and heeded it. Among other things, this helped ensure that the next adrenaline kick, the one that came as we reached the objective, would not produce gas expulsions that could tip off the enemy to our whereabouts.

At night, smell and hearing are your two most useful senses. The technicians testing my hearing during my annual dive physical used to accuse me of cheating. It turns out I have the hearing range of a dog. I can hear tones well above and below the frequencies audible to the average person. Maybe it's nature's way of compensating for my astigmatism. The Navy doesn't care how well you can smell and doesn't test for it, but on operations I could easily smell things that indicated Vietnamese activity. Other SEALs developed similar acuity. Hearing and smelling could keep you alive.

The VC used the same senses, of course, though for some reason their hearing was never impressive, and their eyesight was notoriously poor—probably a diet thing. But they could smell, and we accounted for that. We never used deodorant before an operation, and we applied mosquito repellent only as a last resort. Many of our guys consumed copious amounts of the famous Vietnamese condiment *nuoc mam,* a sauce made from fermented fish oil. The Vietnamese put it on all their food and, like garlic, it permeates the body. You could smell a *nuoc mam* factory ten miles downwind.

We sat in our perimeter for about twenty minutes, listening for activity around us; then I gave the word to move out. Dick Cyrus was my point man. In the field, he was a lot like my old point man Charlie Bump. Five nine, weighing about 150 pounds, he had dark brown hair and a smirk that was born of his natural cockiness. He was a super operator, another guy who couldn't get enough time in the field. He'd have been out every night if he could. Dick was from Norfolk, Virginia, and I used to tell him he was the second-best SEAL from the Tidewater area (I was the only other one). I was second in line, with the National Police officer right behind me. Next in line behind the cop was my radioman, Clay Grady, carrying a PRC-25 and an M-16. I always kept the radioman near me in case we got in trouble, since I usually ended up directing helo fire if we needed it. At about five feet ten inches tall and 190 pounds, Clay was a very solid guy, but so low-key you had to keep looking to be sure he was there. The rest of the men spread out behind in a file, as far apart as visibility would allow. SOP was not to lose sight of the man in front of you. Ken McDonald brought up the rear with his M-60 machine gun. Ken was a squad-leading petty officer, a very good operator and a quiet man. The rest of us carried M-16 variants, M-79 grenade launchers, or the over-and-under M-16–40mm grenade launcher known as the XM-148.

We crossed two rice paddies and their boundary tree lines without incident. Despite conventional wisdom to the contrary, many SEALs preferred to travel in the middle of rice paddies. People, dogs, and geese lived in tree lines, and it was unusual to go any distance through the trees without encountering one or all of the three.

We moved quickly through the paddies and very cautiously through the two tree lines we had to penetrate. As I've mentioned, Vietnamese always leave a candle burning in their hootches overnight while they sleep. I think it's to keep evil spirits away. The candles helped us to avoid populated areas; then, when we got to our objective, the candles would help us find the hootches. In a sense, we were the evil spirits, being drawn to the candle light.

As we passed through the tree lines, we could hear sleep sounds in the hootches we passed. Hacking and coughing were the norm. The Vietnamese made so much noise in their sleep, we could have joined the symphony unnoticed. Yet if we banged a rifle barrel against an ammunition pouch, they would wake up in an instant.

Past the second tree line I turned the patrol to enter the larger canal that would take us to the target area. We moved along the bank, as usual. We were in a tidal region near the South China Sea, where tidal ranges could run six to ten feet. You might enter a canal at low tide with the canal bank five feet over your head, and find yourself unable to move in the incredible delta mud. Three hours later you could be swimming along, even with the bank. Tonight, conditions were good. We were moving on an ebb tide. Wading and swimming to the objective, we hugged the shadows of the brush above us. We all wore the standard UDT life vest, partly inflated to compensate for the weight of the equipment we carried. All remained quiet. The only noise was the sucking of the mud as the water receded around us.

I began to pick up the smells of the target area about 0430. I wanted to hit the target at first light, about 0515, and hold reveille on the bad guys. About a hundred meters from the target, I stopped the patrol. No noise from the hootches or anywhere above us along the canal bank. Dick and I moved slowly forward to reconnoiter. Dick had great operational sense. He knew when to push and when to back off; you couldn't teach that.

We slipped through the water until we were right outside the hootch area. It was still night, and there was almost no illumination. We listened.

Just above me was what looked like a short pier. I had moved under it without really seeing it. Whatever it was, it offered good cover.

Then I heard someone walking toward us. I squeezed Dick's shoulder. He bobbed his head, acknowledging he'd heard the movement too. We hunkered down in the water and waited to see what was going to happen. Whoever it was approached along the canal bank. We'd seen no sign of any sentries, but that wasn't unusual in our operations. We usually went into areas where the VC felt so secure they didn't post sentries. Still, I wasn't sure about whoever was approaching. Had we made some noise apart from the normal night noise? I was sure we hadn't. Had one of the men behind me made a noise I couldn't hear in the water?

All these things went through my mind as the person got nearer. It appeared he was heading right for us. Now we couldn't move—he'd see or hear us. I slipped my knife from its sheath at the top of my equipment harness. Dick did the same. We didn't need to talk. We'd rehearsed the procedure. Whoever was closest to the person grabbed, and the other one killed. But we weren't in the best position to do that, so I wanted to remain undetected. No matter what you see in the movies, a silent knife kill requires perfect positioning: a quick slash of the vocal cords followed by a perfect knife strike in the upper spine. Even then the victim may gurgle loudly enough to disturb sleepers through the ambient night sounds. I didn't want to try a knife kill unless we absolutely had to.

The person moved right onto the "pier." I could no longer see him, and he couldn't see us, so I relaxed a little. I heard what sounded like rustling clothes and heavy breathing. What the hell was he doing? It reminded me of the time I had slipped into a hootch and heard, before I saw, some VC screwing his wife. Listening intently, I heard a loud plop, and water splashed my face. The plop was quickly followed by a loud fart.

The structure above us wasn't a boat slip, it was a crapper, and I was right in the line of fire. In front of me, Dick was struggling not to laugh, while all I could do was keep from looking up and hope for the best. After an eternity, the VC got up and left.

Dick and I moved farther down the canal to see if we could get a look at the target. We saw no activity and heard nothing other than our friend getting resettled in his rack. In front were two hootches, larger than the standard family hootch, and behind them two more, slightly smaller. There were probably more behind those, but we couldn't see. Our friend had gone into one of those directly in front of us. It was starting to get light. I left Dick in place and slipped through the water back to the rest of the platoon.

The cop was certain the two larger hootches housed the VC we were after. We moved ahead to where Dick was, and prepared to get out of the canal. We had to move slowly and let the water drain out of our gear.

I didn't have to go over the plan or make any changes: things were about as we had expected. My objective on this mission, in addition to killing bad guys, was to take prisoners. If our intelligence was close to being correct, we should be able to snatch someone fairly high up in the local VC infrastructure.

I found it was better to take VC prisoners and interrogate them than to kill them in a firefight. We usually got information upon which we built future missions, and occasionally we could turn a guy and have him lead us to his former comrades. This was risky, but we kept informers isolated until we used them, and often, we could act so fast, his comrades hadn't yet changed their routine. My policy was to keep the "turnee" just in front of me on the patrol, and at the slightest hint he was leading us into a trap he was history.

We climbed silently out of the water and stayed prone while Ed Bowen and Doc O'Bryan moved to cover our rear. Quartermaster Third Class E. C. "Ed" Bowen was, without a doubt, one of the best operators I've been in the field with. Quiet and wiry, under fire he was cooler than cool. He was my main Stoner man. He slept with his machine gun, as most successful Stoner men did in those days. And he did talk—on full automatic.

Hospital Corpsman First Class Charles "Doc" O'Bryan was our medic, but he wasn't a SEAL, since in those days medics were not allowed to go through UDT basic training. Our corpsmen were some of our best operators, and they had to kill in self-defense all the time. Doc O'Bryan was great in the field, but when I got to the platoon he was badly out of shape: at about six feet tall, he weighed over 220, and too much of that was fat. On one of our first missions I threatened to leave him behind if he didn't keep up with the platoon. He quit smoking and got in shape, and we never had another problem.

Slowly, the men took their positions. Ed and Doc would stay to our left and right rear, moving with us as we went to the hootches. The rest of us broke into two-man teams for the hootch entries. Dick and I headed for the largest of the first two. The other men moved quickly to the rest. Ed and Doc came up just in front of Dick and me, so they had clear fields of fire over the rest of the complex.

At the front entrance of our target, I could hear snoring within. Perfect. As each entry team approached its assigned target, I heard no other sounds. I burst through the entrance and shifted left. Dick was immediately behind me, moving right. Nothing stirred. Sleeping pallets were laid out, but no one was in them. Where had the snorer gone? The noise must have been coming from the hootch just behind ours. Dick and I were looking at each other when I heard a commotion from that other hootch. One of my guys yelled, "Lai dai" ("Stop, come here"). Dick and I charged back outside. As I cleared the doorway, I heard an AK-47 open up on full automatic, followed immediately by an M-16 on single-shot fire. I thought, "Oh shit, here we go." So much for taking prisoners.

Two VC carrying weapons ran out of one of the rear hootches, about twenty-five meters away. As they stopped to fire, I raised my M-16 and got them in my sights just in time to see them nearly cut in half by some of my men. I yelled for the guys to start sweeping the complex. Ed was at five o'clock behind me, about five meters away, but Doc had gone just behind the hootch at my one o'clock, about ten meters away—not where he was supposed to be. I later found out he had moved up because he couldn't see the hootches well enough from where I'd told him to go—good call on his part.

As I started down the hootch line, a VC broke through the wall of the hootch to the right of Doc and threw something at him, hitting him on the left cheek. Doc went down like he'd been hit with a sledgehammer. I saw no weapons in the gook's hands as he headed blindly toward me.

Things started moving in slow motion. I saw what had hit Doc—an M-26 fragmentation grenade. After ricocheting off Doc, it was now rolling toward me. I kicked the grenade toward the hootch Dick and I had just searched. For some reason, I dismissed the grenade as a threat. Instead I concentrated on the guy, who was racing toward me, unarmed. I turned to butt-stroke him with my M-16—I hadn't given up on taking prisoners. Dick was moving toward Doc at my ten o'clock. When the VC was three meters from me, I could see he was scared and running on automatic. Thinking, "This is going to be easy," I swung my right arm forward, aiming the butt of my rifle directly at his face.

The guy stopped dead in his tracks. At the same moment, I heard Ed's Stoner open up. It happened so fast I almost fell on my face as the butt of my M-16 passed where the VC's chin should have been. Ed had taken him right out from under me. I yelled, "Holy shit, Ed, what the hell are you doing?" I didn't expect an answer, and I didn't get one. He, Dick, and I ran forward, toward the firefight.

The fight was over almost as fast as it had begun. I reached Chuck Newell just as he called, "Cease fire." He'd set security to our front, and I turned to assess the situation. Doc was on his feet, taking over rear security. Ed moved back and did the same. The area was as quiet as it had been when we got there. I decided we owned the turf and told Chuck to have the men start searching to see what we could find. We found and captured four men hiding in the hootches.

Chuck and Ken McDonald had killed three guys running from the last hootch in line, one of whom had had his AK-47, on full automatic, firing over his shoulder as he ran. Then they took some fire from the tree line behind the hootches. Apparently there had been a sentry, but he had been stationed to the rear of the complex.

The cop said an old woman they found in one of the other hootches told him the meeting had been held late the night before, but that all participants had spent the night in the complex. The cadre I was after had been sleeping in the hootch Dick and I entered. She didn't know where he was now. He had probably gotten up early and left; maybe he was the guy who'd almost dumped on me. The woman also told the cop that there was a large group of soldiers in a hamlet about 500 meters to our rear. The cop was scared and said we ought to pull out.

I told Chuck to continue the search, then called Clay over, got on the radio, and told the boat officer on the LCPL to scramble our Seawolves. They'd have been pissed if I hadn't gotten them overhead, and if the woman had told the truth, we might need them.

I also told the boat officer to send the LSSC downriver and position it well northeast of our extraction point—closer but not so close it would give away my intentions to any VC force on the small island. Then I sent Ed and Doc back to the canal to establish security on our intended line of withdrawal. Doc said he was okay, though he had a huge welt on his left cheek, and the left side of his face was so swollen he looked as if he'd just gone a few rounds with Muhammad Ali. Chuck told me the grenade that hit Doc was a dud. The pin had been pulled, but it didn't detonate—luck. They'd found four dead VC, the three he and Ken had greased and the one Ed had nailed. The hootch search had revealed two weapons, some M-26 grenades, several containers full of 7.62 short ammo, and various documents. The cop took a quick look at those and found that they were lists of supplies, weapons, and people. He thought they might also reveal the location of the matériel. Stuffing the documents in his butt pack, Chuck allowed as how we'd been in the complex for about thirty minutes and it might be time to move out. Clay told me the Seawolf leader had checked in on our net; the helos were about ten minutes away. I gave the word to move out.

Dick and I went up to the canal, while Chuck went back to get Ken. It was now daylight; we crossed the small canal running north beside the complex and turned left toward the main river. There was no trail, but moving just inside the canal bank proved easy and it gave us cover. When the Seawolves came overhead, I called them to ask what they saw behind us. The team leader said it was all clear, but they'd keep looking. I told them to stay over the hootch complex. I didn't want them over us because we couldn't hear a thing through the noise of their rotating blades.

I heard the swoosh of rockets leaving one of the birds, and the Seawolf team leader came up on the radio to tell us they had spotted movement in the trees about 300 meters behind the hootch complex. So the old woman had probably been telling the truth about the proximity of the enemy troops. With the helos around, though, I wasn't worried.

We were about 200 meters from the river when Dick stopped us. There were some irrigation ditches ahead, and he wanted to take a look before we crossed. I told him to go ahead, but I kept the patrol moving slowly forward. When Dick gave me the all-clear, we picked up the pace.

We'd crossed three ditches and were about fifty meters from the river when I heard an M-16 fire just behind me. I turned to see the cop pointing excitedly down at the dike by the last ditch. A bloody foot poked out from under the dike: one of our guys had shot a VC hiding in a concealed bunker. I told Clay to get the Seawolves overhead, and Chuck dragged the guy out of the bunker, pulling him to his feet in front of us. The VC never uttered a sound. His left foot had been nearly blown away, but he was in shock.

Doc threw him on the ground and started doing corpsman magic. Our corpsmen never ceased to amaze me. When someone got wounded, they seemed to go into overdrive. Doc had the guy patched up in thirty seconds, gave him a shot of morphine, and pronounced him fit for travel. Chuck held the VC's arms in front of him, cuffed him with plastic "tie-ties," then handed his CAR-15 to Doc and threw the VC over his shoulder in a fireman's carry. We found three more males hiding in the bunker, took them into custody, and headed for the river.

We reached the extraction point five minutes later. I set a perimeter and told Clay to get the LSSC over to pick us up. We sat there looking at our prisoners, and I wondered if the rest of the VC nearby would be stupid enough to follow us with a Seawolf fire team overhead and our little battleship now about 200 meters offshore. They weren't.

I was the last to board the LSSC, just after Ken. I always boarded after everyone else, probably out of some misplaced macho desire to be the last off the beach.

The wounded prisoner, accompanied by Chuck, the cop, and one more man, went by LSSC to the Vietnamese hospital in Can Tho. I told Chuck not to turn the guy over to the National Police until after we'd had a chance to interrogate him back in Binh Thuy.

Next order of business: I called Ed over. "What were you thinking when you cut loose on that guy?"

"Protecting your ass, boss." He had simply reacted—he'd seen the guy throw a grenade and hit Doc, and he figured the best thing to do was kill him before he got to me. I wasn't about to argue with that logic.

"Good job, Ed, but next time try to shoot a little sooner."

I reflected on what we'd accomplished. We'd done well, reaching the objective without being detected. The men had been aggressive and decisive. We'd killed four VC, captured eight, policed up a few weapons and some documents, and not gotten anyone seriously hurt. Doc O'Bryan's pride hurt more than his face, although we later learned the grenade had fractured his left cheekbone. I expected we'd get some useful intelligence from the prisoners. The troops were feeling good, and that was very important to me. All in all, a satisfying operation.

13

GOT THEM RIGHT WHERE WE WANT THEM: BAC LIEU

Toward the end of June 1968 I started picking up reports that the enemy was planning another large operation near Saigon. There seemed to be an increase in troop traffic on the Ho Chi Minh Trail. Since the Tet Offensive had depleted the VC of anything larger than company-sized units, they needed to bring regular NVA troops from the North in order to launch a large operation. We'd been picking off VC along the coastal "Secret Zones," and I figured we ought to do something to welcome the NVA to our part of the delta.

I flew southeast from Binh Thuy to Bac Lieu, where the PRU adviser was Gary Gallagher, a West Coast SEAL I had met on my way over in May. Gary met me at the helo pad and took me to his headquarters for a situation brief.

When he finished, I said, "Gary, I want to go someplace and do something that'll really screw the VC."

Bac Lieu Province, being situated just north of the U Minh Forest, was a major assembly area for units and logistics that had infiltrated from North Vietnam. There were large rest camps containing hospitals where troops recovered from their long journey and got ready to fight in the Saigon area.

"No problem," Gary replied. "I've got plenty of targets. In fact, I've got a perfect place for you guys, but you're going to need slicks."

He pointed out the area on his map. The only way to reach it was by helicopter, because the bad guys had a lock on all land and water communication.

I went back to Binh Thuy and started the ball rolling. My plan was for an extended reconnaissance-ambush. We'd lay up on the large canal that serviced the biggest camp in Bac Lieu, survey the situation for a day, pick a target of opportunity, hit it, and get out. I'd insert by helo at last light (the Army couldn't fly too well at night without using landing lights).

We moved to the LST at the mouth of the Bassac River and prepared to go the following day. I wanted the guys to get a good "shipboard" meal before we left because it might be the last time they'd eat well for a few days. Two Army helicopters arrived early in the morning, and I went over the plan with the pilots. For fire support, I would use the Seawolf Light Helo Fire Team stationed on the LST. I hadn't worked with them before, but they had a good reputation. One helo, I was told, was flown by John Abrams, the nephew of General Creighton Abrams, who had recently relieved General William Westmoreland as Commander, U.S. Forces Vietnam. John Abrams's copilot was a Cuban expatriate, a Bay of Pigs veteran who liked to fight.

We launched the helos from the LST in time to land at last light. The Seawolves accompanied us in case we got into a fight as soon as we touched down. Helo insertions were as hairy as boat insertions, particularly since we'd be landing in an open rice paddy. The two Seawolf gunships flying low over the area would keep enemy heads down, I hoped, long enough for us to get out of the slicks and go to ground near a dike. To confuse the enemy, I had the slicks and the Seawolves do dummy landings in two other rice paddies, a thousand or two meters away. This sort of deception had worked in the past.

Our destination was easy to recognize from the air—or so I'd thought, on the basis of an air recon on the way back from Bac Lieu. The target area was at the confluence of the major canal and a smaller canal running from the east, five canals in from the Bassac. All we had to do was count canals and land between the fifth and sixth. Both I and the lead pilot miscounted, though: we got out between the sixth and seventh canals. Fortunately, this turned out not to matter. It was a really target-rich environment.

With the helos hovering about three feet over the rice paddy, we jumped out, raced to a dike, and set security, waiting for possible fire from the tree line a thousand meters to our rear. I sent two of the men crawling to the edge of the small tree line next to the canal. I needed them forward in case the VC sent someone to investigate from the base camp across the canal. I thought we'd gotten in undetected, but you never knew.

Just after we hit the ground, darkness descended like a curtain. Here in the middle of the Mekong Delta, there were no lights, and the moon had not yet risen. I kept the rest of the platoon by the dike while Clay Grady got on the radio to Gary at Bac Lieu and the TOC on the LST. Once we got good communications with both locations, I moved the platoon to the main canal and formed a perimeter. Dick Cyrus and I headed north along the canal, looking for a good place to stay for the next thirty-six hours.

We found a small, apparently abandoned hootch about ten meters from the canal, partially hidden in a grove of low trees and brush. Alert for any sign of enemy activity, we entered it and looked around. There was no sign of habitation, so I sent Dick back to get the rest of the patrol. I'd be rotating the guys on ambush; the hootch offered good concealment and a place to catch a few winks. We moved in and set up, expecting to be there for a while.

I deployed the platoon by squad in two locations about fifty meters apart on either side of the hootch. The squads would handle their own rotations. We set a perimeter of Claymore mines to our rear, toward the rice paddies.

At first light, I was in the hootch with Clay Grady, Andy Hayden, and Dick Cyrus. Andy manned the doorway, looking through binoculars at the tree line a thousand meters away. Suddenly he said, "Hey, boss, look at this." He handed me the binoculars. "Look at that tall tree in the tree line behind us." It was twenty-five meters taller than any tree around it. "Do you see it?"

"Yeah, I got it."

He told me to look at the top. I moved the binoculars slowly up the trunk. In the foliage at the very top of the tree was a guy perched precariously on a branch. He had a set of binoculars to his eyes, and he was looking right at us. I had to resist the impulse to wave. He stayed in the tree another fifteen minutes, then disappeared. I was troubled, but did nothing more than pass the word to stay alert. There had been absolutely no traffic on the canal all night. I was beginning to wonder if we'd drawn a blank.

No sooner had that thought crossed my mind than Chuck Newell ran into the hootch and said the squad on the right flank had spotted three men in khaki uniforms headed our way. Two were carrying AK-47s and one had an M-79 grenade launcher, but they didn't appear to be on alert.

Chuck asked, "What do you want me to do?"

"Shoot 'em when they get to the edge of our ambush line." Off he went.

The men were more than likely doing a routine check of the area, but it was possible that our friend in the tree had reported seeing something strange by the canal and that these guys had been sent to check it out. We knew the VC communicated by VHF radio in this area, so we all got a little more alert.

I had gone outside the hootch for a better view when I heard the unmistakable *chung* of a round leaving an M-79 grenade launcher. A 40mm grenade exploded in the water in front of me. Another one followed. I figured the VC were reconnoitering us by fire; if, as they hoped, we returned fire, that would enable them to fix our position. I still wasn't convinced we'd been spotted—if we had been, I figured, they'd do more than just recon by fire. No mortar rounds were exploding in our midst. I told the men to hold their fire until the enemy got closer. This might be part of an NVA battalion. I got on the radio and told the LST to send the helos our way.

The next sound I heard was an M-16 on full automatic fire. Chuck had decided they were close enough and opened up. The next sight I saw was a khaki-clad figure literally running on the water toward the opposite canal bank. Rounds were hitting all around him, but he must have stayed on top of the water halfway across the canal. When he emerged on the other side he kept on running.

Our fire had told them our position. Suddenly we were taking heavy automatic fire from what seemed to be all directions. My guys shot back, but when the incoming rounds stopped, I yelled, "Cease fire." For a few minutes all was quiet. I knew it was the lull before the storm. I figured they were maneuvering to cut us off from the rice paddy.

I got on the radio and asked the status of the slicks and Seawolves; the ship reported they were right over the place they'd dropped us in. Andy Hayden spotted the four birds circling about 2,000 meters north of us, which was how I learned that we were south of where we wanted to be. We were right across the canal from the large camp, and we were probably surrounded. As my old squad chief Jess Tolison used to say, "We had them right where we wanted them." Rounds started coming in again from all directions.

I radioed John Abrams; the helos immediately swung in our direction and started looking. Normally, to help them find us, we'd throw out a smoke grenade, the helo would tell us what color smoke they saw, and we would confirm it. (We didn't say the color first, because the enemy had been known to listen in on our frequencies and lure helos to them with smoke of the same color.) On this occasion, I didn't want to use any smoke—it would pinpoint our position for the bad guys as well as for our helos. Instead, Andy stood in the little clearing around our hootch and made himself conspicuous by waving a large water jar we'd found inside.

There wasn't room for the birds to set down where we were. I decided to go through the bushes to our right rear to the paddy, where we could be extracted. I passed the word that I was going to fire the Claymore mines, and we'd haul ass through the smoke and debris. I figured if anyone had penetrated from our rear, the Claymores would get their attention and, if not kill them, stun them and enable us to kill them as we headed toward the pickup point.

I yelled, "Fire in the hole!" and squeezed the firing device. There was a deafening explosion, and the bushes erupted in black smoke and debris. We charged. Either no one had been close by or the mines did the job, because we took no fire on the way to the paddy.

We quickly set up behind a dike; it shielded us on only one side, but there was no place that gave us all-around protection from the ever-increasing volume of incoming fire. I figured the slicks would come right down to pick us up, so all we had to do was hold on for a little while.

The Seawolves started a pattern around our position, putting M-60 minigun and 3.5 rocket fire into the suspected VC firing positions. The minigun put down a heavy stream of fire. As long as the Seawolves fired, the other guys lay low.

But the Seawolves couldn't fire continuously, and during the interval after the first firing run all hell broke loose. We came under increasingly intense fire from 360 degrees, with rounds smacking into the dike between Clay (who was carrying the radio) and me (who was talking on the radio). I was trying to convince the slick pilots that we had things under control on the ground and that they could come get us any time, but they weren't buying. Yet whenever we returned fire heavily, the other guys stopped shooting. For about twenty seconds out of every minute it got really quiet.

Then the rounds would come in again. And my guys would open up again. Ed Bowen firing his Stoner machine gun. Ken McDonald lobbing 40mm grenades toward the canal. Andy Hayden putting down heavy fire from his M-60 into the tree line a thousand meters behind us. The heaviest volume of incoming fire seemed to be originating from the tree line along the canal, so two men fired LAWs into the trees to keep the enemy down. The LAW, a very lightweight antitank rocket, had a shaped-charge warhead that I liked for punching through the caked mud of bunker fortifications. Fired into a tree line, it would explode as it hit the heavy foliage, scattering tree shrapnel. On previous missions LAWs had proven to be good "area" weapons. We used them almost like we'd use mortars.

I began to get concerned about our ammo status. We'd come in with a lot of bullets, but we were also expending a lot. I yelled for the guys to ease up and told the slicks to come down. There was a pregnant pause. They still weren't buying.

Then a Cuban-accented voice came on the air. Soto, the Bay of Pigs veteran, told the slicks' pilots they had two choices: go down to get us, and risk getting shot by the VC; or keep dawdling, and be certain of being shot down by the Seawolves. Both those pilots were also running low on ammo, and there was no way they were going to leave us on the ground while they went to get more.

The slicks killed collective and auto-rotated down. I watched as they hurtled through the air directly over our heads. The two Seawolves laid a fierce curtain of fire all around us. Rockets came screaming over our heads and exploded into the area by the hootch. The friendly fire was so heavy, I began to wonder if we'd survive it. Yet without that volume of fire, the enemy would probably shoot down the slicks as they landed. Pick your poison.

The slicks got to fifty feet and flared. Their rotating blades grabbed the air and kicked up a tremendous downdraft. Dust and debris from the dry rice paddy flew around the birds. They seemed to disappear, then hit the ground about ten meters to our right.

My squad put down covering fire as Chuck Newell's sprinted for one of the two helos. When the last feet disappeared into the bird, I yelled, "Go." Clay and I fired to our rear as we ran for the second bird. The two door gunners on both choppers were firing their M-60 machine guns toward the canal behind us—they must have spotted enemy movement there as they came down.

Clay reached the helo and threw himself in. I was right behind, dodging the fire from the gunner's M-60. The bird was already lifting off the ground as I dove headfirst through the door. As it hurtled forward, I landed half in and half out, and someone grabbed my shoulders to pull me the rest of the way in. I sat up in the door and resumed shooting. Clay squatted just behind me, firing his M-16 out the open door. Off we went, firing everything we had, rounds slapping the sides of the birds. That slick rose faster than any helo I'd ever been on. We kept firing until we were at 1,500 feet. Our door gunners didn't stop firing until they ran out of ammo.

Back at the LST, I thanked John and Soto and took the platoon below for debriefing. Our ammo inventory revealed that everyone but Clay and I had fired everything. I had three full magazines; Clay had two. And that was only because we'd been so busy with the radio. Good thing Soto made his pronouncement when he did.

After our adrenaline stopped pumping, we had a chance to evaluate what had happened. I told the troops we'd had a good mission. True, we'd jumped a much larger unit, been outgunned and surrounded, but we'd killed a few and gotten away with no casualties of our own. Plus, we'd accomplished two things: we'd rattled the gooks in their backyard, and we'd scared the shit out of ourselves. Actually, while we were in the firefight, none of us were scared. We were too busy fighting. We had taken on a large force of VC (or NVA) and fought our way out of a sticky situation. We were damn good.

I never learned the identity of the people we killed. Intelligence officers told me they were probably NVA regulars. Gary Gallagher told me later that he had gotten good information about our battle from some of the locals. Seems many new graves were being dug in that area the next day—more than enough for the four I knew we'd killed.

Gary was so excited by our success he took his PRUs into the area about a month later. Operating on more precise intelligence than we'd had, he captured a high-ranking VC leader. As his unit was leaving, they got into a fierce fight with a battalion of NVA regulars. Vastly outnumbered and without any helo gunship support, they fought a hasty retreat away from the enemy. Gary's PRU chief wanted to kill their wounded VC prisoner, but Gary refused. In the next wave of heavy fire the PRU chief himself was seriously wounded. Gallagher picked him up and carried him as the team fought its way back to a road where the PRUs had stashed its trucks.

Amid a hail of fire they all got out. For his heroic action, Gary Gallagher was awarded the Navy Cross.

As for us, we'd done what I'd set out to do—only sooner, and with a little more excitement. Most important, we'd penetrated an area in which the VC felt absolutely safe and created havoc, once again showing them that with us around they didn't have any real refuge.

14

SOMEBODY HAD TO DO IT: PULLING BODIES

Much has been written about the Seawolves, the Navy helicopter gunship squadron that worked under CTF-116. I don't know a single SEAL who operated in Vietnam and wasn't saved by those guys at least once. They were the best helo crews I'd ever seen. Land-based throughout the delta and aboard LSTs at the mouths of rivers, they'd fly anywhere, any time, to support us. Night or day, good weather or bad, they were there. As my old Seawolf buddies used to say, "We like to get down low and root around," and they did. I can't count the number of times I could feel the heat from their 3.5 rockets as they passed over our heads toward the enemy. Often Seawolf fire teams made dry runs on the enemy after they had expended all their ordnance in order to give our guys a chance to break contact and get the hell out. And they were just as likely to land and pick our guys up if things really got serious. The Seawolf crews were real heroes.

Because of my gratitude to them, I ran a very distasteful mission not long after the Bac Lieu operation. I went to retrieve the remains of a Seawolf and its crew that had been shot down over Dung Island while coming back to the LST near the mouth of the Bassac, the same LST from which we'd staged our Bac Lieu operation.

When we arrived for the retrieval, I asked who had gone down. The CO told me it was John and Soto, who had pulled us out of Bac Lieu. I couldn't believe it. They had been on final approach to the ship when a burst of Chicom (Chinese Communist) 12.7mm machine-gun fire hit them. The people on shipboard watched as the rotor blades locked and the helo plummeted a thousand feet to the ground. They immediately launched another bird, which found the crash site and reported that there was no hope for survivors. The CO said they wanted to retrieve the bodies and what was left of the helo.

A Popular Force (PF) company from the Junk Force base had been waiting for us to get to the LST; they'd provide security while we worked at the crash site, but they wouldn't go in until we got there. Popular Force companies, which resembled militias, mostly defended the areas in which they lived, though some units sought out and aggressively fought the VC. I'd worked with a few PF units upriver and found them to be as good as their leadership. Usually, though, Junk Force PF weren't very aggressive toward the VC. On this operation they could at least provide lookout service while we policed up the helo and the crew.

I got the men together, gave a quick brief, and headed for our boat. The ship put up another Seawolf fire team to cover us from the air. We inserted on the island and patrolled about a thousand meters. Just after first light, we found what was left of the helo.

It was a mess. The helo lay on its left side in an irrigation ditch six feet across and three feet deep. Except for the rotor assembly, the entire helo was squeezed into the ditch, its left side underwater. It had landed with terrific force. We could see the right door gunner hanging out of the door, still strapped into his seat. I saw Soto still in the right seat, staring straight ahead. We couldn't see any of the left side of the helo below the water. I made sure the Popular Force company was in place around us, and we started the grim task of getting the bodies out.

Andy Hayden took over at this point. He had an engineering rating and had salvaged aircraft before. We got the bodies on the right side of the helo out and on the ground next to the bird. Both of them were like jelly.

I think every bone in their bodies had been crushed. It took us six hours to disassemble the helo to get at the other two men. We all were in the ditch following Andy's directions, and quickly much of the helo was in pieces on the ground.

Soon after we had started, I got a call from the Seawolves overhead saying they had taken fire from about 300 meters farther in on the island (I hadn't heard a thing with them circling over us). The pilot told me they were going to go into a wagon wheel to return fire, but since he couldn't see our perimeter forces, would I mark their positions so he wouldn't hit them? I rogered.

I got out of the ditch to look for the Popular Force company commander. Walking about a hundred meters from the helo in the direction he'd said he'd be, I saw no one. They'd apparently run away. I hurried back to the guys and told them I wanted everyone but Andy and one other out of the ditch. Then I radioed the Seawolves to tell them to break contact and circle back over us. I figured the fire they'd taken was meant to draw them away.

I set a perimeter and waited for an attack. The helos started taking fire from .51-caliber antiaircraft guns. They broke contact and came back over us. When nothing else happened for about twenty minutes, I put three more guys back to work on the helo. It was now about 1400, and I wanted to be out of there by nightfall.

Finally, Andy got down to the left side, and we dragged out the other two bodies. John Abrams had been killed instantly. An aluminum crosspiece from the helo's frame had pierced his chest and pinned him to the seat. It took us nearly an hour to free him and put him in a body bag next to his mates.

The ship CO sent in an Army heavy-lift helo with cargo nets for the bodies and whatever parts we'd salvaged from the crash. They'd drop the full nets on the ship, then lift out the rest of the helo and carry it to Can Tho for evaluation. (We later learned investigators had found just one hit on the helo. A .51-caliber round had entered the gear box and frozen the rotor almost instantly—a freak hit.)

We ended up with three nets full of helo parts. Out of respect for our fallen comrades, I put their bodies in the first cargo net by themselves. About 1700, we finally got the rest of the Seawolf attached to the hook, then watched as the remnants of our efforts lifted through the trees and headed upriver. It got really quiet.

I stood at the edge of the ditch and stared into the muck, my men in line next to me. We were all exhausted and emotionally drained. In the silence we paid tribute to the brave men who had died there. After a minute I turned away from the ditch and said, "Let's get out of here." All we had to do was reach the river, where our boat would pick us up. On the way I hoped some dumb-ass VC would take a potshot at us: we were tired, but we were also pissed off. Our buddies had been killed, and we all wanted to kill the assholes who did it, though I knew finding them was next to impossible. Our boat was waiting for us when we arrived at the river, and we boarded without incident.

Later, I found out the PF company had decided to return to their base for lunch. Their U.S. Navy adviser was furious when they showed up, but he couldn't get them to return to the island. They hadn't wanted to go in the first place. They were scared to death of Dung Island—because, they said, evil spirits lived there. The only spirits they were afraid of wore black pajamas, but that was the nature of the war. The Junk Force chief had obviously reached an agreement with the local VC hierarchy, and having his people on the island wasn't part of the agreement.

Back on the LST, I noticed that all of us had been burned by the spilled aviation fuel that had collected in the ditch. Andy was worst off, since he'd been in the ditch for nearly twelve hours. He looked like a cooked lobster. None of the men complained, though. They all knew that if it hadn't been for John and Soto, we might all be dead in Bac Lieu Province. We all felt sick about the shoot-down.

We slept on the ship that night and went back to Binh Thuy the next morning. In a few days we'd put the episode behind us. John, Soto, and their two gunners had been doing their jobs. The same thing could happen to any of us.

15

ANOTHER CLOSE CALL: NUI COTO

On July 23, I loaded the platoon into Huey slicks and headed for Chau Doc. A week earlier, I'd flown there to meet the U.S. adviser to the Provincial Reconnaissance Unit, a Special Forces sergeant by the name of Drew Dix. Drew, about to be awarded the Medal of Honor for his heroism during the Tet Offensive and given a field promotion to second lieutenant, was one of the coolest operators I ever worked with.

His role as PRU "adviser" was actually CIA cover. All the Army commands he worked with were told he was an Army major seconded to the Agency. Six feet two inches tall and a lean 175 pounds, with light brown hair and intense eyes, he not only looked and acted the part, he was a better officer than any major I'd ever seen. It amused me that, while Drew accepted the idea he was going to get the MOH (I don't think he really liked it—he just accepted it) he was very apprehensive about being promoted to lieutenant. He wasn't sure he could be a leader in the "regular" Army.

At the time he commanded a force of over a hundred former Vietcong and Vietnamese mercenaries, conducting operations throughout the province for the CIA.

Drew met us at the helo pad and told me he was going to put us up at the villa, where he lived, because it was the only place he felt security was sufficient. He had a guard force composed of Nungs, Vietnamese of Chinese descent and very loyal to whoever employed them. After settling us in, he gave us an intelligence briefing on the activities around the Seven Mountains, which rise out of the Mekong Delta near the Cambodian border. He had been to one of them, Nui Coto, two weeks earlier as part of a combined operation that had met with little success. The U.S. Army colonel commanding the operation proclaimed the area free of Vietcong, but Drew suspected otherwise. He figured we could have all the trouble we wanted—and probably a hell of a lot more success—if we went back to the very same area. He had good intelligence through his PRUs that there was a huge weapons-and-ammo cache in a cave at the western base of Nui Coto, and he had a guide who could lead us there. I said we'd do it.

We needed a few days to clear the operation. Drew had to convince the corps commander that there was still a good target; I'd have no problem clearing the operation through the Navy side, except for the fact that Nui Coto was not near any water and the staff pukes at CTF-116 might get heartburn over that. I knew CTF-116 captain (later rear admiral) Art Price wouldn't have a problem with SEALs attacking the enemy inland, because he was an aggressive commander who liked our previous results. But, if I didn't make an issue of it, I could save him from having to go to the corps commander, his operational boss, to explain what SEALs were doing in an area the Army had "pacified." So I fudged a bit on the coordinates I sent in.

Drew and I both wanted my platoon to become more familiar with the area before the mission, so we set up a series of recons, which gave an understanding of what we'd face on Nui Coto. We conducted patrols all around the mountain, to the Cambodian border, and on the nearby canals. We drew fire and noted positions but for the most part had no trouble. I began to think that maybe the area really was "pacified."

Drew suggested that we begin the operation at the base camp of an Army Mike Force (a Vietnamese or Cambodian unit commanded by a member of the U.S. Special Forces) that was located at the top of the eastern knoll of Nui Coto. The mountain itself resembled a giant rock pile some ancient giant had assembled. Through the ages parts of it had become heavy scrub brush and jungle. With its natural labyrinth of caves and tunnels, capable of holding forces of regimental size, it was a perfect spot for defensive positions. Onto this huge rock pile a contingent of my platoon and Drew's PRUs went by helicopter on August 2, 1968.

The available intelligence made it clear that this was a high-risk operation, though with equally high potential for gain. To lessen the risk we decided to confer with the Mike Force before we headed for our target. Unfortunately, it soon became apparent they knew less than we did. They were having a hard time convincing their mostly Cambodian contingent to venture beyond the base camp perimeter defense positions.

They had been there for three days, mortared every night by the bad guys on the western knoll of the mountain, where our objective was located. The Army captain and his NCO, who were Special Forces troops, asked if we would allow them and part of their Mike Force to accompany us on the operation. In almost any other situation I would have said no, but after realizing we might have bitten off more than we could chew, I agreed. The twenty or so additional troops could come in handy for their firepower.

The first night we hunkered down among the boulders to get out of the way of mortar rounds and a driving rainstorm. I spent the night with Warrant Officer Ed Jones, my assistant on this operation. Ed was a good operator, really calm under fire. He had come through UDT training as a chief petty officer and impressed everyone with his ability to hack training at his age. His nickname was Carbon Copy, because he was the second Ed Jones to come to UDT. The first Ed Jones had been white. It's interesting that, while the rest of the military was having all kinds of racial problems, we didn't. We didn't care what color a man was, only that he could do his job. On Nui Coto the first night, as we huddled together sharing a poncho and avoiding incoming mortar fire, Ed and I didn't check our pedigrees—we were SEALs, and that's all that mattered.

We headed out early the next morning. Movement in that terrain was extremely difficult: it took us about two hours to go 500 meters. So we decided to risk using the trails, figuring the increased speed offset the increased danger of booby traps and ambushes. Also, while we believed the enemy knew we were on the mountain, we guessed that after observing three days of inactivity by the Mike Force, they might not expect us to be moving, and the faster we moved the more time we had before they realized it. Anyway, going against conventional wisdom was what we were about.

We moved quickly but cautiously, and by midafternoon were near the objective. About 1530 our luck ran out. My point man sighted what proved to be the first booby trap in a diabolically clever defensive perimeter. I stopped to assess the situation. We had expected to encounter a platoon-sized unit in defensive positions and had plenty of air support laid on to help. When we found the first booby trap, and then the next and the next, we considered calling in an air strike to destroy as many as we could. But closer examination revealed the traps had been there for some time, probably set two or three weeks ago when a group of Vietnamese rangers had been on the mountain. At any rate, they hadn't been set for us, and we had seen no other sign of enemy activity, so we decided just to move cautiously and preserve "tactical" surprise as long as we could. Our pace slowed drastically as we changed point men frequently and marked all the traps that we found. Soon, it became clear that we were in the midst of the most complex booby trap system I had ever seen. There were grenades, antipersonnel mines (of U.S. manufacture), mortar rounds, unexploded bombs from past air strikes, and punji pits—just about everything imaginable. For actuation devices they'd used trip wires, pressure-release wires, and pressure and pressure-release foot detonators. They'd put buried mortars in the lee of large boulders so that they would be activated by anyone diving for cover from a mortar attack.

We took so long to cover a few hundred meters that darkness overtook us well short of our objective. We decided to lay up for the night in ambush formation. About 0200, when the first mortar rounds fell near our position, we realized we had lost tactical surprise. At that point I would have scrubbed the operation, but it seemed more sound to proceed than to retrace our steps. We decided to move back just clear of the booby traps and call in an air strike at first light.

A few hours later, we took cover behind enormous boulders (first checking very carefully for booby traps) and said, "Let 'er rip." As the F-100s screamed in on their first run, I remembered the ripe smells we had encountered early on in the patrol: VC killed in the caves by B-52 strikes before the Vietnamese ranger operation. We were so close to the F-100s' target area I wondered if we would meet the same end. I felt as if I could reach up and touch the first plane that came in. It was right on the mark. As the 250-pound bombs hit, we heard numerous secondaries. The mines were being decimated.

The second F-100 rolled in to a steady stream of antiaircraft fire from two positions right in the middle of the drop area. I couldn't believe it! We lobbed some 40mm grenades as the first plane started its second run, but couldn't touch the gun positions—they were too well protected by the rocks. The F-100s made enough runs to drop all their ordnance and expend all their 20mm cannon ammunition; then, with the flight leader wishing us luck, they returned to base to refuel and rearm. As the planes disappeared into the sky, the VC kept firing. The flight leader's parting words seemed ominous.

We moved out. After about 300 meters we began finding more booby traps; the system was even more extensive than we'd imagined. It took about another hour to get to the knoll over the cave we were after. From there we could see across the Cambodian border to the west. We could also see the bottom of the mountain where our target was located. No sign of activity did we see. I told Ed Jones to get our force into defensive positions. We were all physically and emotionally drained from the stress of moving through the booby traps, and the mortar fire the two previous nights had deprived us of sleep. I didn't want to be caught napping. There were enemy forces on the mountain, and by now they knew where we were. I figured they hadn't attacked for a couple of reasons. First, they didn't have to; they could fire mortars at us whenever they wanted. Second, they probably recognized Drew's PRUs and were not in a hurry to tangle with them. They also had one other reason they were waiting, but at the time I didn't know about it.

Drew and I advanced about fifteen meters from our guys to get a better picture of what we'd have to move through to get to the bottom and our cave. We wanted to pick a route through the rocks that would offer us the best cover. As I've mentioned, the VC had established a labyrinth of tunnels and firing points, using the natural formation of the boulders. By now we knew getting to the cave was not going to be easy.

Drew and I were standing in front of a boulder, looking down, when I caught movement out of the corner of my eye. I shoved Drew toward cover on the other side of the boulder and we both dove backward. Without our knowing, Drew's interpreter had been following us, and we ran over him taking cover. As the three of us hit the corner of the boulder, I heard the unmistakable sound of AK-47s firing. Rounds plastered the rock as we crawled for cover, Drew on top of his interpreter and me on top of Drew.

Lobbing 40mm grenades toward the fire, our guys quickly suppressed it. Once we'd unpiled, Drew and I found we were covered with little nicks from the rock shrapnel but were otherwise uninjured. We'd "dodged the bullet." Drew's interpreter had taken two rounds in the back that had exited his chest. He was having a little difficulty breathing but, in all, wasn't in terrible shape. We were assessing the situation when it suddenly got worse.

What I feared most had happened: one of my guys, Joe Albrecht, stepped on a mortar booby trap, even though it had been marked with aluminum foil. The explosion also wounded Andy Hayden, who was directly behind. The guys in front escaped the blast because they had just turned the corner of the boulder where the booby trap was located. Joe—a good operator, who had been in one of my platoons in UDT-22—was in bad shape. His leg had been nearly torn off at the knee, and he had bad internal injuries.

En route to the knoll we had identified a place for a helo MEDEVAC site. About a hundred meters back down the trail. It was the side of a bomb crater—there were no flat spots anywhere. I called for a helo. The voice on the other end of the radio told me one was thirty minutes away from our position. Clay Grady and Doc O'Bryan volunteered to carry Joe to the bomb crater. He was still conscious and joking with the guys about how stupid it was for him to have stepped on a marked booby trap, so I was hopeful that he'd live.

Clay and Doc maneuvered Joe back through the booby traps to the crater. The helo came in, balancing one skid on the side of the crater, and Joe, Andy, and Drew's interpreter were put aboard. The helo literally fell off the side of the mountain to gain airspeed. Fire erupted from below and behind us. Green tracers went zinging by the helo as it lost altitude, and I thought it had been hit. It sailed toward the rice paddies below. Just as I thought it would hit the ground, the helo straightened out and raced across the paddies like a low-flying hawk.

I realized I had pushed too far. It was unlikely we were going to be able to fight our way to the cave without taking significant casualties. Worse, Drew received a radio message from the PRUs we had stationed in the first village off the north side of the mountain just in case we needed help. They'd detected a battalion-sized Vietcong force hurrying toward Nui Coto from the Cambodian border. That was probably why we hadn't been attacked: the VC on the mountain were waiting for reinforcements. The PRU chief said he would hold the village but that we really ought to get off the mountain—now. Drew and I agreed. We decided to head quickly down through a narrow pass on the north side of the mountain that we had passed on the way to the knoll. It would be risky in daylight, but after weighing the alternatives I decided rapid movement was better than going the long way around. The bottom of the ravinelike pass emptied out into rice paddies about 2,000 meters from the village where the remainder of the PRUs were located. I told the Mike Force captain the plan, and he asked to come with us.

We called for an Army Cobra helicopter fire team to cover our descent. The Cobras had just been introduced to the delta, and this was the first time they'd supported any of our operations. When they came in view overhead, we started down the pass. One of my guys and one of the PRUs took the point.

The pass was narrow, and the walls offered natural cover for anyone wishing to lob grenades on us from above. We kept the Cobras tightly overhead. Two-thirds of the way down the pass, the PRU on the point tripped a grenade booby trap. Fortunately, my guys reacted fast enough to avoid injury. When the grenade went off, I thought it had been thrown down on us. I contacted the Cobras and told them to start giving us fire support. They started "wagon-wheeling" and putting down fire on the tops of the walls of the pass.

But the PRU couldn't walk and was losing blood. Doc O'Bryan patched him up, Drew slung him over his back, and we continued down through the pass out into the rice paddy, with the Cobras keeping up a steady stream of covering fire.

As we reached the rice paddy, Drew staggered under the weight of the wounded man, so he and I alternated carrying him as we ran. (Fortunately, this was not the rainy season so the paddy was relatively dry.) Halfway to the village I heard rounds overhead—then, a split second later, the unmistakable sound of a heavy-caliber machine gun, from probably a Chinese 12.7mm, from somewhere on the mountain. I remember thinking, "What next?" The Cobras bought us enough time to reach the tree line at the village, where we linked up with the rest of the PRUs. They were really glad to see us. They were getting nervous about the reported battalion and wanted to get out of there before dark.

We were all exhausted, but our troubles weren't over yet. The Mike Force captain came to me and said his Cambodians were about to mutiny. He wanted to disarm them. Would I help? The Cambodians were sprawled on the ground talking, so I had my guys quietly surround them and hold them under guard while the captain and his NCO took their weapons. They were apparently planning to capture the two Mike Force Americans and turn them over to the VC battalion approaching from Cambodia, as a "token of goodwill." When all the weapons were collected, we left the disarmed Cambodians to come up with another token and boarded the PRU trucks for the ride back to Chau Doc.

Back at the villa, I learned that Joe had been worse off than we thought.

With massive internal injuries, he had died on the operating table aboard a hospital ship in the Bassac River. He was the only guy I lost in my two tours, and I felt like shit. Being aggressive was one thing, but I had pushed too far on this one.

Back at Binh Thuy the next day, Art Price said our battle on Nui Coto had really stirred up a hornet's nest at IV Corps Headquarters. The commanding general had read my after-action report and wanted to see me as soon as possible. We got in Art's jeep and headed for Can Tho.

Outside the general's office we met a very nervous Army officer, the IV Corps G-2 (intelligence officer), whose reporting was being called into question by the results of our operation. The operations officer, a personable Army colonel with whom I'd worked before, gave Art and me a quick brief. Then I repeated for the general what I had written in my after-action report. He asked a couple of questions, one of which was "What the hell were you SEALs doing on Nui Coto?"

I let Art handle that one. He said he'd personally endorsed the operation because we were going after the weapons the VC were using to shoot up his PBRs. This was a bit of an overkill response as it turned out—the general just laughed and said it was a good thing we'd gone because he now had an accurate picture of the area. We exchanged a few more pleasantries about Army and Navy matters and left.

A few days later, the operations officer called to tell me what happened afterward. The minute we walked out of the office, the general was on the radio to the colonel who'd been in charge of the Vietnamese ranger operation on Nui Coto, telling him to report to IV Corps Headquarters ASAP. When he arrived, the general asked him to explain the differences between his reporting and mine (and Drew's). Apparently, instead of just fessing up, or even saying that the situation had changed in the two weeks between operations, the colonel tried to bullshit. He complained that Drew and I, a sergeant and a Navy lieutenant, were not to be believed over an Army colonel. Wrong answer. The general fired him, telling him to proceed immediately to Saigon and await orders. By the time the operations officer called me, the colonel was already back in the States pushing paper.

Nui Coto was a viper's nest. We'd made the IV Corps commander realize that, providing the information he really needed to deal with Nui Coto and its strategic place in the VC resupply effort. When IV Corps finally decided to act, it became a regiment-sized operation, and it took them a week of heavy fighting to gain control of the mountain.

I'd learned a valuable lesson on this mission: SEALs need to stay near water. I remembered that for the rest of my career.

16

BOLD DRAGON: LONG TUAN REVISITED

In late August 1968 the 9th Platoon and Lieutenant Dick Anderson finished their six-month tours and left Vietnam. I became the officer-in-charge of Detachment Alpha.

Now that I was handling the three platoons from SEAL Two, I decided I'd try to find more gainful employment for our young tigers. Bill Early and I had talked about it, and we decided that one of the more strategic things we could do, without making the Saigon staffies too nervous, was to make life difficult for the enemy in the coastal Secret Zones. Admiral Elmo Zumwalt, the commander of naval forces in Vietnam (COMNAVFORV), also wanted the VC and NVA to feel uncomfortable in their "safe havens." NAVFORV wanted to run sustained operations in the Zones, and since I'd spent time in the Long Tuan Secret Zone during my first tour, I was asked for advice. Although there still wasn't much intelligence to operate on, I gave them a plan: give me a couple of naval gunfire support ships, and I'd take two SEAL platoons and create hate and discontent in the Secret Zones.

NAVFORV liked this, so they assigned the U.S.S. *Weiss* to us as a platform from which to conduct our operations. Like the *Ruchamkin*, on which I'd deployed for the Dominican Republic crisis in 1965, *Weiss* was an old World War II APD. It had plenty of room for two SEAL platoons and two of our LSSCs.

The LSSC had been introduced in-country in June 1968, the result of a crash project begun during my first tour. In May 1967, engineers had come to us in Binh Thuy and asked us to describe the best boat to support our operations in the delta. Then they went back to the States, designing, building, and testing the LSSC in less than a year. A squad-sized boat, with two inboard Ford Interceptor gasoline engines and twin out drives, it had ceramic armor on the interior and mounts for machine guns and grenade launchers. It ran about thirty knots with a load of SEALs, and its modified planing hull was seaworthy enough to allow us to use it along the coast. It was a good boat to support the types of operations we envisioned. We could launch over the horizon and have enough sea-keeping capability and speed to get the squads to a launch point on the coast. The LSSC could also come up the canals and rivers that emptied into the South China Sea.

We kicked off Operation Bold Dragon on October 5, 1968, with two platoons—one from SEAL Team One and one from Team Two. It was the first time we had ever done an operation together. I decided we'd maximize the assets we had and run squad-sized missions every night, weather and the enemy permitting.

Weiss's commanding officer was a senior mustang lieutenant commander and one of the best ship handlers I'd seen. COMNAVFORV had designated me task group commander; the captain told me he was there to support me and, although I was very junior to him, that I was the expert and he'd do whatever I said as long as it wouldn't endanger his ship. I couldn't have asked for more. He told me his combat information center (CIC) gang was good at handling gunfire-support ships and aircraft and that his deck force had removed their boats and modified the davits—cranes—needed for the LSSC. They were a can-do outfit.

The operations officer, Lieutenant Grant Telfer, and I got together and started planning. I saw immediately that Grant knew what he was doing, and I decided my going ashore with one of the squads would be no problem. Once our operations started, Grant stayed in CIC as long as we had troops in the field, sleeping on a cot and having all his meals brought to him. (He must have liked what he saw in our operations, because after his tour on the *Weiss*, he applied for and went through BUDS training. He was almost a lieutenant commander when he graduated and took a platoon to Vietnam. Grant later worked for me when I was the operations officer for Naval Inshore Warfare Command Pacific.)

We picked up the SEAL Team One Vinh Long platoon and went to sea to rendezvous with the two gunfire-support ships. I wanted to brief them in person on our operations. The U.S.S. *Dupont*, a Norfolk-based ship, was the senior of the two. Both ships had been on the northern gun line, where they'd been providing long-range, indirect fire support for the Marines in I Corps. They were experienced shooters but their targets up north had been well beyond the Marines' lines, so damage assessment had been vague. They were looking forward to providing direct, close-in gunfire support for us.

I decided to have the Vinh Long platoon concentrate on the Vinh Long and Binh Dai Secret Zones, while the Binh Thuy platoon took the Long Tuan. The two areas were about equal in size. Our platoon would kick off the operations, and I'd lead the first mission. One of the officers in the Binh Thuy platoon had accidentally wounded himself on a previous mission, so I took over his squad.

On one of the missions, I decided to insert at the mouth of one of the canals emptying into the South China Sea. We'd patrol up the canal to see what we could find, then establish an ambush site about a kilometer in, where the canal joined another canal running from the Bassac to the Vinh Long River. This looked like a good place for interdicting any traffic between the two rivers.

We loaded an LSSC and headed for the beach, some fifteen miles away. I stopped the boat just off the small surf zone, and we swam in, but stayed in the water observing the area for about fifteen minutes. After seeing no activity, we waded over to the canal and started moving inland. Canals afforded the best way to move in the Secret Zones. If I'd thought we could get away with using a sampan, I would have done it. Wading along the bank, we could conceal our movement.

Staying in the canal also meant we left no tracks going across the beach. On a previous mission I had mistakenly concluded the VC didn't use beach patrols, so we'd walked from the surf to the dune line, hurriedly brushing our footprints as we'd been taught in UDT basic training. Ten minutes later we sat in the dunes watching two VC puzzle over what the marks meant. They must have figured them out, because about an hour later we heard H & I mortar fire landing in the dunes.

When we'd gotten about 500 meters up the canal, I heard a sampan coming our way. I got the patrol out of the water, and we set up an ambush facing the canal. Soon we saw a sampan and two people with weapons cruising slowly toward the sea. Slung over my back was a recently developed, silenced M-16 for taking out sentries. It used special down-loaded ammunition; the round's speed stayed subsonic in order to eliminate the ballistic crack. That made the weapon really quiet; a *phft* was the only sound you heard when the rifle fired. But because the bullets were down-loaded, they didn't expel enough gas to move the bolt back automatically to load another round. To get another round in the chamber you had to operate the bolt manually. To keep quiet you had to do it slowly; otherwise you got the same clanging or clacking sound you normally heard when an M-16 bolt went back and forth. I decided to test our new weapon on the two VC.

Fred McCarty whispered that he'd like to do the honors. He was an old squad mate from my first Vietnam tour, and I owed him the opportunity. I gave him the weapon, and when the sampan came within fifteen meters of us I signaled him to fire. No reaction from the boat. Fred must have missed, even though the rifle's front sight was coated with illumination paint so the shooter could see it come on target.

He carefully moved the bolt back and forth, putting the next round in the chamber, sighted the rifle again, and fired. This time I saw one of the VC grab his side and mutter something to his buddy. Neither of them appeared to realize that they had come under fire by a highly trained SEAL squad and their state-of-the-art weaponry.

Fred loaded another round and fired. The other VC grabbed his chest and looked down. Both of them just kept standing in the sampan. Neither one made a motion that would indicate that he knew what was happening.

I'd seen enough. Signaling to the squad to hold fire, I opened up with my M-16. The two VC were launched over the side. I fired just two three-round bursts, and the air was quiet again in less than five seconds. After listening awhile for any VC reaction, I decided to continue up the canal. But before leaving, I told all the guys to go ahead and get the laughs out of their systems. They thought Fred had flat missed the VC, but I knew better. The rounds were so weak they had no killing power. That was the problem with a truly silenced weapon: you had to make a head shot to do any damage.

We set up an ambush at the point I'd picked in advance. After four hours, when we'd heard nothing, I decided to push off, cross the canal, and patrol back to the beach north of the canal we had inserted on. We moved uneventfully through the mangroves and reached the sandy area, 500 meters inland from the water, about 0400.

In the middle of the dunes, the point man stopped and signaled "danger front." With me crouched beside him, he pointed to a group of three dugout shelters in the dune line. I hadn't seen anything like them before. Candles were burning inside the dugouts, so they were inhabited. The structures appeared to be reinforced with wooden beams. They would be virtually invisible from above. We moved forward and set up a defensive perimeter. The point man and I went to the closest shelter and looked inside. A woman and a child were asleep on a mat. In the next one, we again saw women and children asleep. No men were to be seen.

It would soon be daylight, but I didn't want to pass up this area. I decided we'd hold reveille and see what happened. Shelter by shelter, we pulled the people out. Still no sign of any males. When we finished, ten people stood in front of us. I told the troops to look around. I didn't like the fact that there were no men in what should have been a secure area for the VC. The women were very nervous, but I figured they'd never seen any "round-eyes," at least none as ferocious-looking as us, in our cammies and war paint.

One of the guys signaled he'd found something: elaborate bunker works constructed along the dune line. I crawled to the top of the dune and looked out to sea. Exploring the bunker works, we found the VC had dug trenches connecting all the bunkers and reinforced them with wooden beams and mud. All the bunkers—they were about 200 meters from the water—had firing slits overlooking the beach. I was surprised at the effort that had gone into their construction. It was as if they'd been built with the expectation that someday they'd be needed to repel an amphibious landing.

It was nearly sunrise. I picked up the radio handset and called the LSSC to come get us, telling them to hustle. We'd stayed longer than I'd intended, and I wanted to be out before it got daylight. I was still worried about the absence of men. Not only did my sixth sense warn me we were being watched, but the bunker line seemed to go on forever, and we hadn't had time to search it all. One of the guys reported finding a recently extinguished cigarette butt in one of the bunkers. That made me certain we weren't the only armed men in the area.

And after getting over their initial shock, the women had become unusually belligerent. One of my semi-Vietnamese-speaking SEALs said he'd overheard one of them tell another that the men would be back soon to kill us. I called *Dupont* on the radio, told them where we were, and gave them the reference point to the bunkers to our south. The ship called back in about ten minutes, saying they were in a good position to shoot. By this time, it was light enough to see the LSSC clearly—it was on its way, about a thousand meters offshore. I signaled with my flashlight.

I got the squad moving toward the water. We were about fifty meters away when all hell broke loose—heavy automatic-weapons fire from the bunkers in the dunes to our south. We hit the deck returning fire, but we were in a bad position. We had no cover, and even though the guys were putting effective fire into the bunker line, I knew we weren't bothering the VC, as well protected as they were.

Rounds were hitting all around. Rifle-fired grenades, automatic weapons—the whole nine yards. Sand was being blown into our eyes by the rounds hitting near us. We were in a bad spot out in the open, but we were close to the water and our boat was on the way. Miraculously, no one appeared to have been hit yet.

I'd crawled over to the radioman right away, and now I called *Dupont* to tell them to fire on the bunkers. The radio crackled, "Shot—out": they'd fired a salvo. Yelling to the guys, "Hunker down—incoming!" I watched the dune line, the radio handset at my mouth, ready to correct fire as necessary.

A fraction of a second later, the shells, sounding like small freight trains, flew over us. The dune line erupted. I heard a tremendous explosion, and bodies flew about a hundred feet into the air, along with sand and debris from the bunkers. The whole line of dunes to my left just disappeared. I couldn't believe my eyes: a dead-center hit. In the sudden quiet, I told the ship, "Cease fire—target eliminated." In disbelief, *Dupont*'s gun boss asked me to verify that order.

None of us had been hit. We headed for the boat, which lay just beyond the surf shooting everything it had into the dunes, giving us cover as we waded out.

In the boat, I grabbed a set of binoculars. Body parts and weapons lay scattered where the bunker line had been. Suddenly, a round cracked over our heads and then another. Apparently some fool thought he could still turn the day for Uncle Ho. I called for another salvo from the ship and watched it tear into what was left of the dunes. The firing stopped. On a notion I told them to fire another salvo, this time 200 meters inland. I figured that might hit any VC bugging out of the area. I sent another few salvos north and south, too, as we headed to sea.

Instead of going to *Weiss*, I told the coxswain to go to *Dupont*.

When we came alongside, the CO leaned out over the bridge and told us all to come on board. We tied the LSSC to a boat painter and I led our contingent of field-dirty SEALs up the ladder. Most of the ship's company seemed to be on deck.

The executive officer (XO) and the gun boss met me as I came over the rail. I'd never seen grins like theirs. The crew members started cheering and pounding my guys on the back as they came over the rail behind me. They were so exuberant, I thought they were going to knock us back over the side.

I was a little embarrassed by all this attention. I'd only meant to come over and thank the ship in person for pulling our asses out of the fire. I didn't feel like a hero at the time, more like a fool for staying ashore too long and giving the VC a chance to set up on us.

I followed the XO to the wardroom. The CO was there, and he started pumping my hand and slapping me on the back as I gave him a quick-and-dirty on our mission. They hadn't realized we were in such a predicament. He said it was the finest day in the history of the ship, and the first time they'd fired for troops actually engaged in combat. I thanked him for his incredibly accurate fire and told him I'd never seen anything as beautiful as all those bodies being blown into the air.

I showed him on the map exactly where the rounds had impacted and where we'd been. He started shaking his head; we were about 150 meters from the impact point and only a hundred meters north of the gun target line. It was definitely a "danger close" situation. If the *Dupont*'s gunners had been just a little less accurate, we might have been the ones blown to pieces.

I told them that, judging both from the body parts I'd seen from the boat as we were leaving and from how many men seemed to be firing at us, I figured they'd probably killed about twenty-five VC. The gun boss was ecstatic—it was the first time they'd been credited with a fairly accurate body count.

Aboard *Weiss,* I got the other squad leaders together and went over what happened. I told them we'd have to be more alert, particularly during insertions, because chances were the word would spread fast that Americans were operating along the coast.

The mission got a lot of good press at NAVFORV—we'd killed VC and continued our campaign of harassing them in their safe areas. Zumwalt sent a BZ message (Navy code for "Well done") to me as the task group commander.

In the two weeks we operated along the coast, we accomplished the main purpose of Bold Dragon: to unsettle and harass the enemy in areas he thought were under his exclusive control. In the overall scheme of SEAL operations in my two tours, Bold Dragon contributed as much to the larger war effort as anything we did. Plus, we'd established a task group commanded by a SEAL officer. It was the first time that had been done in Vietnam, or anywhere else to my knowledge. The fact that I was junior to all the commanding officers in the task group also spoke volumes. It was clear recognition on the part of COMNAVFORV that the experts needed to be in charge. Unfortunately, the lesson wasn't learned; on other operations I did later, the idea of allowing Special Operations Force commanders to run their operations without having to bend to the demands of conventional commanders didn't fly.

On November 6, 1968, I said good-bye to Vietnam. At the time I planned to come back as soon as I could. My CO Ted Lyon and I had gotten into a small pissing contest over who would take my place as OIC of Detachment Alpha. I didn't think the officer he'd picked to relieve me was qualified; he'd been a failure in UDT-21 and left it for duty on a ship. When SEAL Two needed officers for our Vietnam operations, he'd been ordered in, he didn't volunteer. I offered to take a thirty-day leave in Little Creek and then return to Vietnam for another six-month tour as OIC; the SEAL Team One Detachment OIC agreed to cover for me during the leave, and Art Price approved the plan. But Ted said no, and he won—he was the CO. Still, I figured I could talk him into sending me back.

On my way through Saigon I debriefed Bill Early over numerous beers, then went to Tan Son Nhut to catch my flight back to the States. When I got back to Little Creek and I walked in to the Team, the petty officer standing quarterdeck watch said, "You again, asshole." I said something like "F— off and stand a taut watch, slipknot." Then we laughed and hugged each other, and he said he was glad I was back in one piece this time. We all loved each other in SEAL Two in those days, and the troops treated officers with such respect! The truth is, I wouldn't have had it any other way. The troops respected officers who were "operators," and I truly loved the troops. There wasn't a better group of men anywhere.

The watch told me the XO had left word that I was to come see him as soon as I got back.

When I went in to see Jake Rhinebolt, the door to the CO's office was closed. Jake gave me a cup of coffee and I gave him a quick rundown, telling him I'd go into more detail when I briefed the CO. Jake started looking a little uncomfortable. The CO, he said, was awfully busy getting ready for an MTT (military training team) that SEAL Two had been told to provide somewhere. This was strange. Bill Early had personally debriefed each officer returning from Vietnam, and he'd drop anything else he was working on to do it. But Ted was different. I told Jake, "No sweat, I'll wait here until he has time to see me." He kept looking nervous. He told me to go home and start leave. I just looked at him. I couldn't believe the CO of SEAL Team Two didn't want to see his returning-from-combat detachment officer-in-charge. I figured I'd pissed him off more than I'd realized when I argued with him over my replacement. I was just a young, gunslinging lieutenant. Ted was the CO. What did I know? (Sure enough, I never did get called in to debrief Ted.)

Before I left his office, I told Jake to put me down to go back as the next OIC. He said Ted had already picked someone else. Then I asked what I would be doing around the Team, expecting Jake to tell me I was going to be the operations officer, number three in the chain of command. He said that Ted had told him to follow seniority strictly in making assignments. There were three other lieutenants senior to me, and even though I had more combat experience than any of them, there was nothing he could do. He said I'd probably be the assistant operations or training officer. I just looked at him, shook my head, and walked out.

I'd come from a place where I'd commanded a task group, because I was the most qualified, to a place where experience and qualification didn't seem to matter. There was no way I was going to work for a CO who thought like a staff officer, not an operator. Also, I wasn't going to work as an assistant for any combat-avoiding officer. Two of the three lieutenants senior to me were late arrivals from UDT, having stayed in their old commands as long as they could to avoid going to Vietnam. I thought any UDT officer who didn't want to go to combat ought to stop drawing a paycheck. The third lieutenant had been an abject failure in Vietnam and was getting out of the Navy. I made a snap decision: it was time for me to leave SEAL Team Two.

I went into the administrative office, called the UDT/SEAL officer detailer in the Bureau of Naval Personnel, and asked what he had available for me on the East Coast. I didn't want to go to SEAL One, because there I would have been a very junior lieutenant. And I was still a reserve officer, with roots in the East.

I'd called at a good time. The detailer was looking for someone to relieve the executive officer of UDT-22. I took the job and signed an extension-of-active-duty letter about ten minutes later. I figured I could spend a tour as XO, extend again, and then come back to SEAL Two when the leadership changed. I still hadn't decided to make a career out of the Navy, but I was having such a good time in Vietnam I wanted to go back.

I checked into UDT-22 in December 1968. Becky was glad that I'd be out of the war zone for a while. Though I didn't know it then, I would never go back to Vietnam.

17

VIETNAM: A SEAL'S PERSPECTIVE

I have mixed thoughts about my time in Vietnam. On the one hand, I consider it the defining period of my life; because I'd been successful as a SEAL in combat, I decided to make the Navy a career. But my satisfaction is tempered by a major frustration: SEALs were never employed to their full potential.

The military hierarchy in Vietnam completely failed to understand the SEAL capability. "Bing" West, a RAND analyst who spent a few days with me in 1968 observing our operations, put it best: "SEALs were a tactic in search of a strategy." That remained true from the time SEAL platoons started operating in Vietnam, in 1966, until the bitter end.

For the most part, we were relegated to the Navy river patrol forces. SEALs killed considerable numbers of the enemy, and obtained locally important intelligence. A lot of our men were wounded, but surprisingly few were killed. The latter statistic I attribute to training and the fact that we called our own shots—we simply didn't operate where or when we didn't want to.

In my view, we should have been conducting high risk–high gain operations. Instead of chasing VC who harassed the river patrol forces, we could have been applied to such vexing problems as freeing American prisoners of war. I realize national policy, such as it was, barred U.S.

ground forces from North Vietnam—but had we been given a chance, we would have developed executable plans. Plus, we could have been searching for and freeing Americans captured in South Vietnam before they could be transported to the North.

As it was, in the Mekong Delta we did what seemed to be the next best thing: targeting VC prisoner camps in our areas. But that proved to be a frustrating effort, not because of the VC but because of our own insufferable military bureaucracy in Saigon. I learned that the best way to find and liberate prisoners in the delta was to develop local intelligence sources and react quickly to good information. But an organization called the Joint Resolution Center stifled that modus operandi.

For example, in 1968 it was common knowledge in the intelligence community that the VC were holding American prisoners in mobile camps. These were prisoners the VC didn't want to send to North Vietnam, because the southerners increased their status by having their own prisoners to flaunt. Anyway, for whatever reasons, Americans were being held in the delta. We had fairly reliable information about Americans being held near the Cambodian border, in an area called the Plain of Reeds. I amassed enough information on one such location to launch what would have been a successful recovery operation—had I not needed helicopter support from the Army. When I asked for that support, an Army colonel from the Joint Resolution Center showed up and told me, "Step aside, Lieutenant, I'm taking over." He had a bad plan, it fell apart in the rehearsal, and they never attempted the mission.

The SEAL experience in Vietnam was a microcosm of the larger U.S. military experience. We killed and captured a lot of Communists but never focused on the real problem. The United States fought the wrong kind of war. We were doomed to failure as early as 1964, when political leaders, on the advice of military leaders, decided to increase by an order of magnitude the number of conventional forces in Vietnam and commit ourselves to a war of attrition. President John F. Kennedy had recognized the potential quagmire in Vietnam and insisted that our involvement reflect the situation's overriding political-military aspects. He saw the conflict as one that could not be resolved by overwhelming military technology, but that might be thwarted by properly applied pressure using "unconventional" military force.

As a young lieutenant in Vietnam, I admit I wasn't much smarter than those who saw the solution in search-and-destroy missions. But after a while I realized that the best way to hurt the enemy was to cut off the heads of the political cadres who ran the show. The way to make a difference was not to set ambushes in free-fire zones, but to attack the VC infrastructure. Done early, on the scale of the much-lambasted Phoenix program, that might have changed the outcome of the war. We were fighting an ideology. Killing young men and women who had been forced, by terrorist means, into serving their Communist masters wasn't going to defeat the ideology. The only way to do *that* was to kill or capture the ones spreading the "idea."

America lost the Vietnam War before I ever got there. Should the U.S. have become involved at all? Our motives were pure within the context of the time; we couldn't have done otherwise. There was no doubt that Soviet communism sought to establish its domination over the countries of the world. The only way to do that was to defeat its antithesis—the forces of democracy. That was the picture painted by the leaders of the Communist world in Moscow, and that was the canvas American leaders saw in the 1950s and early 1960s. To argue now that our position then was morally bankrupt is to ignore the realities of those times. What was bankrupt was the failure on the part of our military and political leadership to admit that by 1965 the situation in Vietnam could not be reversed by a massive influx of U.S. military forces. Our military leaders refused to understand that they were facing a political-military situation.

The key to the struggle lay in the South—the Mekong Delta. The Communists knew they had to win there in order to bring down the Saigon government. And the key to victory was the elaborate political infrastructure of dedicated Communists. A direct invasion from the North would have undermined the Communists' position that the struggle emanated from within the South and was being waged by South Vietnamese simply trying to overthrow the corrupt government in Saigon. But to keep the fight going long enough, there had to be an influx of fighters from the North. The Vietcong infrastructure in the South was the mechanism by which that infiltration was carried out. It was the infrastructure that picked up the troops coming down the Ho Chi Minh Trail and successfully moved them into the delta to merge with the local Vietcong main force units. And it held the effort together after the Vietcong main force units were virtually wiped out during the Tet Offensive of 1968.

The Communist movement in the South was much like a giant lizard. Its head was the small group of dedicated Communists who formed the political infrastructure. Its tail was the military force. Each time we hacked off a portion of the tail and proclaimed that we had seriously damaged the creature, the head of the lizard grew more tail. Our strategy all along should have been to go after the head. But our military was not keen on fighting anything but another military force, and as long as the Vietcong could give us a main force unit to kick every now and then we'd ignore the real problem. While we were busy searching and destroying with large U.S. military forces, the political infrastructure was busy setting us up, building the network that eventually paved the way for the takeover of Saigon. The vast majority of Vietcong military units were not made up of the dedicated, fearless fighters portrayed in our news media. Most people in the Mekong Delta were apolitical; they just wanted to be left alone to grow their crops and survive. The Vietcong infrastructure, through coercion and terror, filled its ranks with these average people. Eliminate the infrastructure and there would have been no Vietcong military force.

The Communist strategy for the war was simple—keep fighting until enough political pressure built up in America to get out of the war. Ho Chi Minh and his advisers in Moscow were students of the American way of war. They knew that we liked to enter a war only as a last resort and then commit ourselves to a total military victory, as we had done in two previous world wars. The Communist leaders knew that if they could prolong the war we'd eventually tire and go home—that was one lesson of Korea. Some in the U.S. military did understand the situation and attempted to point us down the right path. But the mainstream military structure couldn't accept any course that didn't include the core of the U.S. military structure—conventional forces. If any of our leaders had read and understood Bernard Fall's 1963 book about the French experience in Vietnam, *Street Without Joy*, they would have seen the error of the conventional strategy.

The correct course of action came too late and with too few resources to have an effect. It was the much-maligned Phoenix program. One of its objectives was to do away with the Vietcong political structure, particularly in the Mekong Delta. In the delta the strategy worked well considering its late start. The Phoenix Program went after the head of the lizard.

But our political and military leaders chose to wage a war of attrition, thinking that sooner or later the other side would run out of fighters and give up. This bogus strategy allowed the Communists to win. They managed to create 58,000 body bags filled with brave young Americans. With no discernible end in sight, our country lost the will to continue the fight. Communists also did a masterly job of working on the folks back home through our news media, which correctly pointed out the futility of killing enough Communists to make them quit. Other Americans with less-honorable intentions aided the Communist cause. The Vietnam War split our country. It gave certain U.S. citizens a platform to actively attempt to bring down our form of government, while being glorified by our news media for "doing the right thing." The picture of Jane Fonda posing with a North Vietnamese antiaircraft gun crew after they had just shot down U.S. airmen doing their duty, is indelibly etched in my mind. No amount of apologizing on her part will ever convince me she wasn't providing aid and comfort to the enemy.

Escaping military service became vogue. In all previous wars, draft dodgers had been prosecuted. This time, draft dodgers fleeing to Canada were excused because they objected to war. I object to war. Many people object to war, but in the past they served, they didn't run. In December 1966 I encountered a former college fraternity brother at a party. He told me, proudly, that he'd conjured up a "hardship" reason to avoid the draft because he didn't want to go to Vietnam. I was furious. I had recently visited a friend in the Portsmouth naval hospital who had been shot down flying an A-6 over Hanoi, and I was on my way to Vietnam. Becky grabbed me as I was about to hit my "brother." Fortunately, she only decreased the force of my punch. If I'd run into the guy a year later, after my first tour, I would have ripped his head off.

When the Vietnam Veterans War Memorial was in the planning stages, I thought erecting a black wall to the memory of the brave men and women who fought and died for their country was the final slap in the face. I avoided going there until I was stationed at the Pentagon in 1988. When I did go, I realized the color made no difference. I was struck by the view of the wall. It came out of the ground on one end, rose in the middle, and went back into the ground on the other—exactly the pattern of our effort in Vietnam in the 1960s. Equally striking was the fact that from the other side, the memorial was virtually indistinguishable from its surroundings. Instead of standing tall like the Marine Corps' Iwo Jima Memorial just across the Potomac River, the Wall was hidden, as if the country were embarrassed by the whole thing.

As I walked the length of the Wall, a strange feeling came over me. I was not the disinterested observer I'd intended to be. Tears came to my eyes as I randomly scanned the names and focused on that of Rick Trani, a SEAL Two officer killed during my second deployment. I went back to the directory to find the names of other friends and teammates. I had a hard time focusing, but I found and touched each name. I was affected by the Wall. It symbolized the bravery and dedication of our military and the incompetence of our political leadership. As I walked back to my car I told Becky, "The memorial is a good thing."

I also remember feeling that the self-appointed guardians of the monument—the grubby, bearded, and camo-clad "Vietnam veterans" selling souvenirs—were not like the ones I remembered from the era. I wondered how many of these had actually served in Vietnam. I thought they provided a final fitting insult by a country seemingly embarrassed to honor its dead from an unpopular and unsuccessful war. I didn't buy a damn thing.

To this day, it's difficult for me to explain to non-SEALs what we did in Vietnam and why I liked it so much. People, including some military friends, think I'm crazy when I tell them I liked being in Vietnam. I know a lot of it had to do with SEAL Team Two, which was such a tightly knit unit in those days. I can't imagine going to war with a group of people who didn't have a background and bond like ours. We all felt we couldn't let each other down. No doubt that was part of the reason SEALs were so successful in keeping battle deaths low even though more than 90 percent of the men from SEAL Team One and Two who served in Vietnam have the Purple Heart.

I guess in the final analysis I found complete job satisfaction in Vietnam. Since we weren't part of a grander strategy, the next best thing occurred: we were left to our own devices. I had total control over my actions and the authority to do whatever I thought best. Not bad for a young Navy lieutenant. For the SEALs of that era, Vietnam was a tough act to follow.

PART 4

Fire Three: SEAL Team Six

The 1970s saw the rise of Arab nationalism: the oil crisis of the early 1970s; the Palestinian effort to gain control of Israeli lands; and the Iranian revolution, which elevated hostage-taking to a new level.

The 1970s also saw the end of U.S. military involvement in Vietnam—indeed, the end of our military involvement "east of Montauk Point, New York," as some pundit said. The Vietnam War left a bad taste in America's collective mouth. We had little stomach to take up the cudgel in defense of anyone. But after the Munich Olympics it was clear that we had to be ready to combat a new and more insidious force—terrorism.

Our military readiness hit a post–World War II low in the 1970s. But, given the need to be able to quickly mount small military operations to protect our national interests, we had to have a force in being. That need became even more clear after the debacle in the desert that was our attempt to free our hostages in Teheran.

What emerged in 1980 was what I'll call the Joint Headquarters, formed in the aftermath of Desert One, the failed attempt to rescue the American embassy staff being held hostage in Iran. It commanded forces from the Army, Navy, and Air Force. I became part of the new "joint" family when I assumed command of SEAL Team Six.

Swimmers on the deck of a submerged submarine moving toward the forward escape hatch to lock into the submarine. (GORMLY COLLECTION)

UDT basic training class 31 at Roosevelt Roads, Puerto Rico, preparing for a hydrographic reconnaissance exercise. Gormly fourth from the left, row two. (GORMLY COLLECTION/OFFICIAL U.S. NAVY PHOTOGRAPH)

UDT basic training class 31 at Roosevelt Roads, Puerto Rico, departing the pier for a demolition exercise. Gormly at left front sitting on MK-8 demolition hose used for channel and reef clearing operations. (GORMLY COLLECTION/OFFICIAL U.S. NAVY PHOTOGRAPH)

SEAL Team Two mustered for inspection by the Commander, Naval Operations Support Group Atlantic, Captain Floyd Simons (walking in front). Picture taken just prior to deploying the first detachment to Vietnam. In the front row, from left, the officers: Lt. Jake Rhinebolt, Lt. Fred Kochey, Lt. Larry Bailey, LTJG "Moose" Boitnot (deployed later), LTJG Gormly, and Ensign Dick Marcinko. (GORMLY COLLECTION/OFFICIAL U.S. NAVY PHOTOGRAPH)

Lieutenant Gormly prior to an operation, February 1967. (GORMLY COLLECTION)

Squad 3 Bravo prior to an operation, March 1967. Front: Jess Tolison and Fred McCarty. Rear left to right: Pierre Birtz, Bill Garnett, Charlie Bump, and Gormly. (GORMLY COLLECTION)

SEAL Team Attack Boat (STAB) on the Bassac River, February 1967. Pierre Birtz stands behind the .50-caliber machine gun. Charlie Bump is at the helm as Bill Garnett supervises, ready to man the MK-19 40mm grenade launcher mounted just forward of the .50. (COURTESY OF FRED MCCARTY)

Vice Admiral Mustin awarding Lt. Gormly the Silver Star and the Bronze Star after first Vietnam deployment. (GORMLY COLLECTION/OFFICIAL U.S. NAVY PHOTOGRAPH)

Below Lieutenant Gormly and men departing through a small pass en route off Nui Coto, August 2, 1968—all smiles are gone. Clay Grady and Ed Bowen are looking for VC above. Minutes later, a PRU was seriously wounded when he tripped a booby trap.
(GORMLY COLLECTION)

Above Lieutenant Gormly on Nui Coto operation just after leaving the base camp, August 1, 1968.
(GORMLY COLLECTION)

The 9th Platoon, May–June 1968. Front row left to right: Dave Purselle, Gormly, and John Rabbit. Rear left to right: Ed Bowen, Ken MacDonald, Joe Albrecht, Billy Coulson, Jack Kennedy, Andy Hayden, Doc O'Bryan, Ed Jones, Clay Grady, and Chuck Newell.
(COURTESY OF KEN MACDONALD)

Lieutenant Gormly relaxing between missions in Vietnam, fall 1968. War is hell! (GORMLY COLLECTION)

Lieutenant Commander Gormly, Commanding Officer SEAL Team Two, and the commander of a foreign counterpart unit discuss tactics at the SEAL training area in Roosevelt Roads, Puerto Rico, circa 1973. (GORMLY COLLECTION)

Commander Gormly, Commanding Officer UDT-12, amidst his troops circa 1980. (GORMLY COLLECTION)

Commander Gormly and Captain Dave Schaible, Commander Naval Special Warfare Group One, enjoying a weekend beer! 1980. (GORMLY COLLECTION)

At Salines airfield, Grenada, October 26, 1983. Capt. Gormly (left) and Army Lt. Col. L. H. "Bucky" Burress discuss the situation just prior to returning from Urgent Fury. (GORMLY COLLECTION)

In command of Naval Special Warfare Group Two, March 1988, addressing the troops at a change of command for SEAL Delivery Team Two. The outgoing CO, Commander (now Rear Admiral) Tom Steffens, looks on. (GORMLY COLLECTION)

SEAL Commander Gary Stubblefield, in charge of the barge *Wimbrown* (smaller but similar to the *Hercules*), briefs Capt. Gormly, COMNAVSPECWARGRU-2, in the Persian Gulf, June 1988. Lieutenant Chuck Chaldekas listens. (GORMLY COLLECTION)

Pentagon bureaucrat Gormly receiving an administrative "been there, done that" medal (Legion of Merit) from Rear Admiral P. D. Smith. Becky, Gormly's wife, smiles because they're being transferred to Florida. Summer 1990. (GORMLY COLLECTION)

Return from Desert Storm, March 1991. Becky greets Gormly with a beer at MacDill AFB, Florida. (GORMLY COLLECTION)

Thirty years later—July 1997. Squad 3 Bravo (minus Jess Tolison, who was killed in an accident in 1971) together again at the annual UDT–SEAL reunion in Little Creek, Virginia. From the left: Bill Garnett, Gormly, Fred McCarty, Charlie Bump, and Pierre Birtz. (GORMLY COLLECTION)

18

BACK IN THE SADDLE

August 1983, 1925 Hours

Thirty thousand feet above the southern Arizona desert, the ramp of the C-130 slowly opened, revealing an amazing sight. Seemingly just behind us was a huge thunderhead reaching higher than we could see. Lightning was flashing behind our plane as the sun dropped below the horizon. The jumpmaster looked at me, and we gave each other the thumbs-up. We would do the jump, thunderstorm or not.

I had taken command of SEAL Team Six a few weeks before, and I was in a phase of my "Green Team" training, learning to do the things that other SEAL teams didn't do. I'd done preparation jumps with the Green Team but was called away before the "high-altitude, high-opening" (HAHO) phase. This was "makeup" training with one of my operational assault teams.

There were twenty SEALs in the plane. We'd been breathing pure oxygen for the last forty-five minutes in preparation for the training HAHO jump. HAHO differs from the free-fall jumping so often seen in military demonstrations. In HAHO, just as the name implies, you open your parachute high. Tonight we would open our canopies in five- to ten-second intervals after leaping from the open stern ramp of the C-130 into –45° air. We would be "in the saddle" at about 28,000 feet above the ground. From there we would gather into a formation and follow the lead jumper to our target on the ground.

Jumping from a plane at 30,000 feet is never routine, no matter how experienced or capable you are. It's dangerous. The air at that altitude is low in oxygen. In order not to be asphyxiated, jumpers must breathe oxygen, first in the plane before jumping and then from self-contained rigs. Without the oxygen a jumper under canopy loses consciousness within seconds of leaving the plane. He may suffer severe brain damage or even die before he reaches 15,000 to 18,000 feet, when the oxygen content of the atmosphere will bring him around.

Our self-contained rigs, consisting of a mask, regulator, and bottle, provided enough oxygen when all functioned well. Problems can occur as the jumper leaves the plane and begins his free fall before opening. In a normal free fall, the jumper maneuvers against air resistance, and thin air is not very resistant.

The air at 30,000 feet is much less dense than that at sea level; it's easy to lose control, tumbling or spinning instead of falling chest first. Because the air is thinner, the jumper is also traveling faster, leaving the plane at about 180 miles per hour rather than the 100 or 120 miles per hour of a low-level jump. Under these conditions, getting into a stable (chest to the ground) position before opening the parachute is critical, because if you open in a tumble or a spin or while out of control, there's no telling what will happen.

Finally, in military HAHO jumping you don't have the option of waiting until you get control before you pull your rip cord. You are part of a team whose members must pull at specific intervals in order to get into formation and stay together till you reach the ground. So you'd better be ready when you leave the plane, because when the time comes, you will pull.

The opening shock at that altitude is incredible even when you are in a perfect body position. You feel as if your head is going through your feet as you go from about 180 to 0 miles per hour in a matter of one or two seconds. When a jumper's position is not good, all kinds of funny things can happen, none of them pleasant. At best, he will have a harder than usual opening. At worst, he may get so entangled in the chute as it comes out of its deployment bag that he'll be jerked around violently. Even worse, his oxygen mask may be ripped from its attachments on the helmet; in that case, the jumper has to cut away his main canopy and free-fall to around 18,000 feet, where he opens his reserve chute and hopes for the best when he gets to the ground. Tactically, he is lost to the group. Although the group has a prearranged rendezvous site for such emergencies, in an actual operation the jumper would be on his own, having landed miles from the rest of the formation.

A jumper who is knocked unconscious by the opening shock and has lost his oxygen supply faces a grimmer reality—without oxygen and floating downward under canopy, he may die before he gets low enough for breatheable air. So HAHO, even in a training situation, is never ordinary and never safe. Add a large thunderstorm to the equation, and it really gets interesting.

I left the plane third, behind Mike, the lead and most experienced jumper in our stick. In our business, experience, not rank, has privilege, and although I was the commanding officer of the team, this was my first HAHO jump. Before making his final decision, Mike contacted our drop zone (DZ) crew to learn what the conditions were there. Even though my unit trained as it fought, there were realities to HAHO operations no amount of experience or determination could overcome. Altitude winds were not a problem, but ground winds had to be taken into consideration. Our canopies could give us about 35 miles per hour of forward speed, so theoretically we could land in winds a little stronger than that. But we kept some safety rules. My policy was that if we would do it for real, we would do it in training. I would not plan a HAHO infiltration if the expected ground winds were higher than 30 miles per hour, so that was our cutoff velocity tonight. The ground crew assured Mike the winds were no greater than 20 miles per hour. And the thunderstorm was moving away from our intended track. So we jumped.

I dove off the ramp headfirst, trying to relax as much as possible while maintaining a "tight" body position. When you jump from the ramp of a plane, the first wind you encounter is the flow from the bottom of the plane; if you aren't properly positioned, it will start you flipping head over heels. Past that initial flow, the next thing that can happen, if you are leaning left or right, is that you may start a flat spin. Tumbling and spinning are very possible even for an experienced jumper, because the body position "error tolerance" as you leave the plane is slim. If you know what you're doing, though, you can to some extent overcome a spin or a tumble in the five to ten seconds you have before opening. Since I was third in line, I had to pull at eight seconds—plenty of time!

I was fortunate enough to go out of the plane in good position, slowly starting a heels-over-head tumble that I easily corrected. I pulled at eight seconds, got through the negative Gs, and checked my canopy, which looked good. I took a quick look around to ensure I wasn't on a collision course with another jumper, and then freed my control lines.

Looking around again, I saw we had ten good canopies and started maneuvering into my position in the "stacked" formation. Mike came on the net to check with all of us and ensure no one had a problem. Attached to the left side of his harness, each man had a Motorola MX-360 semisecure VHF radio with earphone and throat microphone. A small rucksack, containing ammunition and food, was attached to the front of the harness between each jumper's legs. Just above the rucksack was a control board containing an altimeter and a compass. Each jumper also had a weapon (assault rifle or submachine gun) attached to the right side of his harness, plus a pistol in a holster for immediate action when we hit the ground.

We were around 26,000 feet at this point, and I looked around to enjoy the incredible view. The thunderstorm was now south of us, but it seemed to be closer than when we had left the plane. To the southeast, I could see the Tucson Mountains and lights from the few houses there. By this time it was dark on the ground, but we could still see the sun setting in the west, just past the Gulf of California. I turned to look north toward the DZ. We had expected southerly winds at about 50 knots, so our ground speed should have been around 65 or 70 knots. It didn't seem we were moving over the ground that fast, but so high up it's difficult to judge.

I wasn't concerned. Another reality of HAHO operations is that the winds aren't always as forecast. I used to tell my bosses that I couldn't guarantee we'd always land where we planned, but I could guarantee we would land together and we would know where we were. So even though we seemed to be moving more slowly than we'd planned and would likely land short of our objective (the airport DZ), I wasn't worried—we'd just patrol back to the DZ.

What *was* beginning to worry me was the thunderstorm. It seemed to be moving north, not south. I got on the radio and told Mike we'd have to keep a close eye on it.

Meanwhile, a Boeing 727 was also headed our way. It appeared to be well below us, but, having just taken off from Tucson International to the east, the pilot was probably headed for his cruising altitude, 30,000 or 40,000 feet. The 727 was headed right at us. Mike came on the net and told everyone to be ready to execute an emergency cutaway so we could fall below it if necessary. The turbulence produced by the 727 could cause us serious problems if it came too close, to say nothing of what would happen if he hit the formation. Finally the plane passed by—directly under us, but a good distance away. We all instinctively pulled up our legs, then turned our attention to the storm, which had crept closer.

Lightning was the least of our worries. Our real concern was strong updrafts. Found in all thunderstorms, these winds could easily carry us up to 50,000 feet before spitting us out of the top of the storm. Then our oxygen wouldn't last long enough to get us to the ground. Recently, two civilian jumpers caught in a local thunderstorm had found themselves going from 2,000 feet to 30,000 feet before they had the presence of mind to cut away, fall through the storm to about 1,000 feet, pull their reserves, and land safely if not soundly.

I was thinking about this as I saw the storm overtaking us. Mike came on the net again and said we were going to forget our original flight plan and head immediately for the ground.

We started executing a tight spiral descent, still in good formation. But we didn't seem to be descending fast enough. Because we were no longer flying away from the storm, it started to gain on us—quickly. The winds picked up, buffeting our canopies and making me wonder if I shouldn't tell Mike to have us cut away. Still, no jumper wants to cut away from a good canopy, and I trusted Mike's judgment completely. I kept my mouth shut.

We kept spiraling toward the ground. The winds from the north kept increasing—a solid sign the storm was overtaking us. Mike came up on the net and told the ground crew we'd land about eight miles short of the DZ. We didn't hear a response; the storm was probably interfering with the signals, and as we got closer to the ground we were losing our line of sight with the DZ.

Around 2,500 feet, the winds really increased. Mike came on the radio and told us he was going for an into-the-wind landing on a northwest heading. We came out of the spiral headed south, running with the wind to bleed off more air. At 800 feet we turned east and then north. It was pitch-black by this time, but as we turned north to face into the wind, I could see we were moving south at a pretty good clip. It was going to be a very interesting landing.

We were underneath MT-1X canopies, which as I've mentioned could move us forward at about 35 miles per hour at full speed with no wind. We controlled the speed with our control lines, called brakes. Normal landing procedure for these high-performance canopies was the same as that followed by aircraft: fly a downward leg; turn right or left to the base leg; then, for an into-the-wind landing, turn again, in the same direction. The last maneuver is called "turning final."

As we turned final, we could all see what was in store for us—a landing in more than 30-mile-per-hour winds. The normal procedure for landing the canopy is to stall the chute as your feet touch the ground, reaching zero altitude and zero speed simultaneously. Tonight a stand-up landing wasn't even on my mind—a no-bones-broken, semicontrolled crash was what I was hoping for.

Mike came on the net to recommend that we pull our trim tabs (located on the front risers) down to the retainer, a maneuver that dumps more air out of the rear of the canopy, increasing forward momentum but also increasing the rate of descent. Jumpers normally use this maneuver at higher altitudes when they want to lose height quickly. It is not usually done on landing because it's very hard to judge the trade-off of forward movement for increased rate of descent. Each of us had to decide for himself whether to do it. I did it.

I looked down at about 500 feet to see where I was going to land, but it was pitch-dark; the thunderstorm had taken care of any ambient starlight. We seemed to be in the middle of some farmer's field. I saw a fence fly between my legs, but there was no more I could do to control the situation—I was flying full out, my trim tabs at the retainer. I was still moving backward. Fifty feet off the ground, I saw another fence fly beneath my legs. I figured I'd land between that one and the next.

My feet, butt, and head seemed to hit the ground simultaneously. I pulled my canopy-release mechanism and did a somersault. The canopy took off in the wind, impaling itself on the next fence a hundred meters away. I took a quick inventory and found my body parts in the right places, with nothing broken.

Two other guys were being dragged in their harnesses at a good clip. I intercepted one and jumped on his canopy, collapsing it with my weight. The jumper was stunned, so I ran up and released the canopy for him.

We mustered once everyone was down. Incredibly, nobody'd been hurt. One man had been dragged through a fence before he was able to get rid of his canopy, but he appeared okay—SEALs are hard to hurt. We had all landed together in the space of a football field. Even Mike was impressed.

Back at the DZ, where we'd been driven by a friendly farmer, we figured we had landed about five miles short. It turned out that the DZ officer realized, just after he told us it was good to go on the ground, that the thunderstorm was approaching, not moving away. He stopped the second stick from jumping. They were now in the debriefing room, waiting to hear our stories. There were 30-knot winds on the DZ, gusting to 40 knots about the time we hit the ground. I told him to keep that information within the command. Some higher headquarters folks thought we were pushing the safety envelope as it was; I didn't want word getting out that we were doing night jumps in 40-knot winds, even if it wasn't on purpose.

Being back in the saddle, in command of a SEAL Team, was great; I hadn't enjoyed myself this much since Vietnam. As I look back on my Navy career I realize the time between my last combat tour in Vietnam and my next combat tour, at SEAL Team Six, was a period of hiatus, in which I did what I had to do to get by. I didn't plan it that way because I had no way of knowing the future. I once told my old friend and mentor, Dave Schaible, that there were only two good jobs in the Teams. As the commanding officer, he had one of them; and as a platoon commander, I had the other. The corollary is, it gets better when you have those jobs in combat.

After I left SEAL Team Two in November 1968 and before I assumed command of SEAL Team Six in July 1983, I had many less interesting assignments, but each made me a more proficient SEAL officer and prepared me for a senior leadership position in my community. I had three operational tours, three staff tours, and a stint at our institute of higher learning, the Naval War College.

Operational tours were always more pleasant than staff assignments. As executive officer of UDT-22 from 1968 to 1970, I had an opportunity to learn administration. I even got the chance to "command" a small joint task group during an exercise with Army Special Forces. I stayed busier than hell in my first "administrative" job. Despite what Ron Smith had told me in 1962, XOs didn't get to surf anymore. I never did understand how he managed to take so much time off; he must have been a lot more organized than me.

Commanding SEAL Team Two from 1972 to 1974 gave me my first real taste of service politics and also showed me I was right in my assessment of jobs: it was the next best thing to being a platoon commander. I was the first former SEAL platoon commander to command a SEAL Team, and the first CO to have commanded a platoon in combat. My counterpart at SEAL Team One at the time had not even been in a SEAL Team. He spent his "combat tour" on the staff of the Naval Special Warfare Group Vietnam, headquartered in Saigon. I was full of piss and vinegar when I took over SEAL Two. I knew we had to wean ourselves from our Vietnam missions and make ourselves invaluable to other commanders. We focused on the European theater, on keeping the Soviet bear in his cage. Language training and running escape-and-evasion (E & E) networks became a high priority, and we also conducted numerous mobile training teams in South America.

Commanding UDT-12 on the West Coast from 1979 to 1981 was an extra treat for me. In the midseventies we'd managed to get our organizational act together. Under the reconstituted Naval Special Warfare Groups, the Team commanding officer slots were upgraded to commander level to put us on a par with the rest of the Navy. I had the good fortune to have made commander and be available when it came time to change command of Team Twelve—which not only allowed me to be operational again for the first time in five years but also gave me a chance to work for Dave Schaible again. He took command of our group soon after I joined UDT-12. Together with Dave and my old swim buddy Chuck LeMoyne, who became his chief of staff, I had the pleasure of being able to turn around the malaise that had developed in the West Coast SEAL-UDTs. Dave gave me the go-ahead for realistic and demanding training, and my SEAL values were reborn under his expert leadership. We had a push-the-envelope training mentality, for which SEAL Team Six was later to become notorious. Our rationale was, if you didn't push hard and make mistakes in training, you'd make those mistakes on a real mission and pay a tremendous price. We made great progress in swimmer delivery vehicle operations and submerged reconnaissance. My guys became almost as good in the water as my old UDT-22 platoon had been back in 1966.

The three staff tours were less exciting. These tours are to be avoided at all costs, even though they play an important part in officer development. I was lucky in that two of my assignments were on the Pacific Naval Special Warfare Group staffs. As a young operations officer from 1970 to 1972, I commanded a small task group during an exercise in Korea. Here I learned that tact and diplomacy (heretofore not two of my more renowned skills) are crucial to working with allied troops.

On the staff of the commander-in-chief of the Atlantic command (CINCLANT) from 1976 to 1979, I gained an appreciation for life near the top of the military food chain. Then, after a year at the Naval War College learning the theory about how the services run, at CINCLANT I learned the practicalities of war planning, programming, and funding—all of which were invaluable to me later on.

My second stint on the Pacific Naval Special Warfare staff came just after my tour as CO of UDT-12. As the chief staff officer I had the opportunity to learn how to manage a large organization and how to deal with female subordinates (carefully). The job also put me in the right place at the right time to become the second commanding officer of SEAL Team Six.

SEAL Team Six, formed in 1980, was the Navy component of a permanent joint operational headquarters (with Army, Navy, and Air Force), which enabled the U.S. military to react quickly to various contingencies. Other SEAL Teams still worked near the bottom of the food chain, but SEAL Team Six was in a very short chain of command; the commander of the Joint Headquarters reported directly to the chairman of the Joint Chiefs of Staff. And all units under the Joint Headquarters were required to deploy, ready to fight, within a few hours of notification—the highest alert status in the defense structure of the entire conventional force.

Toward the end of my assignment as chief staff officer, Captain Maynard Weyers, the administrative commander of Six, asked if I wanted to command Six after Dick Marcinko.

Dick and I were old friends. We went way back; he was an enlisted man in UDT-22 when I checked in after basic training. We made a recruiting trip to the Great Lakes Naval Training Center shortly after I arrived and did a demonstration parachute jump to impress the young recruits.

The plane we borrowed wasn't equipped with an anchor cable (needed to attach my parachute static line to begin the opening sequence). So, I jumped out with my static line wrapped around Dick's arm as he braced himself against the side of the plane to take the eighty-pound pull that would open my canopy. As soon as I had full deployment, he jumped using a free-fall rig. It's not as dangerous as it sounds but it illustrates the great confidence we had in each other. I was young—what the hell.

After Dick was posted on the staff of the Chief of Naval Operations—the right place at the right time—he became the first commanding officer of SEAL Team Six. He did a good job getting Six off the ground. But, over the three years he'd been in command, he'd pissed off both his administrative and operational commanders so much that they wanted him to go do something else.

It took me about a millisecond to tell Maynard yes. I was going back to command for an unprecedented third time—and to a command that would be the first to go to war. Nothing could have been better except a chance to turn back my personal clock and be a platoon commander at Six.

Getting back in the saddle proved to be very interesting. On May 2, 1983, Master Chief Petty Officer "Johnny" Johnson, the senior enlisted man at SEAL Team Six, paid a call on me. He got right to the point: I shouldn't relieve Dick. Why? Because Dick had a lot of initiatives about to come to fruition. Johnny, as the voice of the enlisted men at Six, felt that no one coming in could finish what Dick had started. He told me Dick needed another year; after that, it would be okay if I relieved him. I listened, but Johnny was pissing me off and he sensed it, so he quickly added that as far as he was concerned, if anyone had to relieve Dick now it should be me. I told him I had no qualms about coming in and continuing what Dick had started. We parted amicably, him saying he'd support me fully "if" I showed up—Dick, he intimated, would probably use his pull in Washington to get the turnover quashed. Johnny was a "stalking horse," sent by Dick to see how committed I was. But I had a lot of respect for Johnny. He was a super operator in Vietnam, was well thought of by all who knew him, and he helped me considerably when I got to Six. Sadly, he died of a heart attack during my tour.

On May 9, Dick called to say he'd "heard" what Maynard had in mind. Normally, at least in the SEAL community, the prospective CO contacts the man he is to relieve to coordinate the turnover. I'd planned to do so as soon as Maynard gave me the go-ahead. (In fact, I had called Maynard as soon as Johnny had left my office to tell him that someone had penetrated his cloak of silence, but Maynard had asked me to not contact Dick yet anyway. I hadn't been comfortable with the subterfuge, but out of respect for Maynard and his position I'd complied.) Dick seemed resigned to my relieving him that summer; he told me he wanted to leave about July 9, to give himself some time off before he reported to his next assignment at the National War College. Two weeks, he thought, would be plenty for the turnover; I should also spend about three days at Joint Headquarters meeting people. I said all that was fine with me, and I'd be there when he wanted.

I still hadn't received orders, though I'd been told they were "in the mail"; then, on May 25, the SEAL officer assignment office called to tell me that my orders were on hold. The civilian assistant who made the call thought there was "flag" interest in the situation. I learned why from her boss, a hot-running young SEAL lieutenant commander named Tom Moser. Dick knew Vice Admiral "Ace" Lyons—who was commanding Second Fleet in Norfolk and was rumored to be the next Deputy Chief of Naval Operations for Plans, Policy and Operations (OP-06)—because they had both worked together in OP-06. Before Dick left the Pentagon to form Six, he made OP-06 the OPNAV guardian for Six, and now he'd asked Lyons to use his influence to keep Dick in his job. Moser said he'd let me know as soon as he heard something.

The next day, Maynard called saying that Lyons had met with Vice Admiral Briggs, Maynard's boss, who was Commander, Naval Surface Forces Atlantic. Marcinko had apparently told Lyons I hadn't been interviewed like everyone else who went to that command. Lyons asked Briggs about my "quals," Maynard said, and then Briggs called *him* and said he wanted to talk to me ASAP but that I had to go to the Pentagon first, for an OP-06 interview. Maynard asked if I could be in Washington the next day to start the process. I said no sweat.

Captain Irish Flynn, my boss and Commander, Naval Special Warfare Group One, told me to do whatever it took but please be back in time for the farewell party he was giving me on May 27, since a lot of out-of-town folks were coming. It would be nice if the guest of honor were present. I figured there'd be no problem, since we were three hours behind East Coast time.

I grabbed the red-eye to Washington that night and was in the OP-06 office at 0800 the next morning, May 26. Lieutenant Commander Joe Quincannon, the resident SEAL in OP-06, took me to meet with Rear Admiral Dudley Carlson, whom I'd first met when he commanded U.S.S. *Grayback*, an old Regulus missile submarine that had been reconfigured to conduct swimmer support operations. Carlson apologized for the situation; he knew I'd have no problem handling the job, he said, but the face-to-face interview had to be done for the sake of form. He said he'd recently visited Six, finding a group of very dedicated and capable men in need of some discipline; Dick had done well establishing the command but had run his string and was becoming counterproductive in his ability to influence the chain of command. It was time for new blood, and I was the best man for the job. I took all these platitudes for what they were and said, "Thanks, I'm looking forward to the challenge," or something appropriate to that effect.

Next Joe took me to meet Rear Admiral Packer, who reiterated what Carlson said. I thanked Joe for the hospitality and left the Pentagon for Washington National Airport to catch an afternoon flight to Norfolk. I'd kissed the OP-06 ring and been sprinkled with holy water. It was time to repeat the process.

I arrived in Norfolk about 1800, got a room at the airport motel, and called Maynard to let him know I was there. He said he'd be by to get me around nine the next morning, and then we'd go see Vice Admiral Briggs. He asked that I not let anyone know I was in town. Things were really getting mysterious.

On the way to see Briggs the next morning, Maynard told me all he knew about Dick's machinations. Apparently, Lyons had vehemently insisted that Dick remain in place until he, Lyons, took over OP-06. Then Lyons would decide who would relieve Dick. Maynard and I agreed that the whole process was bizarre; he said it only served to illustrate that Dick had gone off the deep end.

Briggs welcomed me and apologized for dragging me across the country to go through the interview; he said he'd promised Lyons he would touch all the bases. We had a short conversation, which would probably have been even shorter if he hadn't felt bad about me being there in the first place. He asked me about my career, I gave him a synopsis, he asked how I got my Silver Star, I said something about being stupid but lucky, he laughed and said being lucky was better than being good. The interview ended, and Briggs said I'd receive my orders in a few days.

Maynard took me to the airport to catch an afternoon flight back to San Diego, and I got to my farewell party at Irish's house only two hours late.

I checked out of Special Warfare Group One on June 10 and hit the road to Norfolk. A few days before that, Dick had called to say he knew what had happened in Norfolk. Very nicely, he told me I shouldn't sell my house in San Diego (I hadn't intended to) or move Becky and the kids. (I hadn't intended to move anyone just yet; Kevin was staying to attend San Diego State University, while Becky and Anne would follow as soon as Becky got our house rented.) I thanked him appropriately for his interest in my welfare and said I'd see him about June 17.

Stopping only for food, gas, and sleep, I drove straight through from San Diego to the Joint Headquarters. There, I heard that Six was composed of good people and Dick had done a great job . . . But it was time for him to go. As one Army colonel put it, "Dick took the hill—now it's time for someone to come in and solidify the position." As I learned later, more than half the hill remained to be taken.

I arrived at the gate outside the SEAL Six headquarters at about 1600 on Friday, June 17, 1983. Lieutenant Commander Pete Stevens, the Team's XO, brought me inside and introduced me to a few people. Men I'd worked with before came by the office and welcomed me. My old shipmates said they were really glad to see me. But Pete was the gladdest of all, it seemed. I found out why the next day; meanwhile, though, it turned out I had a party to attend, at a local watering hole. Dick had called and was sending his car to get Pete and me.

In a few minutes, Pete and I were in a gray Mercedes sedan, equipped with all the accoutrements of a police car, on our way to Virginia Beach. The party was in full swing, and the troops were anxious to meet me. Seems Dick had told them a lot about me and the men wanted to see for themselves.

At the bar, we found Dick ensconced in a rear booth with a group of longhaired men. He welcomed me aboard the command and told someone to get me a drink. I had a beer and looked around. Besides Dick, I recognized only Duke Leonard and one other young officer, whom I'd known from a distance when he was an enlisted man in UDT-21. Duke had been a young seaman in SEAL Team Two when I left in 1968. Now he was a lieutenant and one of the assault team leaders at Six.

It was an interesting evening, a good opportunity to meet some of the men in Six and to ask and answer questions. A few of the men made some insubordinate comments but I blamed that on the booze. Also, except for a few minutes before I relieved him, it proved to be the only "turnover" I was to have with Dick.

The next day Pete told me he'd about had it working for Marcinko. He'd tried to insert some discipline and integrity into the command, only to have Dick cut him off at the knees. Pete said Dick ran the place in a libertine style: anything the troops wanted was okay by him, and he routinely misled his superiors in the chain of command under the guise of OPSEC. If the officers attempted to assert themselves, Dick backed the enlisted. Pete went on: Dick insisted upon everyone drinking with him whenever he wanted and as long as he wanted. Pete was concerned about the readiness of the command; on exercises they seldom finished the entire scenario because as soon as things got tough, Dick would step in, abort the exercise, and take the troops drinking.

I listened but probably didn't hear as well as I should have. I knew Pete had extremely high operational standards. And I also knew exercises were meant to uncover flaws in training and tactics. Besides, I'd just come from the operational commander's headquarters, where everyone told me how great the command was in the field.

I should have paid more attention to Pete.

On Monday, June 20, 1983, I arrived at the command to begin the turnover and learned that Dick had left for Europe on Saturday, taking an officer and three enlisted with him, ostensibly to visit a counterpart unit in Italy for some training and familiarization.

Though I figured I didn't need Dick, I had no idea why he hadn't told me he was going. Maybe it had something to do with the real purpose of the trip—as I later learned, a last attempt to keep me from taking over. Vice Admiral Lyons was finishing up a Second Fleet exercise in Northern Europe, so Dick and the troops met him in Germany and provided him bodyguard services while he was out bar-hopping on liberty. Dick and his guys were all illegally carrying concealed weapons, and to make matters worse, Dick imposed upon a German "brother" unit to help by keeping them out of jail if they were caught.

Apparently Dick figured his services would give him some more chips with Lyons, so that when he took over OP-06 he would retain Dick and send me away to some cushy job. A couple of years later, the commander of the German unit told me it was one of the most distasteful things he'd ever had to do; he was embarrassed for Six. Two of the three men who accompanied Dick also told me they were embarrassed at being used in this way and embarrassed by how Dick had treated me. In fact, I heard the latter comment from about 99 percent of the troops during the three years I was in command.

On June 22, Maynard asked me to come see him and asked how things were going. I said, "Not bad." I figured I owed some loyalty to my new command. I wasn't going to go into the details of the previous Friday night because my first day at the command convinced me that the behavior I saw then wasn't a fair sample of the command. I told Maynard there was nothing I couldn't handle. All the men needed was some good leadership and adult supervision, and I could provide both. We did, however, discuss the events that transpired after I left the bar.

After Pete and I left, Dick had told his driver to drive him around Virginia Beach. At a stoplight, they rear-ended another car, driven by a "little old lady." The accident did considerable damage to both cars, but fortunately no one was hurt. Dick had his car spirited off to a local Mercedes dealer for repairs.

Pete and I learned about the accident at the same time Monday morning. Normally the duty officer would have notified Pete at once, and Pete would have sent a standard SITREP—situation report—to the chain of command. In the military, the rule is clear and uncompromising: you report such events immediately, so the hierarchy doesn't hear about them from the news media. But Dick had ordered the duty officer to notify only the operations officer, Lieutenant Bill Davis, and specifically *not* to tell the XO or me. And he'd told the OPSO not to send any reports or tell anyone, including Pete and me. But Bill Davis, being a good officer, found he couldn't follow such an order; he came in first thing Monday and told Pete, who immediately sent the required reports and initiated an investigation.

Now Maynard told me that Vice Admiral Briggs had ordered him to take over that investigation. Apparently Briggs was angry that Dick had used one of the four Mercedeses "owned" by Six to go to the watering hole. Some background about these cars: Claiming that they were needed for operations, Dick had used "procurement" money to buy them in Germany, despite being told not to do so by both his operational and his administrative commanders. Then he shipped the cars to the U.S. in a "mission" C-141. Both chains of command investigated the incident but since no one knew what else to do with the American taxpayers' new vehicles, Six was allowed to retain them, and Dick was told not to do anything like that again. Actually, the purchase really was a good idea. All four vehicles were police configured, and two were off-road "Jeep" types that proved to be very useful in later mission planning. The real problem was, Dick used one of them, a gray sedan, as a personal vehicle, although Maynard told him not to. He argued that the command's high alert status required him to have an appropriately equipped vehicle with him at all times. Again, the argument had merit but he never took the time to send a proper request through the chain of command to CNO to get a waiver. And Maynard was in the hot seat with Briggs because it appeared he had no control over Dick.

The investigation lasted about three weeks. Dick wound up being taken to "captain's mast"—this is the lowest-level discipline system in the Navy, for minor offenses that don't warrant a court-martial—and getting a letter of reprimand from Maynard. Usually that's enough to end the career of a Navy officer. In the course of the investigation, Dick tried to blame the entire incident on his driver. I couldn't believe it. And when word leaked out to the troops, most of them were really pissed.

During our June 22 meeting, Maynard asked if I would be ready to relieve Dick by July 8. He was concerned that, if we didn't transfer the command by then, Dick might find a way to keep it from happening. I said that although I had found the job much more complex than I had imagined, I could take over that day, only I'd need his support if I uncovered any rats' nests. He said not to worry, and the change-of-command ceremony was scheduled for July 8.

Normally an outgoing CO spends a lot of time with his relief, explaining the nuances of the command. Dick and I met in his office on July 8, about ten minutes before the ceremony. He showed me the safe, the refrigerator, the gin, and the gin glasses, and that was it. The formal ceremony, before the assembled troops, took no more than twenty minutes. Usually, the officer immediately senior to the CO will tell all assembled how great a guy the outgoing CO is and how all should support the new guy so there will be a seamless transfer of responsibility. The operational commander spoke for about one minute, telling the command how great they were. Maynard said nothing. Dick spoke disconnectedly for a few minutes, but he did say that even though he didn't want to leave I was the best person to relieve him. I think he still believed Lyons would intervene and put him back in the saddle by October.

I was in command of Six—let the fun begin.

19

ONE MORE CLOSE CALL: URGENT FURY

In 1983 the leftist, Cuban-backed government of Grenada, with the help of Cuban engineers, was hastily constructing an airfield at Point Salines; ostensibly, the airfield was intended for civil aviation, but it was capable of handling military aircraft. In the Cold War era, to have a military airfield built and supported by a country aligned with the Soviet Union was unacceptable to the United States.

On October 25, the U.S. military launched Operation Urgent Fury to rescue American medical students attending classes at the Grenadan Medical University just outside the capital, St. George's. To carry out that mission the forces were ordered to take over the island and rescue the former governor general, who was being held under house arrest by the new regime.

I'd been in command since July but most of my time had been spent trying to garner operational funding; the coffers had been depleted by my predecessor. On the Friday afternoon four days before Urgent Fury, I received an odd phone call from the chief of staff of the Joint Headquarters, who told me to be ready to come see him the next day for briefing on an operation. I asked my operations officer, Lieutenant Bill Davis, what was going on, but he said he didn't know. I had a feeling my first exposure to Joint Headquarters procedures might be a real operation.

The next morning I was eating breakfast in my kitchen when the phone rang and the chief of staff told me to get to a meeting at CINCLANT headquarters as fast as I could. This surprised me; Joint Headquarters normally took direction from the secretary of defense, through the chairman of the Joint Chiefs of Staff, so having CINCLANT in the operational picture seemed strange. But what the hell—I was a new guy in the organization. I called Bill Davis and told him to meet me there.

Commander Dick "Andy" Anderson, a SEAL officer assigned to the operational commander's staff (and an old SEAL Team Two, Vietnam compatriot), was at the security station when I arrived. We went directly to a briefing room on the second deck. There was a buzz of activity. Army Lieutenant Colonel Dick Pack, from the Joint Headquarters operations division, told me briefly that JCS wanted us to "take down" an island in the Caribbean—Grenada. He said we would be working with CINCLANT; the commanding general (CG) of the Joint Headquarters had objected to that, but was overruled when CINCLANT convinced the chairman that because Grenada was in his area of responsibility he should be in charge. This was to be the first time the Joint Headquarters had ever conducted an actual operation and the departure from the planned chain of command proved to have a big impact on it.

Showing my keen geographic knowledge, I asked, "Where *is* Grenada?"

Pack pointed to a speck on the map, then explained that the CG wanted us to get an Air Force combat-control team into the Salines Point airfield that night or the next. They were to determine if the runways were clear so U.S. Army Rangers, tasked to seize the airfield, could land in C-130s. If it were blocked they would have to parachute instead. He had to brief CINCLANT in five minutes and needed my concept of operations. Andy said there was some planning going on in the room behind us, so we joined in.

I asked what Navy ships were near Grenada and was shown the order of battle. There was a destroyer in port at an island just east of Grenada that also had a civilian airfield. I turned to Bill Davis and told him we'd simply throw our guys and the two-man combat-control team in a C-130 along with a couple of rubber boats and fly them to the airfield; from there, they could board the destroyer. The ship could then launch our people for the reconnaissance of the Grenadan airfield. It sounded simple and effective. Whatever gear the men needed to take would fit easily in the C-130, and they'd get there in a hurry. I told Bill to get on the secure phone and recall our standby assault team, then went to the briefing room and filled Pack in. The briefing had already begun, and I took a place off to the side.

When Pack explained how I planned to put our people on the destroyer, the CINC objected: he didn't want us tipping our hand by using military aircraft. Someone in the audience asked why we didn't jump the men in, so I spoke up: we could; at-sea jumps were routine for SEALs. But since we had Air Force people involved, I'd rather keep it simple. At that point, Pack introduced me to the crowd and I said I'd continue working on the problem. I knew the Joint Headquarters had access to "civilianized" military aircraft and I figured it would be easy to get one on short notice. We also had direct access to other civilianized aircraft, smaller than I thought we'd need but easier to arrange.

Bill and I drove back to our headquarters, planning en route. Back at Six, Pete Stevens had everyone we needed on board. The standby team was in and getting their gear ready. I got everyone together and went over the plan. It seemed simple and would require only about six of our guys.

With Master Chief Billy Acklin, my senior enlisted man and air operations expert, Bill Davis and I left immediately for the Joint Headquarters, some 200 miles away. The place was hopping; the Army colonel who was the operations chief told me to be prepared to brief the CG in thirty minutes. Meanwhile, though, Billy Acklin told me the navigation equipment on the small civilianized plane needed parts and wouldn't be ready for another week. The operations chief put his guys to work getting another, larger civilianized plane.

After I briefed the CG, he said he'd gotten permission from CINCLANT to put our people in the next night. "And by the way," he said, "you've got some more missions." My other assault teams would be on standby at Salines airfield for expected rescues and direct-action missions—raids.

At 1800 on October 22, we learned the commanding general had to brief the Joint Chiefs of Staff at 0700 the next morning. Our standby team and some members of another assault team arrived around 2000 and began the struggle to come up with good plans amid a flurry of activity. Davis, Acklin, and I went from pillar to post seeking intelligence to help us. It was at this point that I learned of the Cuban "engineers"—who were probably military advisers.

The civilianized aircraft was to arrive at midnight to pick up our reconnaissance team. Acklin and I went to the airport at 2300 to see the guys off. So far so good.

Back at the command center, things had changed dramatically. The CG, having thus far restricted our operations to the western end of the island, where all the important targets were located, now wanted to take a look at a second airfield on Grenada's eastern end. He wanted another combat-control team in there the next night, because the guys we had just launched couldn't reconnoiter both.

We huddled with the combat-control planners, who finally suggested we "rubber-duck" people in. I asked when they had last dropped inflatable rubber boats (used by all SEAL Teams as their basic insertion craft) by parachute at sea. They said never. Our guys had never done a rubber-duck drop either, but they *had* dropped our Boston Whalers, which had been in SEAL Team Six since the command was formed. Bill and I both believed it would be no sweat to drop our Whalers near the destroyer during the day. This was also a good way for me to get down there to take over. Like all SEALs, I wanted to get to the action, and the two reconnaissance operations were all we had going. I told the standby team leader to get my gear packed in one of our boats.

Then plans changed again: we'd been taken off the standby mode and were going to have some real targets. The CG told me to get with the Army component commander and divide up the targets.

The colonel and I looked at the target list. Our two units were to liberate political prisoners and rescue the governor general. The politicals were in a prison that looked very formidable—a good job for the Army, I thought, and he agreed. We'd handle the governor general as well as another target, the Radio Grenada broadcast station, located near the sea at Beausejour, about seven miles north of the governor general's mansion. Also, I said we'd plan for two other targets at the eastern end of the island that the general wanted covered.

We were to seize the governor general's mansion and the radio station and hold both targets for about four hours, until we were relieved by elements of the 82nd Airborne Division, who were to land at Salines airfield soon after it was under Joint Headquarters control. They would transport the governor general to the radio station so he could broadcast to the world that the U.S. presence in Grenada was legal and desired by the legal government.

The Whalers were rigged for parachuting. We planned to drop them to the destroyer about 1600 the next day at a point about forty miles northeast of Grenada, well away from the airfields but also on the opposite side of the island from the routes used by local merchant ships. I didn't want to risk being seen by them.

By now it was becoming clear to me that I wasn't going to be able to jump; I'd have to stay at the Joint Headquarters to plan the other missions. But because the mission was so important, I would go with the assault team to rescue the governor general and establish my command post at his mansion. The boat-drop team was ready and the planes were being loaded. They pulled my gear out of the boat and, after a brief delay in loading because of power failure on the base, the C-130s took off. I told the men to do good.

On October 23, while the CG was at the Pentagon briefing the Joint Chiefs of Staff, they learned that the Marine barracks at Beirut Airport had been bombed.

Up till now, the Marines had not been involved in Urgent Fury; the initial assault was a Joint Headquarters show, with the 82nd Airborne Division and other forces coming in after. But now that the Marines had been bloodied in Beirut, they wanted an active role. Politics took over and the island was divided down the middle, with the Joint Headquarters retaining the southwestern part and the Marines given the go-ahead to make an amphibious landing at the smaller airfield in the northeast. The chain of command changed as well. Instead of reporting directly to CINCLANT as the task force commander, our commanding general was made subordinate to a joint task force commanded by a Navy admiral, who would now be the on-scene commander for the entire operation. This was a dramatic change to make only hours before we were supposed to launch. And there would be more.

The Joint Headquarters had planned for an 0200 H-hour on October 25. SEALs were trained and equipped to operate at night, under the cover of darkness. All our tactics were based on that. The problem was, the Marines, like most conventional military forces in those days, weren't trained very well for night helo operations. So they wanted a daylight H-hour. After much gnashing of teeth and our CG threatening to pull us out, H-hour was set at 0500—first light—to accommodate the coordinated assault. At least we'd have *some* darkness as we approached our targets.

Finally, the new command structure dictated new targeting. We lost two targets we had been planning for at the eastern end of Grenada. And, though I didn't learn it until the next day, the Marines didn't want us doing a reconnaissance at Perles, the smaller airfield, which was in their OPAREA.

Bill Davis and I went to the Joint Headquarters Tactical Operations Center at 1600, October 23, to get news of the boat drop, scheduled for 1600. But 1600 came and went—no drop. Bill learned the drop had been rescheduled for 1800 because the planes had to fly a longer, circuitous route to avoid detection. The air planners said not to worry because there would still be plenty of daylight at 1800.

At 1800 we listened on the SATCOM radio as the planes reported their drop runs. Normally, the two planes would approach the drop zone (the destroyer) in tandem formation from downwind, with the trail plane just above the lead. Both would turn into the wind on final heading to drop the boats and jumpers right next to the destroyer. My guys on the ship sent a radio report that they were ready and the weather was okay. The planes turned final and dropped. Then things went to shit.

First, it wasn't daylight. It was pitch dark, with no moon. Urgent Fury had been planned on "local" time. Eastern Daylight Time was the same as Atlantic Standard Time, which applies in Grenada. That is, it *was* the same, until 0200 of the day we launched the reconnaissance team: the Atlantic time zone didn't observe daylight saving time. When we "fell back," they stayed the same. Instead of an easy daylight drop my men had to do a more complicated night drop. I didn't know it at the time, but SEAL Six had never done a night boat drop—or *any* night water parachuting, for that matter.

Second, the trailing C-130 missed its turn point and dropped our men some two miles away. The destroyer's pickup party had to split into two groups and the ship had to maneuver accordingly. (In the aftermath, the Air Force couldn't really explain why the second plane had gone astray, except that the pilot had made an error. The real problem was that the C-130 crews, though well trained, were not familiar with water drops.)

Third, the jump took place in the middle of a rain squall that apparently came out of nowhere. Such squalls are not unusual in the Caribbean but, for some reason, no one noticed the shift in weather until it was too late.

Alone, night drop and the separation of the two groups might not have made a difference, but the squall combined with them did. Four of my men died. To this day I don't know for sure what happened to them. We never found their bodies. I can only surmise that the four men couldn't get rid of their canopies, were dragged through the water facedown, and drowned. In a matter of minutes the weight of the chutes would have dragged the bodies to the bottom. All the gear was rigged for a daylight drop, so no strobe lights were attached to the jumpers or the boats. A jumper with a problem would have had to solve it himself, because no one could see him. Strangely, the four lost men came from the plane that dropped next to the ship.

Four good SEALs drowned, and one of the two pickup boats capsized, apparently also because of the squall. I was devastated. I blamed myself (and still do) because I hadn't done something to prevent it. We searched for hours but couldn't find the missing men. When it was time to start the insertion to the airfield, I had to tell Lieutenant "Pat," the assault team leader, to stop looking and go. A larger air search began the next morning and continued during daylight for three more days. Though they located the capsized boat the next day, they never found my men. And in the aftermath I learned of the Marines' decision that we wouldn't be doing a reconnaissance at Perles. The additional shooters need never have left Norfolk.

Pat, some of his men, and the Air Force combat-control team departed the destroyer for Salines airfield in the one good boat. Encountering a ship with a spotlight, they assumed it was one of the two patrol craft in the Grenadan "Navy" and took evasive action, which slowed them down. (Later, we learned that it hadn't been a patrol boat at all but a U.S. Navy ship conducting electronic intelligence. Because of secrecy, the Joint Headquarters wasn't informed of its presence.)

Pat's boat started taking on water. It was getting late and Pat rightly judged that he couldn't get to the airfield in the dark. He didn't want to run the risk of being spotted and giving away the larger operation, so he decided to return to the destroyer. They had time to do the operation the next night and still get the information back well prior to H-hour. Meanwhile, since SOP called for operating the whalers in pairs, we dropped a second one to him the next day.

At this point I still wasn't concerned about the Salines mission. I figured that with two boats, unreliable though they were turning out to be, Pat would get the combat-control team to the target. But then the first boat, being towed behind the destroyer because it had no way of lifting the Whaler on board, capsized in the heavy seas. So that night, instead of two boats, the men were back to one. Wary of what they still thought was a patrol boat operating near their target area, Pat had the destroyer move to the south side of the island. They launched, and Pat decided to go to a small island just off the south side of the airfield. There he planned to load his personnel into a rubber boat for the short transit to the airfield. But again they encountered heavy weather; the Whaler took on water, flooding one of the engines, and the Air Force lieutenant colonel decided it was in no condition to proceed. Pat, being a good SEAL and at home in the water, felt they could continue but the lieutenant colonel was adamant. They finally returned to the destroyer.

At 0500 on October 25 the rangers parachuted into Salines. It turned out that they would have had to jump anyway, because the Cuban "engineers" had blocked the runway with a bulldozer, but that didn't lessen the embarrassment and depression I felt. We hadn't completed the mission, and we'd lost four good men in the process. The damn boats weren't capable of doing what we needed to get done—they weren't seaworthy.

Meanwhile, back at the command center, confusion continued to reign. While attending a meeting at CINCLANT, the commanding general had met a U.S. State Department representative who showed him a three-week-old hour-by-hour plan for taking the island. Approved by the White House, it assigned target priorities different from those we had established. I fought off the target changes, but I didn't win on another issue.

The commanding general called me aside to tell me the State Department representative would be in the command center within the hour and I had to meet with him.

"Why?"

"Because he's going with you to the governor general's house," the CG replied.

I protested vigorously. The general told me to figure it out and walked away. He'd made the same argument at higher headquarters earlier, to no avail; the White House–approved plan called for our State Department to hold the governor general's hand to make sure his radio broadcast said all the right things.

When I met him later, the State Department representative offered me some interesting information: that the Cuban "engineers" on the island wouldn't be a problem, because their government had informally agreed to keep its people in their barracks during our incursion. (In other words, the Cubans knew we were coming.) I asked how he could be so sure of their cooperation. He said, "Don't worry about it," or something like that.

As we were finalizing our plans, the commanding general told the Army component commander and me he was very concerned about all the last-minute changes, and asked if we wanted him to request a twenty-four-hour delay in the operation. The colonel and I agreed: No way. Any delay would only give higher headquarters more time to make more changes. The troops were ready, but if I had to go another twenty-four hours without sleep I wouldn't be.

Still depressed over our lost guys, I had to keep reminding myself that my troops were depending on me and that I was one of the few people in the command who had seen combat. I decided I needed to talk to the troops, so at about 1800 I took a helo to the remote site, twenty miles from the command center, where they were in isolation planning their missions.

I got them in a briefing room and saw before me a sea of anxious but determined faces. They were ready. I don't remember exactly what I told them. I gave them what information I had about the missing men; I was still expecting them to turn up, because the wet-suit tops they'd worn for the jump would protect them against hypothermia. I told my men we had to go on, and I went over the rules of engagement. They were to shoot only if shot at or threatened, and they were to give Grenadan troops a chance to surrender before firing, because the higher-ups were trying to avoid hurting any islanders. Even though we had been told not to expect resistance, I told the troops to be ready.

I do remember thinking I wasn't worried about my guys—they were among the best in the world at picking the right target and shooting accurately. I think I mumbled something about how everyone is scared their first time in combat and not to worry, they'd do fine. A couple of years later, one of the men who was there told me he remembered everything I said that night and that it inspired him. When I looked at him as if to say, "Don't b.s. me," he protested, "No, really, you said just the right things for the time." I'm still not sure about this.

By this time I had managed to round up the third assault team, which had been training in California. The SEALs in Six had trained hard for three years and now they wanted part of the action. So I did my best to ensure that all of our shooters had a role. Since I was going to the governor general's mansion to establish my command post, I sent Pete Stevens with the reserve team to establish an alternate CP at the airfield after the rangers had secured it. I didn't think we'd really need a reserve force at the airfield, but I felt much more comfortable having them, and that proved to be a good decision.

At 2100 on October 24, the assault teams bound for the governor general's mansion and Radio Grenada, and I with my small command element, boarded a C-5 aircraft along with our UH-60 Blackhawk helicopters. We were settled in for the flight, and the plane had begun to taxi, when suddenly there was pounding on the fuselage. The Air Force load master opened the side door, and there was one of our men, Larry Barrett, running alongside with his rucksack. A couple of the guys grabbed his gear and pulled him aboard, and the plane kept rolling. Larry had been in an independent training course when one of the guys called to tell him he'd better get back to the Team without telling him why. When Larry got on the plane, he had no idea where we were going. He only knew he wasn't going to miss out.

I was exhausted. As soon as the C-5's wheels cleared the ground, I drifted off to sleep, thinking, "Here we go again." At 0330, we landed at a commercial airport near Grenada. We were more than an hour behind schedule, so as soon as the C-5 touched the ground, the Army helo guys were in the well deck undoing the shackles that held the helos in place. Some bureaucratic flight crew member started yelling at them to keep their seats "until the plane has finished taxiing and the captain has turned off the seat belt sign." Duke Leonard, the assault team leader for the governor-general mission, told him to sit down or he'd shoot him. The man sat.

The helo guys figured they needed an hour to get the Blackhawks ready to fly, but it turned out longer. We took off for Grenada just after 0500.

The eighty-minute flight to Grenada was uneventful but terribly uncomfortable. We had only three Blackhawks available for our missions. I had dedicated two for our primary target, the governor general, and the other for the radio station. We had to get all our troops plus the State Department weenie into the three birds. Then another change came up.

At the staging island, we'd been met by two men with a portable broadcast radio. The State Department guy told me they were part of his team and had to go with him to the governor general's mansion. The broadcast radio was so the governor general could start transmitting as soon as we seized his residence, instead of waiting till we reached Radio Grenada. Of course, that was the first I'd been told of this part of the plan. I decided two more people wouldn't matter, and that was how I ended up with fourteen combat-loaded SEALs, my radioman, and three State Department people in my helo.

Fifty minutes after leaving the staging island, we were over on the eastern end of Grenada. By now it was daylight, I could see the Marines ensconced at their airfield waving at us as we passed. We waved back. As we flew down the south side of Grenada, islanders on the ground continued to wave at us. It seemed they were glad to see the Americans. We made our way west, keeping the main mountain chain between us and our targets, then turned north and crested the mountains. The helo with the radio-station assault team, under the command of Lieutenant Kim Erskine, broke off and headed for their target.

As soon as we had crossed the mountains the friendly Grenadans disappeared. We began taking ground fire. The air seemed to be filled with aircraft and tracers. We were just east of our airfield when I spotted a firefight going on between the Rangers and the islanders. I remember thinking what a difference the mountains made. But I didn't have much time for reflection—rounds zinged by and slapped into the Hawk.

Looking down at the heavy canopy and steep terrain, I thought we'd have a hell of a time finding the mansion, yet somehow the crew managed. I have to admit I didn't see the place until they flared the bird to begin the insertion.

I had decided to go to the governor general's mansion because his recapture was the "political" key to the operation. But to take the State Department officers I had to change my insertion plan. Originally, we'd planned to have the Hawks drop us at the front and rear of the mansion, using our special rappelling technique. I go in at the rear, with the group securing the grounds, while Duke's group, at the front of the mansion, would rescue the governor general. But rappelling down a ninety-foot rope in the dark with forty pounds of gear on your back was not something I could allow the State Department people to try. To get them on the ground safely, we would have to land one of the helos or get it low enough so they could jump. One of Duke's guys, Bobby Lewis, volunteered to go in with a chain saw to cut down two trees at the front of the mansion to give us room to land, or at least hover low.

I wanted Duke to have enough people to overcome any resistance he might encounter as he assaulted the house, so I took the State Department guys with me in the bird going to the rear of the mansion. After dropping off our assault team we'd fly the Blackhawk to the front. By then Bobby would have cut down the trees; if he hadn't finished, we would hover till he did.

When our helo flared at about seventy-five feet, my guys bolted down the rope and were gone. I leaned out to help the crewman pull the rope back in so it didn't get sucked up into the rotating blades and turn the helo into a rock.

We began to take heavy fire from the top of the hill, just above our eye level as we looked out. I couldn't hear any gunfire—the high-pitched whine of the helo in hover and the *whop*ping of the blades as they spun just over the treetops drowned out all other noise—but I *could* hear the rounds slapping the helo. Just as I got the rope into the Hawk, I glimpsed some large muzzle flashes through the trees at the top of the hill, too bright to have come from small arms.

Just as I registered "Antiaircraft weapon," the Hawk was pushed horizontally through the air, away from the hill. It shuddered and tilted left. The pilot yelled that the copilot was hit and the helo lurched out of control and started falling downhill, toward the mansion.

For a few seconds all was chaos. I was pressed into the left door of the bird—if it hadn't been closed, I would have fallen out—and all I could see was sky as we picked up speed. We almost inverted, but somehow the pilot managed to regain control and keep flying. As the helo came upright I fell on the floor. My radioman's eyes were saucers, but otherwise he looked okay. The State Department guys were on the floor next to me, also okay. I took inventory of my own parts and determined that I hadn't been hit either. In the few seconds it took me to do all this, the helo screamed sideways past the mansion and down the hill toward the harbor. I saw trees and buildings flash past. I remember thinking we were going in, and I only hoped we made it as far as the water.

By this time, the helo crew chief was half in the front seat, trying to stem the copilot's bleeding. I yelled to my radioman and the State Department guys to prepare for a crash and started unlacing my boots, thinking we were going to be swimming—at best. A peaceful calm developed within me. I'd survived two "controlled" crashes in Vietnam, but this bird was out of control and badly shot up.

The ground rushed past the door—then, as we broke over the pier area, I saw muzzle flashes: we were still taking heavy fire, this time from the harbor. Just before it seemed we would hit the water, the pilot leveled the bird. Scant feet above the water we hurtled out of the bay, tracers zinging past and into us until we cleared the harbor.

The crew chief was still giving first aid to the copilot, who was in shock and losing a lot of blood from a massive wound in his thigh. I thought a round had severed his femoral artery and I told the crew chief to get a tourniquet on immediately. The pilot said he wasn't sure how long he could keep us flying. We knew the operation's flagship, *Guam*, had hospital facilities, but could the pilot keep the Hawk in the air long enough for us to find it? To compound our trouble there was a mist in the air at sea, so visibility was poor.

The pilot cleared the harbor, started a slow climb, and turned east, toward where we figured *Guam* would be. After what seemed like an eternity, I saw a few destroyers below us. The Hawk was still jerking and pitching, and the pilot kept yelling he didn't know how long he could keep us in the air. I'm not a helo pilot, but I'd flown in enough of them to know the sounds of a good one. This one wasn't making any good sounds. We kept flying east, seeing more and more gray shapes in the water. Through the morning mist we finally spotted a large gray shape that looked like the *Guam*. As we headed in, a helo took off and another approached. Our pilot radioed *Guam* and we received permission to land immediately.

Our helo came out of the sky like a wounded bird. The pilot was fighting the controls, and the Hawk kept trying to heel to the left as *Guam*'s deck came rapidly toward us. There was nothing I could do to help and I just figured we were going to crash. The bird's tail was swinging back and forth as we fell toward the flight deck. I yelled for those of us in the back to brace for landing. Somehow, the pilot managed to slam us into the deck hard but not too hard. We bounced once and came to rest, the blades whopping furiously and the engine screaming.

I jumped out immediately and helped pull the copilot out of his seat as ship's corpsmen converged on us. He was still bleeding heavily and I didn't think he was going to make it. Then I headed for the flag bridge—I had men on the ground and I had to talk to them. When I hit the flag bridge, I encountered Lieutenant Colonel Digger O'Dell, the Joint Headquarters liaison officer on the task force staff. I left my radioman and told him to establish contact with our guys on Digger's SATCOM.

I ran into the Army brigadier general who was the deputy task force commander, and gave him a quick brief. After listening intently he asked if I had managed to deliver the letter to the governor general.

"What letter?"

He said it was their understanding that I had a letter for the governor general to read over the air, welcoming us to his island. I told him that was the first I'd heard of any letter and that I had three State Department guys he could talk to, but that I'd really like to start arranging transport back to the mansion and my men. He agreed to get me the first flyable helo.

Digger took me aside and explained the situation as he knew it—basically, a mess. All but two of the Joint Headquarters Hawks were out of commission. The ship was trying to save the one I came in on, but it didn't look good—the deck crew had had to turn a fire hose into the intake to get the bird shut down, and *Guam*'s captain was considering pushing it over the side to make room for incoming casualties. (They wound up not doing so, and a later count came up with forty-eight holes in the helo, including one round in the gearbox. I don't know how it kept flying.) And, Digger told me, a Hawk had just come in with Army casualties from the prison attack. Things had not gone well for them either. The team leader had taken a round in the chest and was in bad shape. Ground fire had been so heavy they couldn't land, and the colonel had ordered them out.

My radioman came up and told me he couldn't raise our guys. It seems that just as we were loading the C-5s, the staff communicator had changed the frequencies for secrecy reasons, so now my guys at the two target sites couldn't talk with anyone. I thought it was strange we couldn't raise them, since we had the same wrong frequencies, but my radioman explained that it had to do with the satellite: when we changed frequencies, we also changed satellites, and our guys were pointing their antennas in the wrong direction. At that point all this sounded to me like radioman babble; I figured the guys on the ground had been too busy to set up their SATCOM radios anyway.

Back to the flag bridge, I learned that my pilot had been injured and couldn't fly another helo back.

Meanwhile, I told Digger I wanted to talk to our commanding general, who I thought would be at our airfield by now. Instead he was still in the Airborne Command, Control and Communications (ABCCC) plane. I called him on Digger's radio and passed him the code word meaning we'd secured the governor general. This was assuming a lot, but I had complete confidence in Duke and his men. The CG told me the situation at our airfield was still undecided, with the locals putting up stiff resistance. He wasn't going there until we had control. I told him I was trying to commandeer a helo to get me back to the mansion. If I couldn't get one, I'd go to the airfield and set up my command post.

Finally, about 0830, Digger found me another helo. I grabbed my radioman and headed for the flight deck. The Blackhawk that had just brought in the casualties from the prison was getting a hot refuel. My radioman and I jumped on board. I grabbed a headset and told the pilot I wanted to get back to the governor general's mansion. A medic from our Army counterpart unit who had come in with the helo leaned in and asked me if I minded him coming along. I said, "Hell, no—get in." We lifted off and headed for the island.

I told the pilot to circle off the radio station: I wanted to try to contact Kim to see how he was doing. We tried both the MX-360 and the SATCOM radios, but there was no response and now I was getting really worried. Given the resistance the Rangers had encountered at the airfield, what were my guys facing? On the *Guam* I had learned the pilot who flew Kim in hadn't reported taking any fire, so I knew they were on the ground okay but that was all I knew. We circled for twenty minutes while my radioman and I tried everything we knew to contact them. Finally we gave up and I told the pilot to head for the governor general's mansion. He flatly refused, saying another helo had been shot down near there and he'd received orders to go to the airfield to support the Rangers. At this point, I figured one fight was as good as another and the best place for me to influence the action was at Point Salines airfield. That's where the Joint Headquarters advance control element would be located, and there I could get support for my troops at both targets.

As we landed at the airfield, I heard scattered small-arms fire. The Rangers were still fighting, but C-141s were landing. My third assault team, led by Lieutenant Steve Seigel, had landed and were all sitting on the ground near the runway with the XO, wondering what to do. After a quick briefing they started planning a way to get to the governor general by road.

I left them to it and went to look for the Joint Headquarters command post, which turned out to be in an unfinished building next to the unfinished control tower. There, the Joint Headquarters operations chief in charge of the CP told me the plan had fallen apart. The lead battalion from the 82nd Airborne was supposed to be on the ground, but he didn't know where they were. The Rangers mopping up had found mortar positions without weapons all around the airport. Apparently the Cuban "engineers" hadn't had a chance to man them, or we might not have been there. He suggested I talk with a Ranger battalion commander about help getting to the governor general's house.

Chief Dennis (Denny) Johnson, the assault team's senior enlisted man, came up and told me they'd managed to establish MX-360 communications with Duke at the governor general's place. I said "great." The MX-360 had a transmission range of about five miles over water. Any trees or buildings between us would have reduced that considerably. Fortunately, the airfield was about three miles as the crow flies across a small bay from the mansion in the hills surrounding the bay. We could hear Duke loud and clear.

He told us they had everything under control. Two of the guys had received minor dings during the helo flight, but there had been no friendly KIA and no serious wounds. The troops holding the area had simply thrown down their weapons when they saw our guys. One of Duke's men had shot and killed two uniformed soldiers who were coming in the gate to the grounds, but he didn't think anyone had heard the shots; at the moment all was quiet. As for the governor and his wife, they were unharmed and in good spirits.

Suddenly, though, three armored personnel carriers appeared at the front gate of the mansion. Duke said they were just looking at the moment, and he had told his guys not to fire.

I got real worried. We had enough men in the mansion to resist a good-sized infantry force, but they didn't have the weapons to deal with Soviet BTR-60s. I ran to the Joint Headquarters CP and told the operations chief I needed air support at the mansion, *now.* He told his guys to get an Air Force AC-130 gunship overhead. The gunship was a modified C-130 troop transport, with 20mm cannons, a 105mm howitzer, and a lot of ammo—basically, a fixed-wing weapons platform.

My radioman ran up to report that Duke had just called: the BTR-60s were trying to enter the gate. Duke was still holding fire because they hadn't yet fired and he didn't want to start anything without air support. I told him an AC-130 would be overhead in five minutes.

Unfortunately, the group's SATCOM had never made it out of the helo, so we'd have to set up a radio relay—we were the only ones who could talk to Duke with the MX-360. The operations chief suggested we contact the AC-130 with a PRC-77, a rugged military VHF radio that had been around since Vietnam. Army helicopter gunships and the AC-130 gunship used VHF as the primary means of coordinating close-air support. We didn't have one, but our army counterpart unit did. This was our relay system: Duke called us on the MX-360; our radioman turned to our Army counterpart unit's radioman and passed the message; the Army radioman relayed to the gunship over his PRC-77.

By now, the AC-130 gunship had started circling slowly 10,000 feet over the mansion, like a hawk flying slowly above its intended prey. The AC-130 was well above the range of the antiaircraft guns, and so far no ground-to-air missiles had been fired at any of our aircraft—apparently the Grenadans had neglected to get any from the Cubans. The BTRs were now inside the gate, headed slowly for the house, as if they weren't sure what to do. The first one got nailed by 20mm cannons from the AC-130 just as he was swinging his turret toward the mansion. The next two were hit immediately afterward. Duke brought the gunship's fire to within twenty meters of the mansion's front door. The BTRs probably didn't know what hit them. I got more comfortable, but we weren't out of the woods yet. At least Duke had control of his situation.

I began to think that the bad guys didn't know what was going on at the mansion, and that as long as Duke lay low they couldn't be sure we had anyone in there. We kept the gunship overhead. The situation was stabilized—as long as Duke's radio batteries lasted.

Meanwhile, Denny Johnson had been looking for a better place for our CP. For the sake of reliable communications with Duke, we needed to be higher. Steve's assault team took over an abandoned house overlooking the airfield, with a line of sight to the mansion. By this time I figured the best place for me to be was at the operations chief's elbow, since he controlled all the assets I needed to support Duke. So I kept in touch with my CP by MX-360 and shuttled between it and the Joint Headquarters' CP for the duration.

The Ranger battalion commander had agreed to help my guys get Duke and his charges out of the mansion and to Salines airfield; his guys and mine were planning the operation. The operations chief said we probably couldn't get too far outside the airfield before encountering real resistance, and to underscore the point a report came in that a BTR-60 had penetrated Ranger defenses on the east end of the runway and was headed our way.

We heard a loud explosion—a young Ranger sergeant had nailed the BTR with his shoulder-fired 75mm recoilless rifle. After the BTR attack, the operations chief said he wanted to keep most of the Rangers at the airfield for security. Since we figured it would take all of the Rangers plus my reserve assault team to break through to the governor general's mansion, I abandoned that plan. We had Duke covered with the AC-130, but I still had to figure out a way to get through to the guys at the radio station, and the reserve assault team would probably have to do it.

By this time the commanding general was on the ground. He assessed the situation, took one of the operable Blackhawks, and flew to the flagship to meet with the task force commander. The Marines had encountered no resistance and were looking for something to do, so he convinced the commander to commit a reinforced Marine company to relieve Duke. They would make an amphibious landing that night and be at the house by early the next morning. I passed the news to Duke and told him we'd keep an AC-130 over his head until the Marines got there. He said, "No sweat."

At this point I was really proud of Duke. He had seen action in Vietnam and had been decorated for bravery, but in this situation he'd been more than brave—he'd been smart and cool. He had correctly assessed the situation and figured as long as he didn't open fire he'd probably be left alone. He'd also figured out that the bad guys didn't know what was going on. In fact, I later learned that the police chief, who was aligned with the Communists, had called the house to ask if everything was okay. The governor general's wife took the call and told him they were fine. When the police chief said he would send some of his troops over to "protect" them, she said he needn't bother, because they were already being protected by "a large number of extremely well armed men."

I'd had no radio contact with Kim since he'd inserted. Two AH-6 helo gunships I'd sent up to the radio station during the day had drawn heavy ground fire. Kim had obviously pulled out, but to where? As darkness—cover—approached, we got ready to try again. Our reserve assault team would go by helo to the radio station to look for Kim.

As the force cleared the runway, I got word that Kim and his men were being picked up at sea by the task force ships. Involved in heavy fighting soon after they hit the ground, they'd been constrained to pull back from the radio station by a larger force equipped with a BTR-60. Kim and one of his men had been wounded. After lying near the coast until night, they had made their way off the island, and within an hour all were safe and sound. A weight lifted from my shoulders.

The Marines landed northeast of the governor general's house later that night, and carefully made their way to Duke's location, arriving just after daybreak. The governor general, his wife, and Duke's guys arrived by helo at the airfield about 0800. The governor general thanked me and said the SEALs had been perfect gentlemen; as soon as they burst through the front door, he knew he and his wife were safe. He said even the Grenadan soldiers seemed almost glad to see Duke, for they handed over their AK-47s without protest.

Pat and his men came by boat from the destroyer to the airfield, stopping to pick up Kim's team. The operations chief had a C-141 waiting to take us back to the Joint Headquarters. We got there around 1700 on October 26, and headed for the isolation area to unwind and debrief.

After listening to war stories and drinking a few beers, Billy Acklin and I got a few hours' sleep. We got up at 0400 and headed back to our home base to begin the grim task of informing next of kin that, after two days of searching, we still could not find any of the four missing men. (I had the search continue for another day, to no avail.)

Notifying next of kin that their man is dead is the most difficult task I've ever had. All military wives live with the knowledge that their husbands may be killed—the nature of the military is to go in harm's way—and SEALs stand a greater risk than most. SEAL Team Six trained more realistically than the other SEAL Teams, and their wives knew we'd be the first to go to combat. Yet I doubt that any SEAL's wife ever really expects her husband to be killed, because she knows he's expert at his job. The minute my man's wife saw us, she knew. She took it as well as could be expected.

20

POLICING THE BATTLEFIELD: BACK TO BASICS

After Urgent Fury, one of the first things I had to do was report to my Navy bosses about what we'd done during it. Then I had to solicit their assistance in solving the equipment, personnel, and funding problems highlighted in Urgent Fury. I went to the Pentagon to brief the Chief of Naval Operations, Admiral James Watkins. I took Duke with me. He'd done a great job with the situation he was handed, and I wanted the admiral to meet one of the officers responsible for our success. After we briefed Admiral Watkins about Grenada, I gave him a "status of the command" report. I told him we needed help badly to procure essential equipment and to increase our allowance of SEALs and support personnel.

Admiral Watkins listened closely. After I finished, he told me that Urgent Fury had broken the ice on our use of the military after Vietnam, and I'd better be ready to do the same thing again somewhere else. He also told his staff to get me the equipment, people, and money I needed. And he went on to say we had done a fine job, considering the ad hoc nature of the operation and the obstacles we had to overcome. He was especially pleased with our action at the governor general's mansion.

He and the other Joint Chiefs had watched the battle unfold and had been considering calling off the operation until I sent back the code word saying we had the governor general safe. They were listening on the SAT-

COM net when I radioed from the ship to my commanding general, and a big sigh of relief went around the table. Admiral Watkins said that at that point they all knew the outcome of Urgent Fury was no longer in doubt. When I replied that the credit and praise belonged to Duke, the admiral said something to the effect that since I was in command I should take whatever praise was given, because I sure as hell would have taken all the blame. At any rate, I knew who deserved the praise.

Later, I reflected on what had happened in Grenada. We'd done some good things, but we'd lost four men and not gotten the combat-control team to Salines airport. What really troubled me was the incredible confusion at all the Joint Headquarters units during the planning phase. The solutions to that set of problems were way above my pay grade, but I knew if things didn't change before the next operation, we'd again be at the end of a flailing whip.

I had been surprised at how much resistance we'd met in Grenada. Despite all precautions, the Cubans had known we were coming at least two days before the operation. "Don't worry about the Cubans. The engineers will stay in their barracks!" I still remember those words. The day before we arrived, Cuba had sent to Grenada a very senior colonel, veteran of much combat in Angola. There was evidence that he instituted defensive measures that probably cost U.S. lives. Army Rangers and helo pilots died who otherwise might not have. And with Cubans present the Grenadans offered more resistance than they would have on their own. Left to their own devices they surrendered at the first opportunity, as they did at the governor general's. At the radio station, with Cuban leadership, they fought and maneuvered well.

In retrospect, I think the State Department did all it could to resolve the situation diplomatically, without military force. That's the mission of the State Department, and if they can't succeed at diplomacy they'll try to limit the violence. Some overzealous officials probably divulged more information than they meant to, in exchange for assurances that the "engineers" would stay out of our way.

The State Department thinks it has failed if the military has to be called in. The United States had never come to grips with military force as a part of diplomacy. Rather, the military is a last resort, to be used after all diplomatic efforts have failed. Then the press gets all over the military for "excessive force" and all involved try to cover their political asses and blame each other. The military says it was called in only after the diplomats blew it, and the diplomats say that the military is always spoiling for a fight. In other crises, after Grenada, it always frustrated me that we were never brought in until we were the only option and the bad guys knew it. As a result, we never had the element of strategic surprise.

The confusion was another serious concern. Urgent Fury was planned and executed in a hurry. It was a complex operation, made more complex by the introduction of last-minute command-and-control changes. Urgent Fury, as it turned out, was not the type of operation the Joint Headquarters had been planning for since its inception in 1980. Rather than being a small-scale operation—quick-in and quick-out, with minimal opposition at the objective—Urgent Fury was a fight-your-way-in, fight-your-way-out operation.

It was also the first time since Vietnam that SEALs had seen combat. In Vietnam we had planned and executed our own operations, but in Urgent Fury we were part of a large task force and subject to factors beyond our control. Also, in Vietnam SEALs eased into operations after lengthy predeployment training. The first few times platoons went into the field after arriving in Vietnam were usually "break-in" operations in which they could make their mistakes under controlled conditions. In Grenada, we didn't have the luxury of a mission-specific rehearsal.

In retrospect, I do consider Grenada an overall success for SEAL Team Six. It wasn't pretty, but we got the most important missions done. We lacked essential equipment such as military radios, light antitank weapons, and reliable boats that would have made our task easier. But our people made up for these inadequacies with ingenuity, quick thinking under fire, and plain old bravery. I put a number of men in for personal decorations, and all were approved. The command received the Joint Meritorious Unit Award.

Duke and his assault team rescued the governor general and held his mansion until relieved—about eighteen hours longer than we had been told we'd have to. (Units from the 82nd Airborne Division were to have relieved our assault teams within four hours after H-hour.)

Before they had to pull out, Kim's team knocked Radio Grenada, which was spewing rallying cries for the Communist forces, off the air by destroying the transmitters.

The mission to put Air Force combat-control people at Salines airfield failed because our Whalers couldn't handle the weather and seas off Grenada. Air Force planners had started the chain of problems by not ensuring the first air drop was done in daylight, as we had insisted and they had agreed.

Despite our successes, Urgent Fury showed the command was not as operationally ready as I wanted. Plus, my unfamiliarity with the operating procedures used by the Joint Headquarters played a role in a lot of our problems. Bottom line: I was the commanding officer. I accepted the Admiral's praise and I accepted full responsibility for our shortcomings.

We had to go back to SEAL basics and move forward again.

In taking over SEAL Team Six, I was reminded of SEAL Team Two from 1966 to 1968. Six just hadn't been tested in combat. The men were dedicated and had a clear mission, and I didn't want to make a lot of immediate policy changes just to be making changes. (I did make *one* policy change: we'd do our drinking only after work was done.) I wanted to get to know the command better before I started to "mark my territory." Unfortunately, we were sent into combat before I could do that.

After Grenada, I realized I had to change the command's belief in its own press. I had to foster self-confidence, but within the context of knowing one's limitations. As I was making the rounds during turnover, I kept hearing, "We're so good, we're two years ahead of the state of the art." Catchy phrase—but not the mind-set I wanted.

Urgent Fury also showed shortcomings in our readiness and planning procedures. I told Seal Six's officers and chiefs that our organization had to be ready to plan and fight in accordance with whatever stringent schedule was laid on us by our operational commander. I wasn't going to accept an ad hoc approach to mission planning anymore. We would establish and train a cadre of operations, intelligence, logistics, and communications planners. The planning cadre would go to the Joint Headquarters at the earliest indication that something was up. We had to have communicators who could closely link with our operational commander's communicators. Never again would I accept being cut out of the communications planning, after the problems that had caused in Urgent Fury.

I told my operations officer to keep one of our officers or senior enlisted in the operations section at the Joint Headquarters permanently, not just when the staff down there asked for someone. We had to know what they were doing before the train left the station—this was a key to our future readiness.

In the future, too, I wouldn't run off to the Joint Headquarters before I was sure we had things well covered at Six. At the Joint Headquarters, I was effectively cut off from my planning base and dependent upon the operational commander's staff for information. They had their own business to worry about.

Finally, regardless of what the operational commander's staff did, we were going to go to Zulu (Universal) time for all operations and exercises in the future. In all my years with the SEALs, Urgent Fury was the only occasion on which I saw the standard military procedure of using Zulu time violated. Doing that had caused us to jump in the dark instead of daylight as we had planned.

In the three years before I arrived, Six had been funded at levels well above other SEAL Teams, and at their expense. Given all that money, Six's lack of fundamental SEAL Team mission-essential equipment was baffling.

Within six months after Grenada we had military radios, antiarmor weapons, and a new mix of small arms, designed to deliver maximum firepower with increased accuracy. We had new boats capable of operating at sea. We developed new parachuting procedures for the boats and the men, replacing the MC-1 static line parachutes and their two-point "capewell" release system with MT-1 square canopies and their simple, reliable single-point release system. Then we rehearsed and rehearsed, until I was certain we could do that complex, dangerous operation at night, at sea, without a problem.

SEAL Six also had trouble with command integrity. In the three years since the command had been formed, each assault team had gone its own way, with different standard operating procedures, different emergency procedures, and different equipment. Even their basic patrolling hand signals were different. Going from one to the other was as big a change as going from one SEAL Team to another.

I had to develop a system to ensure we were all singing off the same sheet of music and to tell me if anyone was hitting wrong notes. I needed to review our training and develop standards to measure how well we could do our mission. In June 1983, before relieving Dick Marcinko, I asked to see training records for the two assault teams. The training officer told me they were training so hard, they didn't have time to keep records. Under Marcinko, the Team had been training hard for three years, but I had no way of knowing how well they could do certain procedures. We implemented standards and measured our ability to meet them. The process eliminated bullshit: you either met the standard or you didn't.

As the training standards went up I could see the command improving in all aspects. The Team leaders and chiefs worked the men hard. Like all SEAL Teams, in order to train realistically we had to get out of town. This was a problem. I'd increased the numbers of assault teams to allow the men more training time and time off. But for the duration of my tour the average man was spending more than 280 days a year away from home. They didn't seem to mind; they were there to operate and fight. But we were violating Navy policy, which called for men to be away from home no more than 180 days per year. I had no choice.

At least with three assault teams the men could take leave occasionally. The only one of us who took no time off during my three years in command was me. I couldn't have been comfortable on leave; I'd have spent the time thinking about Larry Barrett tearing down the taxiway to catch the plane. Becky was the happiest person on the block when I left Six in July 1986.

The true measure of any organization is the ability of the key members to make critical decisions without consulting the leader. I knew we were ready when I was paged one night late in 1985 while eating dinner with Becky at a Pizza Hut (big spender Bob). The code on my beeper was the one for real-world immediate recall—drop whatever you're doing and head for the Team, because we're going to war. "What the hell? I'm the only one who's supposed to authorize this code," I thought. I called the Team. My operations officer answered, and before I could ask what was going on, he told me he'd gotten a call from the Joint Headquarters saying that a C-141 would be at a local military airfield soon to pick us up for an operation. Knowing I'd approve, he authorized the code. I took Becky home, and by the time I got to Six, all the gear and people were already loaded on trucks and headed for the airfield, along with our boats—ahead of schedule.

Generally I was in my comfort zone, but not completely satisfied. Satisfaction causes complacency. Complacency causes screwups. At Six, we weren't allowed to screw up. In the years after Grenada, we got very good at doing the things we needed in order to carry out our missions.

21

THEY CAN RUN, BUT THEY CAN'T HIDE: THE *ACHILLE LAURO* MISSION

As a rapid-deployment force, SEALs had to deal with any contingency. In the 1980s that came to include terrorism. During the *Achille Lauro* mission we would also learn a tactic we had no training for: diplomacy.

On October 7, 1985, I was in Washington. It seemed I was always in Washington, trying to push our requirements through the bureaucracy. This day I was in the SEAL resource sponsor's office, trying to get him to help us get the manning increase we'd been promised after Grenada, nearly two years ago.

The good captain listened as I explained why I needed additional SEALs now and said, "Sorry, Bob, the other Teams need people too."

"Don't give me that. You and I know no other Team has the same mission and readiness requirements."

Later, when I remembered that conversation, I thought, "Too bad he couldn't have gone back to my headquarters with me." As soon as I walked in the door of my office, my operations officer came in and told me the *Achille Lauro*, an Italian cruise ship with a lot of American passengers aboard, had been hijacked just after sailing from Alexandria, an Egyptian port on the Mediterranean. Within hours, we were on a C-141 heading that way. En route, we developed a good plan to recover the ship and free all the hostages. Meanwhile, before we reached our forward operating base, the PLO ordered the hijackers to return to Alexandria and turn themselves in to the Egyptian authorities.

When we landed in the afternoon of October 8, the commanding general of the Joint Headquarters and I went over the situation. The *Achille Lauro* was heading for Alexandria, but our orders remained in effect. Simply stated, we were to recover the ship and free the hostages. Ready to go, we continued to refine our plan, but because Air Force transport had a slow reaction time key equipment and people I needed to carry it out had not yet arrived. They didn't get there until it was too late to conduct the mission under cover of darkness. To act in the daytime would have been too risky for the passengers, because the hijackers could spot our approach to the ship.

As the *Achille Lauro* approached Alexandria, we waited to see what would develop. Would the hijackers really surrender? Finally, early in the evening of October 9, they gave themselves up to Egyptian authorities. We had already learned that they'd killed one passenger, Leon Klinghoffer, but all the others appeared to be safe. We were ordered to return to our stateside base; the crisis was over.

At 2000 on October 9, all of my men were loaded on our C-141, ready to return home, and I was waiting for the commanding general to give the word to take off. We were all disappointed at not having had a chance to execute our plan, particularly since the hijackers had murdered a fellow American. I was deep in thought about what I had to do when we got back: go to Washington to continue the fight with the bureaucracy. The sound of the plane's engines brought me back to the present. We were about to begin taxiing when the commanding general came on the radio and told me to keep the engines running but hold the plane. He'd just received word that President Reagan had ordered 6th Fleet aircraft to intercept an EgyptAir Boeing 737 carrying the *Achille Lauro* criminals out of Egypt.

I figured a deal had been cut. The Egyptians probably wanted the hijackers out of their country as soon as possible, because they didn't want to have to bring them to justice and risk the ire of Islamic fundamentalists.

The general said that as soon as the 737 was detected leaving Egyptian airspace, F-14s from the aircraft carrier *Saratoga* were going to force it into Sigonella, Italy, where we shared a NATO base with the Italians. Our C-141 was to land right behind the 737, take custody of the criminals, and fly them back with us.

Sounded like a great idea to me. We would have a crack at getting the bad guys, and the Egyptians would save face. Forcing their plane down at Sigonella seemed particularly fortuitous because I had already rerouted one assault team there after it became apparent we weren't going to launch an operation on the *Achille Lauro*.

I told the troops what was happening. About five of them immediately began forcing themselves to puke in order to get rid of the sleeping pills they'd taken so they'd sleep all the way home. Lieutenant Pat and I (Pat had been my assault team leader during Urgent Fury and was now my operations officer) quickly briefed the C-141 pilot. Then off we flew, in company with the CG's bird, headed for Sigonella. The CG and I planned and coordinated over the radio en route. I learned that in addition to the four criminals, there were two PLO members and Egyptian "guards" aboard the 737. The plane was headed for Tunisia.

Our plan called for my assault team in Sigonella to block the 737 as soon as it taxied off the runway and stopped. One of the two teams with me would board the plane; the other assault team, I'd keep in reserve. I asked for permission for my guys at Sigonella to shoot out the 737's tires as soon as it came to a stop. The general relayed the request, but it was denied. We were told to tread lightly until we saw what the Egyptians were going to do. My guys already on the ground were to do no more than surround the 737 until the CG and I arrived.

I told the CG that we should contact the 737 pilot on the ground-control frequency as soon as we arrived and tell him to turn over the criminals. I figured we could explain the situation to him in terms he couldn't refuse. Either he handed over the criminals, or we were going to take them. If we took them, Egyptians would die. Faced with those options, I figured he'd hand them over.

The F-14s intercepted the 737 as planned, and the Egyptian pilot didn't argue too hard when the F-14 flight leader told him to declare an emergency and land at Sigonella.

We landed in the slipstream of the 737. I ran off my bird to the Boeing's rear, where my Sigonella assault team had established a command post. They had the 737 surrounded, the team leader told me. All of his men were concealed in the weeds nearby.

I told Lieutenant "Bo," one of the two team leaders who flew in with me, to assemble his assault team off the tarmac behind the 737 and to its left, and be prepared to assault the jet on my order. Bo was a hard-nosed former Army Ranger, and his guys were ready to go.

Lieutenant Randy Rhodes put his assault team in position next to our C-141. Randy was a former enlisted SEAL who had worked for me when I commanded Team Two. His guys were ready to do whatever I needed.

As Randy and Bo positioned their assault teams, I tried to figure out where we were on the airfield. The lights from the EgyptAir 737 inhibited my night vision. I could see the shapes of hangars in the distance. I couldn't tell our exact position, but I figured we were on the U.S., not the Italian, side of the field.

The commanding general's plane landed. He raced over to our command post. One of his radiomen arrived with a radio tuned to the airfield ground-control frequency. When we called the 737, its pilot told us there was an Egyptian ambassador, with proper credentials, on board and he wanted to talk to us. This was a new wrinkle.

The general and I huddled. Having an ambassador on board seemed to us a signal that the Egyptians wanted to get rid of their cargo. We figured he'd turn over the criminals to us as soon as we got him off the plane. I also figured the president and the State Department had managed to convince the Egyptians they ought to lose the bad guys, and that's why the ambassador was on board. If they intended to take them to Tunisia as we'd been told, there would be no need for an ambassador. We decided the best thing to do was get him off the plane and talk to him. I told the CG I'd go.

I went to the forward door of the aircraft and waited while the crew lowered stairs. An armed man stood beside the door. I couldn't see very far into the plane from the bottom of the stairs, but behind the crew members operating the stairs, I could see two more armed men. I was unarmed, because I didn't want to spook the ambassador, but I knew my snipers had zeroed in on the door.

The ambassador appeared in the door, turned, and said something to one of the men behind him. I yelled for him to come down the stairs, and he did. He was a well-dressed, short, round man, obviously very nervous. I asked for his credentials, and he produced a letter and a diplomatic passport. The letter said he was an authorized representative of the Egyptian government, and the passport looked authentic.

One of the snipers covering me radioed that he had Abu Abbas, one of the most infamous Palestinian terrorists, in his sights as the ambassador came down the stairs. Pictures of Abu Abbas were scarce, but we knew what he looked like, and we thought he might be one of the two Palestinians on board.

I took the ambassador by the arm and headed for my command post. As I walked up to the commanding general with the Egyptian in tow, I heard one of the radiomen say that one of our intelligence agencies had sent us interesting information regarding the Egyptians. President Hosni Mubarak had instructed the pilot to turn over the criminals. The ambassador's eyes widened in surprise. He said he wanted to confer with Mubarak first. (We later learned Mubarak thought the Italians had the plane.)

The ambassador and the general began a heated discussion. The CG pointed to me and told the Egyptian that if he didn't hand over the criminals immediately, I was going to take my men aboard and get them. I called Bo on my radio and told him to get ready. The ambassador paled and he started arguing that it wouldn't be necessary for us to take them by force if only he could talk to Mubarak. He said he was concerned for the safety of the crew members. The general said if we had to take the hijackers by force, he couldn't guarantee the safety of any of the Egyptians on the plane. The ambassador got more nervous and repeated that he was sure that wouldn't be necessary, if only he could speak to Mubarak.

One of my men came up and grabbed my shoulder, saying we were about to have a problem. A large number of Italian troops and police had arrived on the scene. I had been so busy with the ambassador that I hadn't even noticed. I began getting reports over the radio from all of my guys that the Italians were quietly surrounding us. The situation was getting more tense. I told the men to stay off their triggers because we appeared to be about to get the bad guys.

At this point I was about ten feet away from the CG and the ambassador. A group of Italians walked up to me and demanded to see whoever was in charge of our forces. I told them I was. An Italian general demanded to see my general. I said the CG was busy and he could talk to me. We argued about it for a few minutes. The Italian general stormed off, yelling something in Italian I didn't understand. More Italian police and military began to appear around us. I was worried their egos might take over and they'd do something really stupid.

A Navy captain who identified himself as the commanding officer of the U.S. Naval Air Facility at Sigonella arrived and said we ought to turn over the criminals to the Italians. I said no way; we were conferring with an Egyptian ambassador, and I expected the situation would be resolved soon. He said in return that we were on the Italian side of the base and that he found out what we were doing when the Italians told him. I began to wonder just what coordinating the people in Washington had done. (We later learned our government had tried to coordinate with the Italians, but that by the time they reached Premier Bettino Craxi, we were on the ground.)

My general came up and told me he was going to take the ambassador and a three-star Italian general (not the one I'd pissed off) someplace quieter to negotiate. "Hold down the fort, Bob. Don't let the Italians on the plane."

I said, "Aye, aye, sir," and they drove off.

As soon as he was gone, my radio operator told me we'd just received an order from someone over the SATCOM to assault the plane immediately, capture the bad guys, and depart on our C-141s. I took the receiver and explained the situation: we were surrounded by a large number of angry, heavily armed Italians. They had blocked our planes with vehicles and surrounded our position. Did he really want me to start a battle with them? I heard, "Wait—out."

Earlier, I'd sent my executive officer, Commander Tom Moser, to keep a lid on things at the airplane stairs. As soon as I'd signed off, Tom came on: "Hey, boss, you'd better get over here. The Italians are about to assault my position."

I went. Tom, Chief Petty Officer Rich Peters, and a couple of our troops were blocking the base of the stairs. An angry Italian officer was there as well. He told me he was taking his men aboard the plane. I told him no one was going on the plane until our bosses had reached some sort of agreement. We spent a few tense moments eyeballing each other, and he blinked. He agreed not to push the issue. Good thing, too, because my guys were beginning to get pretty irritated themselves. It was starting to get hot all around.

Back at my command post, I received a SATCOM transmission from the National Military Command Center, where the chairman of the Joint Chiefs of Staff and the secretary of defense carry out the president's orders and otherwise manage crises. They asked for an order of battle. I told them I had eighty-three men with me. As near as I could tell, the Italians had about sixteen hundred troops around the airplane. "But," I pointed out, "it's dark and I can't count heads." The person on the other end thanked me and asked if I thought I could keep the 737 on the ground. I said, "No problem—the 737 isn't going anywhere."

I knew this because earlier I'd sent Bob "Bobby Lew" Lewis, the man who'd taken the chain saw to the trees around the governor general's mansion during Urgent Fury, to the front of the 737 with a truck our Sigonella assault team had borrowed. I told him to take two men and make sure the plane stayed put. Bobby Lew said, "Don't sweat it, Skipper," and what Bobby Lew said went.

Then the situation got even more tense. Bo called on the MX-300 to say that Italians with automatic weapons had surrounded his position to the left rear of the plane. I told him to have his guys face out and stay put. With Italian armored vehicles approaching from the apron in front of the 737, I suddenly heard a loud "bang." Amidst a burst of adrenaline I thought, "Shot fired." Bobby Lew came right up on the radio and said not to worry—one of the armored cars needed a tune-up. When he saw me confronting the Italian at the stairs he'd moved forward underneath the plane; when he went back to his vehicle, he found the ignition key broken off in the lock. Master Chief Billy Acklin told Bobby Lew that was okay, we weren't sending him out for beer anytime soon.

Everyone's nerves were tight as drumheads. The Italians were furious. In retrospect I don't blame them but at the time I didn't have much sympathy for their damaged feelings.

I called the commanding general's communicator on the SATCOM and asked how things were going. Lieutenant Colonel Dick Malvesti, from the operations division, told me it looked as if things were going well. They weren't yelling and they had just sent out for coffee. Dick said he would stay on the radio and let me know as soon as they decided something. One of the coolest officers around, Dick had been in our Army counterpart unit for years before moving to the Joint Headquarters staff. He knew what he was doing, and I trusted his judgment.

More Italians kept arriving at the plane. If shooting started, it was going to get interesting. I wasn't too worried, because we had enough firepower to force a standoff, but I knew we'd take casualties. Over the radio, I kept checking with my team leaders, who all reported that they were doing fine. Randy had refused a request by some Italian police to board and look around our C-141.

After a while I lost track of time. I remember looking at my watch and seeing we'd been in Sigonella about five hours. It seemed a lot longer than that.

Finally, Dick Malvesti called to say an agreement had been reached: we would turn over the hijackers to the Italians, who had agreed to prosecute them under Italian law. I told him I wasn't letting the Italians on the plane until the CG got back.

By the time the commanding general returned, the Italians had heard the news too; they were joking among themselves, and the atmosphere had lightened. The general told me to let the Italians board the plane but to keep my guys in place until the criminals were in the police vehicles.

I stood at the stairs as the criminals were led off the plane in handcuffs and driven away. The Italian general with whom I'd had words came up and shook my hand, assuring me they would be dealt with quickly and severely.

The CG told me he figured things had worked out as well as possible under the circumstances. Now it was time to get my guys out of there. We took off without incident at about 0930 on October 10.

After we were gone, the Italians loaded the criminals back aboard the Egyptian 737 and used it to transport their prisoners to Rome. After the four criminals were off-loaded in Rome, the 737 took off with Abu Abbas and his assistant still on board—so the Italians had apparently cut their own deal with the Palestinians.

The Craxi government fell because we had violated Italian sovereignty and gotten away with it. In fact our actions at Sigonella remained a festering sore in Italian pride for some years. Later, I could understand how they felt. Suppose the Italians landed unannounced at one of our airfields and held our forces at gunpoint. We'd be pissed too.

As soon as we'd gotten back to our base, just after dark on October 10, Vice Admiral Scott McCauley called me congratulating us for a job well done. I also received many calls from people in Washington to the same effect, and the following week the commanding general got an appreciative message from President Reagan. I agreed with these assessments—a few days after we got back. We were all disappointed at not having a chance to take the ship, and I'd really wanted to get the bad guys at Sigonella.

I sent Bo to New York City to attend an FBI debriefing of the American passengers from the *Achille Lauro*. When Bo returned, he told me our plan would have worked, "big-time." We had deduced correctly where all the bad guys were on the ship, a key feature in such an operation. I'm convinced we would have resolved the situation quickly had we had the chance to take down the ship.

During our own debriefing, a few days after we returned, the CG and I agreed that if we had assaulted the 737 as soon as we hit the ground, we might have gotten away with it. But we might also have caused an international incident like we'd never seen before. Given the cards we were dealt, I think matters worked out for the best. Both of us were really proud of the fire discipline and maturity my guys showed. SEAL Team Six was awarded the Joint Meritorious Unit Award (JMUA), and I got some of my key people individual awards for their superb actions at Sigonella.

What we did in Sigonella was unprecedented. Without clearing the operation with the Italian government, we landed two C-141s with combat troops. Then we held the Italian police and military at bay for about ten hours. We were still feeling the repercussions in 1990. While I was working in the Pentagon we were negotiating with the Italian Defense Ministry to allow us to set up a Naval Special Warfare unit at a base in Italy. The Italian military was all for it, but as soon as the proposal reached the Defense Ministry it slowed, and after about five months we learned that it had been refused. A book about the *Achille Lauro* incident had hit the streets about the time our request hit the Defense Ministry. Public pressure was so strong that the government felt they couldn't approve setting up a special operations unit on Italian soil.

To me, the most significant aspect of our action was that it showed the world that the United States of America was willing to take extraordinary steps to apprehend and prosecute international criminals. Forcing down a plane belonging to a friendly government and violating the sovereignty of another, even more traditional, ally are drastic measures. We put teeth in President Reagan's message to criminals that they could run but they could not hide.

As for the Italian prosecution, I was satisfied with the results: all four criminals got prison time. Given the events surrounding some trials that took place in America around then, I'm not sure we'd have even gotten convictions.

My big regret was that the Italians allowed Abu Abbas to leave. He was well known to Western intelligence as the mastermind behind a number of terrorist incidents. Since he had appeared on the scene, I think we can correctly assume he had some role in the planning of the *Achille Lauro* hijacking as well. What the terrorists were trying to accomplish is not clear. The fact that they attempted to take the ship into Syrian waters led some experts to believe that the operation was not sanctioned by the PLO, and so they intended to get off in Syria. Another, more plausible explanation is that they were planning to pick up more compatriots and explosives, after which they would sail into an Israeli port and do as much damage as they could. I don't know. Certainly they didn't have enough men to sustain themselves very long; there were too many passengers for four men to control twenty-four hours a day. (No doubt they felt they couldn't safely smuggle more than four men on board the *Achille Lauro.*) Whatever their reasons, by seizing the ship and holding it for nearly three days, the criminals drew the attention many such fanatics crave. Clearly, they responded to PLO orders, and one can reasonably assume they were not acting on their own.

The *Achille Lauro* operation showed me the command had matured. The men showed extraordinary discipline and professionalism under very tense and politically sensitive conditions. By mid-1985, I knew we were the best in the world at what we did.

22

AUDITS AND INVESTIGATIONS: THE MARCINKO LEGACY

In early 1986, the Naval Investigative Service (NIS) started an investigation that would last four years and sully the reputation of SEAL Team Six. The ostensible subject of the investigation was Dick Marcinko, but many others were drawn into the vortex.

I had known Dick for many years, and until after I relieved him at Six I had always considered him a friend. Throughout my command of Six he was on the OPNAV staff, meaning he worked for the Chief of Naval Operations. There, he attempted to discredit me among senior Navy officers in the Pentagon. He said that morale was suffering in Six under my leadership. I didn't like that, but I considered it part of the service politics one encounters at the upper echelons of the Navy, and no one in my chain of command believed him. However, in trying to get at me, he also questioned the professionalism of the people in the command, and the command's ability to carry out its mission. He denigrated the men of SEAL Team Six in order to further his goal of getting me out of command. Attacking me was one thing; attacking the command was another. I lost all respect for him as a naval officer and a SEAL.

In early February 1986, I heard an investigation had been started in which Dick Marcinko was a "party" (i.e., under suspicion). Soon two NIS agents visited me and asked me questions about Dick, many concerning issues for which he had already been investigated while he was in command. I pointed them toward the investigation reports, on file at headquarters. The agents also asked me about some actions other members of the command had taken before my time—I had no comment on those—and agents talked to many of my Team.

I forgot about the investigation until a few months later when two more agents showed up and asked me about some special ordnance items that had been procured for SEAL Team Six two years earlier by Marcinko while he was at OPNAV. I told them the items had been procured for Dick's OPNAV office, not for SEAL Six. I had arrived at work one day in the spring of 1984 to find a message from Joint Headquarters asking us to validate a requisition that had been submitted to a procurement agency in SEAL Six's name. I'd heard nothing of the request and wasn't familiar with the list of items. Yet, knowing how things went, I told my executive officer to check with our ordnance department; they didn't know anything about the requisition either. I thought some of the items looked interesting, but there was no way I could agree to the vast numbers being procured. Nor had any of the items, to any of my people's knowledge, undergone any type of testing.

Soon, I received a call from Dick asking why I hadn't validated the list. At first I didn't know what he was talking about. Then I realized *he* had written it, and I told him that though we'd be happy to see small quantities of some items we weren't interested in the whole kit and caboodle. He started yelling that I didn't know what I was doing and that the Team needed all the items on the list, et cetera, et cetera. When I asked him about the large quantities of these experimental items, he said that most of them were for the "Red Cell" he was putting together under the auspices of OPNAV.

Red Cell, an organization that tested the security of naval installations, reported directly to the deputy chief of Naval Operations for Plans and Operations, at that time Vice Admiral Ace Lyons. Eight or ten former members of SEAL Team Six had transferred there. Dick had gotten Lyons to agree to the idea but so far no money had been allocated to equip and run Red Cell because it had not been authorized by the CNO. I thought such security testing was a good idea, given the worldwide terrorist threat, and I also figured running Red Cell would give Dick an outlet for his energy. Since they had no money, I let him borrow some SEAL Team Six equipment to get started.

I told Marcinko to say in the procurement document that the ordnance items were for Red Cell and leave SEAL Team Six out of it. He mumbled something about not being able to do that (which was because no one had yet authorized Red Cell). I told him he didn't determine what Six needed—I did—and after we'd exchanged appropriate pleasantries, I hung up. A few minutes later Dick's boss, Captain Bill Hamilton, called to apologize for Dick's outburst. Of course I accepted the apology, but I didn't change my mind about the ordnance items.

In July 1984, my new ordnance chief told me we were about to receive some new, experimental ordnance items from OPNAV. What did I want to do with them? Turned out these were the same items that Dick and I had discussed. Apparently he had found a way to buy them. I told the chief to have them sent to our training facility in Nevada and subject them to some rudimentary safety tests. It wasn't unusual for us to do this, because we were given broad latitude to test and develop special items for our use. Also, we could use some of the items if they proved safe and effective.

Some time later, the chief told me the few items they had tested proved unsafe, having failed the standard military "bullet test": a high-powered round had been fired into the items, and they had exploded. We couldn't dispose of them by turning them in to an ordnance facility, because they had been procured outside the system and no ordnance facility would accept them. I told him to have our explosive ordnance disposal–qualified SEALs destroy them.

Soon afterward, the command was subjected to a series of audits by all levels of the chain, up to and including the auditor general of the Navy. I would have been the first to admit that we did things outside the usual procedures, but we were forced to in order to maintain our readiness because the system moved too slowly to keep up with our changing environment.

My guidance to the members of the command always was to get the job done but not to do anything illegal or irregular without my approval. I was the one responsible. During my three years in command of Six no one ever came to me with anything illegal. I often authorized the breaking of military regulations, but I always wrote a "Memorandum for the Record" explaining why. We kept those memos on file and showed them to every audit team that came by. Though they usually blanched when they saw what I had authorized, never was I told I shouldn't have acted as I did given the circumstances at the time.

Each investigation and audit team came to Six convinced they'd find the smoking gun that would prove Six a bunch of crooks whose only purpose in life was to milk the system for all it could get. Each group left the Team wondering what the fuss was all about. I just wanted to be left alone to get my job done.

That wasn't to be. In late February 1986, a team from the Navy auditor general's office came in, with fire in their eyes just like all the other audit teams we'd seen. They told me they'd be there for about two weeks, but they stayed for six.

Two weeks into the audit, I called an emergency load-out drill and invited the head auditor, Dennis Friend, to stay with me as the troops went through their paces. The drill culminated with a simulated launch. I recalled the alert assault team and had them do a shooting exercise. Throughout, Dennis asked why we did certain things, and I explained as well as I could. He asked, too, whether this drill was for his benefit, and I answered honestly, "I do these all the time." As the night went on, I could tell he was gaining an appreciation for what we did and why we didn't always follow regulations designed for the peacetime Navy. At the end I asked him what he thought, and he said he'd had no idea about the scope of my responsibility.

From that night on, the audit team really was there to help us. Dennis instructed his team to study us, identify our problems, and find a way to fix them. Then he told his people to tell us how to explain our anomalies in "bean counterese," so later audit teams would understand our unique situation. What wound up taking them six weeks was turning over every stone and tidying it so we would never have problems with auditors again.

Dennis gave me the final report, which cited the problems his team had already given us the tools to repair. However, its major finding, one the report itself called "a show-stopper," was that we weren't being properly supported in the present system and the Navy was at risk because of it. Dennis made a recommendation that I heartily endorsed because I'd been pushing it for two years: Six should be taken out of the present oversight system and placed in a special one designed to handle such oddball things as we were doing. Until then, he recommended that we continue as we had been. He told me to carefully document every deviation we had to make for operational reasons and to state why explicitly in "Memoranda for the Record." He recommended that I sign the more contentious memoranda but that my supply officer could handle routine deviations.

The NIS investigation continued through all of this. In fact, two NIS agents were in Dennis's party when he started his audit. They left after two weeks, but in July they were back in force. I later found out someone in the hierarchy at NIS had said that they finally had the goods on SEAL Six, and Gormly was involved up to his ears.

At any rate, the NIS came and we cooperated. They wanted copies of all documents we had made since the command was formed. I explained that 90 percent of what they wanted was classified and closely controlled. We kept only one copy of many of the documents. The head agent said he'd be responsible for their security and promised to ensure that my administrative people could record every document they copied. I told him to go ahead. It seemed to me this NIS team was on a fishing expedition in waters that had been well fished before.

I knew we'd done nothing illegal as a command. The head agent took great pains to tell me they were looking for evidence of Marcinko crimes, and that neither I nor any others in Six were now under investigation.

These words rang hollow when I learned from my guys that one of the first things they asked for was a copy of all my travel claims.

I was at a special warfare conference in Washington when Tom Moser paged my beeper. I called back to find him laughing. He told me the NIS had boxed up all the papers they wanted and had about three U-Haul trucks loaded and ready to go. He had looked out his window and seen five agents with Uzi submachine guns standing by the trucks. Tom found the head agent and had asked him what the hell was going on.

"We know your guys," the agent replied. "We're not taking any chances on the trucks getting hijacked on the road."

"Are you serious?" Tom asked.

"Serious as a heart attack," responded the agent.

I couldn't believe it. My old shipmate and boss Rear Admiral Irish Flynn, who was now in charge of the NIS, was at the conference. I found him and asked what the hell was going on. He said the agent on the scene was overreacting, and he'd speak to him about it. Throughout, I had kept an open mind about how Irish was running the investigation; out of respect for his position as a SEAL running NIS, I never called him to find out how it was going. But there was no reason for what his guys had just done.

The investigation continued. About 0900 on July 16, 1986, the head lawyer (judge advocate general) on Vice Admiral McCauley's staff called to tell me to have my XO, Commander Tom Moser, report to his office at 1300. Around 1100 I was due to see Captain Ron Bell, who had taken over Naval Special Warfare Group Two and was now my administrative commander. I gave Tom the word to go and drove over to meet with Ron Bell. Ron told me someone had accused Tom of telling my people not to cooperate with NIS.

Tom was a most scrupulous officer, and I knew he would never have done anything like that. As soon as I got to my vehicle, I got on the radio and called Six to warn Tom he was about to be blindsided. We agreed to meet at a shopping center on his way to the JAG's office.

When I told him what I'd learned, Tom thought for a minute and said one of our guys, about to be questioned by the NIS, had come to him one day and asked if he had to take a lie-detector test. Tom had told him he should see a lawyer if he was concerned. Apparently, when offered a lie-detector test by the NIS, the man translated this into "The XO said I should see a lawyer first."

Tom came back late in the afternoon, and he was mad. Hearing his side of the story, the JAG had told Tom that if that was all there was to it, Tom had done nothing wrong. The incident told me that NIS was getting desperate for results.

That night Ron Bell called me at home and said he had to see me the next day. In view of Tom's session with the NIS agent, I asked whether I should bring a lawyer. Ron said, "No, just come on over tomorrow."

When I got there, he was looking very uncomfortable, but he got right to the point. Someone had told the NIS that I'd allowed my men to bring back an airplane load of illegal weapons from the Grenada operation. That someone told NIS I even had three AK-47s of my own from the haul. I looked at Ron and said, "That's a bunch of bullshit." I had explicitly forbidden my teams to bring back any weapons.

But I know SEALs, and a few weeks after we had returned from Grenada, I had put out the word that there was a one-week grace period during which anyone who'd brought back illegal weapons could turn them into our ordnance department, no questions asked. Four weapons had turned up. I had sent a message to the Joint Headquarters asking that we be allowed to put the weapons in our inventory and use them for training, and the CG gave permission. I told Ron the weapons had been inventoried weekly thereafter and they were still in our armory.

"Okay, okay," Ron said. He then asked if I had told my disbursing officer to make sure the troops got every dime of Temporary Additional Duty (TAD) money they rated and if I had told him to bend over backward to see that they were well compensated. TAD money is provided to military personnel for their care and feeding when they're away from their home base on official duty. Apparently, NIS had questioned the validity of some of the travel claims my men had submitted.

I said, "Yes to the first part of the question, and no to the second." As I explained to Ron, my guys didn't eat regular meals when they were on the road training because they worked long hours and ate when they could. They couldn't fill out travel forms showing three meals a day because they just didn't eat on that schedule. Right after I took command, I told the disbursing officer (a chief petty officer) that I wanted him to look carefully at each travel claim and bring any funny-looking ones to the XO or me.

I asked Ron, "Do you have any idea who's making these off-the-wall accusations?"

He asked me if I knew a certain ex–chief petty officer. I did. He had worked for me at Six as the administrative officer, having been there when I took over from Marcinko. I "civilianized" the job and hired him for it after he retired from the Navy. He was a personality problem, but I put up with him until, in September 1985, I learned from one of our OPSEC agents that the man was calling Marcinko regularly to tell him what was going on in the command. The XO found this was true—the guy was feeding command-confidential information to Marcinko. I fired him on the spot. Now it seemed he'd found an avenue for revenge. Had Marcinko put him up to it?

Ron was relieved by my answers, and I told him I'd be happy to go see Admiral McCauley and tell him the same, face-to-face. Ron said that wouldn't be necessary; McCauley, he said, was convinced there was nothing behind all the aspersions being thrown at me, but he was getting pressure from someone above him to relieve me "for cause"—that is, in military terms, to fire me. Relief for cause terminates the officer's career.

When I left Ron's office, my anxieties hadn't been allayed. I was now sure that the NIS was getting desperate to hang someone. They were thrashing the weeds, having uncovered so little that they couldn't justify all the money they'd spent. They wanted a Navy captain's head, and I was the only one around.

The other shoe dropped later, when Becky and I returned from a short vacation after I left command of SEAL Team Six. One of the administrative people from Six came to my house and gave me a letter from the

Chief of Naval Personnel. He knew what was in the letter and apologized for having to be the messenger. Inside the envelope was a modification to my orders to relieve Ron as Commander, Naval Special Warfare Group Two. Instead I was ordered to the Naval Amphibious Base to await the outcome of the investigation. It looked as if my next command tour was in jeopardy.

In 1985, Dick Marcinko had nearly convinced Vice Admiral Ace Lyons, OP-06, that I ought to leave Six. I had put in an official request for a one-year extension that winter (normally I'd have been moved on to another job in July 1985). The request sailed through the chain of command and ended up on Lyons's desk. Dick Marcinko was in another section of OP-06, running the Red Cell. When he learned of the letter, he started politicking to get me out. He had not been able to control me, and he still saw himself as the "hot runner" in the SEAL community. With me out of command at Six, he'd be in a more powerful position to run the entire program.

The man he proposed to relieve me in the summer of 1985 was Commander Gary Stubblefield, a great officer and one of our best operators. He was finishing a demanding operational assignment and moving him into Six made sense but for two problems. First, the commanding general of the Joint Headquarters, my administrative boss Captain Ron Bell, Vice Admiral McCauley, and other admirals in my chain of command wanted me to stay for another year so I could finish some things I'd started. Second, Gary was not a captain. Finally, after the CG sent a personal message asking Lyons why I shouldn't stay another year, my extension was approved.

Normally, commanding officers of SEAL teams served two-year tours and moved on. Six was different, though. Our rapid-deployment mission demanded that Six be kept in a much higher condition of readiness than any of the other SEAL teams. Both my operational and administrative commanders thought a three-year tour would provide better continuity at the top of Six, which, in their minds, equaled better readiness. Also, they wanted me to stay on to complete changes in procedures that I'd instituted to counter the Marcinko mind-set. Whatever the case, I wanted to stay and my bosses wanted me to stay.

And stay I did, until July 1986. Then I turned over the command to an old friend and headed out to take command of Special Warfare Group Two. But the turmoil continued.

About ten days before I was to relieve Ron, another bizarre thing happened. I got a call from one of my former Six officers, who was working at the Pentagon pushing our issues through the bureaucracy. He had heard Captain Ted Grabowsky, head of the SEAL resource office on the CNO's staff, telling another OPNAV officer that the Gormly-Bell turnover wasn't going to happen. And, though Gormly and Bell didn't know it yet, he (Grabowsky) was going to be jerked out of OPNAV to relieve Bell, and Gormly was going to jail.

"Thanks for the heads-up, but we're turning over on schedule," I told my former officer. If there was to be a "night of the long knives," they'd better hustle.

Then I called Ron.

He just laughed. "I must have forgotten to send Ted an invitation to the ceremony."

Ted and I had worked together on many different occasions over the years. He was a good SEAL staff officer, but I figured he'd misheard the latest Gormly rumor circulating in Washington and was assuming a lot more than he should have.

I'd already danced this dance. In March 1986 Captain Paul Moses of the Navy Personnel Office had called to ask if I'd like to relieve Ron.

"Sure," I said.

"I'll get your orders cut," he replied.

I thought nothing more about it until Irish phoned about a month later. Would I like to relieve Captain Larry Bailey, who had served with me on my first tour in Vietnam, as commanding officer of the Naval Special Warfare Center in Coronado? I'd stay in the job for one year and then take charge of Special Warfare Group Two.

When Irish was done I said, "Sounds like a plan to me, Irish, but you'd better call Paul Moses because I already have orders in hand to relieve Ron."

Irish was quiet for a few seconds. "I'll get back to you."

Soon after that conversation, I received a heads-up from a friend in Washington. It seems Irish had been seeing admirals at the Personnel Office, trying to change my orders to relieve Ron. Irish was the only SEAL admiral at that time, and he felt a responsibility to assign SEAL officers—particularly senior SEAL officers. Apparently he wanted to put Ted in the job because Ted had selected for major command (Naval Special Warfare Groups One and Two were major commands) a year before me. I saw the logic of this, but the decision was out of my hands.

A few days later I got another call from Paul Moses, who told me not to listen to rumors. It was his job to decide where I went, and if there were any changes he'd be the one to let me know. I never heard any more from Irish on the subject.

A humorous aside. Two months after I relieved Ron, my secretary buzzed me on the intercom and said some captain wanted to speak to him. I told her to put him through. It was Captain Paul Moses, calling Ron to find out what had happened to me. When I answered, Paul asked, "What are you doing there? I thought you were still assigned to the base."

I said, "Ron and I turned over on McCauley's instructions two months ago. The admiral said he'd square it with you guys."

No response from Paul.

I went on. "What I'm doing here, Paul, is commanding Group Two."

He laughed. "I never got the word." He had called the amphibious base CO to find out how I was doing. The base CO told him to call the group. Paul wished me luck and hung up.

The investigation, code-named Iron Eagle, kept up after I left Six and took over Special Warfare Group Two. I think the Navy inspector general (IG) still believed I was part of the problem when it came time to resolve an incident involving Red Cell. Like many senior Navy officials, the IG had a hard time distinguishing between Red Cell and SEAL Team Six. No doubt Marcinko's repeated attempts to commingle the two contributed to that misunderstanding. The Red Cell investigation seemed entwined with Iron Eagle, but the common thread was not the two commands; it was Marcinko.

Under Dick Marcinko's leadership, Red Cell had been testing security at naval facilities worldwide, throwing everything but the kitchen sink at them, going far beyond what the bases might expect from terrorists. That was fine, because by the time they left a base, it had been thoroughly wrung out. Trouble surfaced when team members roughed up the civilian base-security officer at the Seal Beach, California, Naval Ammunition Depot.

A few months later I got word that I would be responsible for adjudicating charges against two former members of Red Cell for their alleged actions at Seal Beach. I received a copy of the investigation report and a copy of a videotape made during the incident. Red Cell normally took elaborate videos of all aspects of each exercise and used them to instruct the facility being tested.

The investigation said Marcinko had ordered his men to capture the security officer at his house and make him a "hostage." Such hostage-taking was a normal part of each exercise, so the order wasn't unusual. The problem, according to the investigative report, was that Marcinko had told his people to work the security officer over a bit, apparently because he had been causing Marcinko problems in the exercise. The security officer felt they went too far, so he filed a complaint. Yet just after the incident, the report said (and a video sequence verified) the security officer was sitting in the postexercise debriefing, laughing with his captors about what they'd done to him. The report also had statements from "hostages" who'd been taken in previous exercises, attesting to how they had been treated. The descriptions of their treatment sounded just like what had been done to the Seal Beach security officer.

My staff lawyer and I went through the investigation and video with a fine-tooth comb. We could see clearly what they had done to the guy, and I will admit they treated him a little roughly—as if he'd been a fellow SEAL. But from what my lawyer and I could determine, they didn't treat him worse than previous hostages.

That, to us, was an important point. It meant that a norm had been established in previous exercises and ostensibly approved by the oversight officer, Rear Admiral Paul Butcher. Also, from the video it was clear to both of us that one of the men charged, a corpsman, had tried to tone down the action. The other man charged had been on the periphery of the action. The two men dealing out most of the blows weren't the ones I'd been asked to punish.

My lawyer and I independently came to the same conclusion. The men weren't guilty of doing anything wrong. In fact, one of them had tried to soften the situation. We couldn't figure out why these two were being charged. Both of them had worked for me at Six and they were outstanding SEALs. As far as I could see, the only thing they were guilty of was poor judgment for going to work for Marcinko again. I told my lawyer to ask the judge advocate general if he could find out what was going on, and what the Navy planned for Marcinko.

Similar charges had been made against Lieutenant Duke Leonard, the assault team leader who'd rescued the governor general during Urgent Fury. Duke left Six in 1984 and went to work for Marcinko at Red Cell. He was at Seal Beach, but not in charge.

It turns out the Navy IG wanted me to hammer the people with the expectation they would testify against Marcinko in exchange for lighter sentences. In other words, they were using a typical investigation method: start at the bottom and hope the juniors will help hang the seniors. I told my lawyer there was no way I was going to ruin the careers of two fine SEALs in an attempt to get Marcinko.

The case against Duke didn't stick either. We all felt the Red Cell had gone too far in their treatment of exercise hostages, but none of us thought it right to punish legionaries for the transgressions of Caesar.

My staff lawyer said that the Navy IG was pressing the JAG hard for convictions. I was supposed to take the guys to a Captain's Mast and give them letters of reprimand, which would have killed their careers. I said I was going to do the right thing, and the hell with the inspector general.

My lawyer agreed, but said I'd better conduct the hearing and dismiss the charges, which otherwise might be brought to another commander who might be more inclined to buckle under to the IG. As usual, he was right. We scheduled the hearing for the afternoon of February 17, 1988.

Duke's hearing fell on the morning of the same day. The admiral who ran it chewed on Duke for a few minutes and then dismissed all charges, saying the wrong person was before him and he wasn't going to ruin Duke's career over something for which Duke wasn't responsible.

I did a repeat performance at 1300. Duke was there to take full responsibility for the actions of the two men before me, and I had to tell him to shut up so I could get on with it. After telling each of them I expected them to exercise better judgment in the future, regardless of what a senior officer might tell them, I dismissed the charges.

Soon afterward the bomb dropped. The Navy inspector general sent three of his lawyers down to find out why justice had not prevailed. They summoned my lawyer, who told me he learned from them that the IG was so mad, he had threatened to have me relieved of command. That was impossible, but my lawyer told me, "Better watch your Six with the IG from now on."

The Iron Eagle investigations finally came to an end late in 1989. With respect to SEAL Team Six, they found no command-sponsored corruption. Three men admitted to bringing one automatic weapon each back from Grenada (and not turning them in during my amnesty). Four other members of SEAL Team Six were charged with submitting false travel claims. One pled guilty and received a slap on the wrist. One was found not guilty at a court-martial. After that charges against the others were dropped. Two non-SEAL petty officers I'd found cheating on travel claims before the NIS investigation were convicted at courts-martial in 1987.

The Marcinko aspect of the investigations had different results. Dick and a civilian associate were charged with conspiring to defraud the government of $50,000 while he headed the Red Cell. The case centered on the grenades and other explosives Dick had contracted to buy in 1984, ostensibly for Six and his fledgling Red Cell. I was subpoenaed to testify that as commanding officer of Six at the time, I had neither requested nor wanted the explosives. The government alleged that Marcinko and the civilian, who manufactured the ordnance, were in collusion to charge twice what it cost and split the profit.

When Dick was charged, he had his lawyers request for his defense documents he knew were highly classified. They hoped the government would drop the charges rather than risk public exposure of classified information. This wasn't an unusual tactic.

I was the head of the SEAL division in OP-06, the OPNAV sponsor for Six, and the senior SEAL on the Navy staff. The request hit my desk at the speed of light. I went to talk to my immediate boss, Rear Admiral P. D. Smith, about how he wanted to handle the situation. Normally, when a request for classified information is received, a "flag review officer"—an admiral—is assigned to go through the material and declassify it or deny access, whichever is appropriate.

I really enjoyed working for P.D. He was a hot-shit naval aviator, one of the Navy's foremost experts on antisubmarine warfare. He'd also spent a couple of tours in the Pentagon and knew his way around the building.

P.D. said to me, "Bob, I'm going to recommend that you be designated the flag review officer."

"You can't do that." I grinned. "The Navy just got finished deciding I wasn't good enough to be promoted to admiral." The latest rear-admiral selection board had reported a few months before, and though P.D. and a lot of other folks hoped I'd be picked, I wasn't.

He laughed. "Everyone knows that's bullshit. Besides, I won't be able to find a flag officer who'll touch this with a ten-foot pole."

I didn't comment on that one.

"Who's better qualified than you to determine which, if any, of the material can be declassified?"

He had a point: All of the requested material concerned Six. None dealt with Red Cell.

Once the OPNAV lawyers determined there was no conflict of interest, I was designated the flag review officer. Since we had to do it, I was determined we would do the review thoroughly and fairly. After reviewing the list of documents, neither I nor the other SEAL officers working for me could see their relevance to the charges, which all had to do with events that took place after he'd left Six. We all considered the request frivolous and wanted to tell Marcinko's lawyers to pound sand. But I had already conferred with the OPNAV lawyers and knew we couldn't do that.

The Joint Chiefs of Staff were the original authority for nearly all the classified information. I called my compatriot at the special operations division of the JCS, and he agreed to set up a committee composed of special operations people from all the services and the joint staff to review all the documents. It took us about a month to wade through them, and the bottom line was that not much could be declassified. I sent a letter to Marcinko's lawyer telling him so. In fact, we erred in Marcinko's favor and probably gave him more than he'd expected.

As for the trials, I didn't think my testimony would be particularly damaging; still, I didn't want to testify against a fellow SEAL, nor was I privy to any of the evidence amassed against him by the U.S. Attorney General. I still couldn't believe he'd been stupid enough to do what he'd been charged with. When I gave my testimony, I simply said what had happened. The single question the defense lawyers asked me on cross-examination seemed irrelevant. I left the witness box, glad to be out of there.

The trial ended with a conviction for the civilian and a hung jury for Marcinko. In 1990, however, the U.S. Attorney General retried him and got a conviction. Again, I had to testify. Marcinko served time in a federal prison.

Dick had once been a good naval officer. When he became a convicted felon, he shamed the uniform he'd worn for so many years. He discredited himself, the Navy, and SEAL Team Six in the process of trying to steal taxpayers' money. While Dick commanded Six, he created an aura of suspicion around the Team. The way he did business made many question his honesty. When his actions at OPNAV brought him under scrutiny again, his former association with Six brought the command under scrutiny, too. Six became known within the upper echelons of the Navy as "the command under constant investigation"—Dick Marcinko's legacy.

PART 5

Fire Four: A New Way of Doing Business

Of all the events that have affected SEALs since they were formed in 1962 nothing has had as much impact as the formation of the United States Special Operations Command (SOCOM) in 1986. SOCOM put the special operations forces of all the services under one command for the first time in military history. That put the "care and feeding" of Navy SEALs, Army Special Forces, and Air Force Special Operations Forces under one commander.

SOCOM didn't happen because all the players thought it was a good idea, and it didn't happen overnight. It was the result of years of frustration with the way the services dealt with their special operations forces. It didn't happen until Congress made it happen.

From 1983 until 1990 I held positions from which I could influence the process. The Grenada operation focused congressional attention on the general problem of conducting joint operations and the specific problem of how special operations forces are best integrated in battle. From 1986 to 1988, while commanding Naval Special Warfare Group Two, I strongly supported the SOCOM concept because I thought it was right for the military and the country. In the Pentagon from 1988 to 1990 I fought hard to ensure SEALs weren't abandoned by the Navy, which had struggled to keep us from participating in the new command. During this period I fought "battles" as intense, if not as bloody, as any I faced on real battlefields.

23

THE OLD WAY OF DOING BUSINESS: PUT THEM BACK IN THEIR CAGES

By late 1968 the country had grown weary of the Vietnam War. Most junior SEAL officers resented the war protests and the denigration of our efforts. But it was clear to many of us that our government's policy was not to win the war. SEALs were still fighting and winning our own battles in the Mekong Delta and the Rung Sat, but "winning" was a function of killing more bad guys than the platoon before you. When Nixon was elected president, he said he was going to get us out of Vietnam. What we didn't know was that he was simply going to declare victory and leave. By the end of 1971 all SEAL combat platoons had been withdrawn. Nothing was left but advisory teams with our Vietnamese counterpart units. When I assumed command of SEAL Team Two in August 1972, we had one team left in-country, and they'd been withdrawn by November.

SEALs, like the rest of the military, were downsized beginning in 1972. For the next ten years we had to scratch out a living in the Navy. The SEAL Teams had grown because of Vietnam, and the military hierarchy accepted the fact that we'd done a superb job there. But there was also a general feeling among the conventional leaders that organizations such as SEALs and Army Special Forces didn't have an application in a peacetime environment. I often heard the line "We need to put them back in their cages." That meant reducing drastically the number of SEALs. SEAL Team One, which had more than quintupled from its original size of ten officers and fifty enlisted, got hit harder than SEAL Team Two, which had only doubled. People and funding were cut. In October 1973, when I commanded SEAL Team Two, we, along with the rest of the military, were put into DEFCON 3 for the Yom Kippur War. I didn't have enough gear to outfit more than two of the seven platoons we had to provide under the war plans. My entire time in command of SEAL Team Two was spent fending off attempts to downsize us further, including one attempt to decommission the command.

Our biggest problem was having enough money to keep our people trained. It was almost impossible to do any realistically rigorous training at our home bases in Little Creek and Coronado, and we had to get out of town for such non-civilian-friendly activities as blowing things up. So we had to send the troops away. The problem was we didn't have any money to pay their expenses. While I was in command of UDT-12 in the late 1970s, we were still doing most of our mission-essential training with "no-cost orders," meaning the men had to pay for their own meals and lodging if they wanted to go. (Most of them did.) I used to explain to my bosses that we used travel money like ships used fuel oil. Most of the time I wasn't successful.

During the Carter administration the military hit a low. The Navy leadership made a decision to fund new technology at the expense of the men and money needed to operate them; we called the result "hollow force." SEAL procurement programs were minuscule compared to those in the rest of the Navy. Often we didn't put a big enough blip on the screen to get noticed. Sometimes, when funding for large programs was reduced, our technology disappeared completely, being absorbed into the overall program reduction.

When I took command of UDT-12 in 1979, I inherited a hollow command. Naval Special Warfare Group One had been forced to consolidate a number of functions under the group's staff that had historically, and correctly, been the responsibility of the UDT-SEAL commanding officers. By the time I took over UDT-12, the consolidation had cost the Teams their control of mission-essential equipment. The equipment was lost because of the philosophy that we needed only enough gear to support the three UDT-SEAL platoons deployed in the Pacific Theater, while the ones in Coronado, preparing to deploy, could share what was left. For example, UDT-12 had only ten of the needed hundred Emerson closed-circuit scuba and twenty parachutes of a similar required number. UDT-11 and SEAL Team One were in like positions because the equipment had been equally allocated by Naval Special Warfare Group One. In other words, we had about thirty of our primary scuba rigs available to support the training of three units, each with a minimum of sixty or seventy people in Coronado at any one time.

By 1980, all special operations forces had similar problems. It's not surprising Desert One was screwed up. There just wasn't much emphasis on special-operations-forces capability in the Department of Defense. In essence, SEALs worked at the lowest level. Their employment was left up to whatever local operational commander they were assigned to—just as in Vietnam.

Within the Navy programming system we were lumped by the surface-force commanders into a funding category with other nonship units such as the Seabees and assault craft units. The group commanders received part of a pie that surface-force commanders divvied up among all the oddball units. We were oddball units.

The point is, not all the money Congress thought it had appropriated for SEALs ever reached our coffers. Our procurement programs for boats and submersibles, though they cost what to us was big money, were peanuts compared to the cost of a ship or plane. I used to tell my bosses we could run our whole program for five years for the price of one F-14 fighter. We always had to take our "fair share" of the routine, across-the-board program cuts mandated by the Navy, but coughing up our "fair share" often meant we lost a whole program. Cutting $500,000 out of one of our programs would essentially kill it. The same amount of money could be absorbed easily in a major shipbuilding program by reducing something like staff administrative travel.

Finally, some admirals thought SEALs were not all that important to the Navy. We needed to be put back in our cages until the next war—but when would the next war occur? For special operations forces, war is sometimes small and fast.

24

HUNTING IN THE GULF: JOINT SPECIAL OPERATIONS AT WORK

One day in January 1985, I heard from the general who had commanded the Joint Headquarters during Urgent Fury. Calling from his new command, he told me I had to appear with him before a Senate subcommittee reviewing the use of special operations forces in Urgent Fury.

When we testified, we said all the problems we'd encountered in Grenada had been fixed. That was true for the problems we could fix. But the fundamental issue of who would be in overall charge of special operations forces was beyond our "pay grades." The senators thanked us for our time and told us we'd performed as well as could be expected in Grenada. Then they sent their staffers off to write the Nunn-Cohen Amendment to the Goldwater-Nichols Act of 1986. As the legislation was being drafted, Congress raised a few trial balloons for the Pentagon to shoot at. And the shooting was intense. The Department of Defense did not want Congress telling it how to command its forces.

The Goldwater-Nichols Act had the greatest impact on the military structure since the 1948 legislation that established the Department of Defense. Goldwater-Nichols made the Chairman of the Joint Chiefs of Staff a decision-maker rather than a consensus-taker. It also directed more power to the commanders in chief (CINCs) of the regional war-fighting commands, giving them peacetime control of the forces assigned to them. In essence it codified what we all had known for years—CINCs, not individual services, fight wars. The Navy was the most vocal in opposing the change, but each service chief knew he would lose a lot of clout in the budget process. And he would lose day-to-day decision making about the employment of his forces.

Special operations forces gained a new lease on life through the Nunn-Cohen Amendment, which directed the establishment of the U.S. Special Operations Command (SOCOM), headed by a four-star officer and with the same stature as the regional commanders in chief. The new SOCOM would have its own money to train and prepare forces for employment by the regional CINCs, but most of all it required that all special operations forces not actually assigned to a regional CINC be assigned full-time to the new SOCOM.

In 1987–88, while I was in command of Naval Special Warfare Group Two, the Navy fought hard to keep from implementing the Nunn-Cohen Amendment. Navy staffers had managed to get the authors of the bill to write some ambiguous "sense of Congress" words into the legislation that gave DoD the option to assign SEALs to SOCOM or not.

Almost as soon as the new commander in chief of U.S. Special Operations Command took command in 1987, he started asking for "his" SEALs. The Secretary of the Navy told him to pound sand, because in the Navy's view SEALs should be exempted from SOCOM. SEALs, the Navy said, were being trained and prepared to support fleet operations, and the Navy didn't need the new special-operations-forces command to tell them how to do it.

The Navy was really afraid of "functional" CINCs generally; they didn't want the assignment of aircraft carriers to an Air Force "CINCAIR" to be the next item on the table. Wanting to squash the notion of functional CINCs, period, the Navy chose as its battleground the assignment of SEALs to SOCOM. But no one was seriously considering establishing a bunch of functional CINCs. The issue was special operations forces and only special operations forces. Congress wanted them to be supported better than the services had been supporting them.

I got caught right up in the fight. I strongly supported putting all SEALs under the new command, and I didn't hide my opinion—not a very popular position with some of my admirals. But I knew putting all special operations forces under one commander was the best thing to do: for the country, because it would provide cohesive organization to the forces and improve their operational readiness; for the military, because it would charge one commander with the responsibility for forces each of the military services found difficult to fit into their core missions; for SEALs, because they would have a commander who appreciated their special support requirements.

Finally, just before he resigned, Secretary of Defense Caspar Weinberger ordered the Secretary of the Navy to put SEALs under the new command. The new joint structure was a done deal. Some of my fellow SEAL officers continued to question the principle of "jointness." I knew joint warfare was viable and productive. In addition to my experiences at Six, I had a joint force in the Persian Gulf combating the Iranian threat to oil shipping.

November 11, 1987, 0300
Northern Persian Gulf

The sixty-five-foot patrol boat pitched and rolled as we proceeded slowly just outside Iranian territorial waters. I was in command of Naval Special Warfare Group Two, and I was in the Persian Gulf to see how my troops were doing. In order to do that I went on a night patrol with them.

It was pitch black, as is often the case at sea when the moon isn't shining, and surprisingly cold. Our Furuno surface-search radar turned slowly over the pilothouse. We were looking for Iranian mine-laying ships, which were creating havoc with the oil-transportation traffic going in and out of Kuwait City, at the northern end of the Persian Gulf. If there were any radar contacts within fifteen miles of us, the Furuno would pick them up and display a blip on the screen located just in front of the boat officer's position.

We'd seen nothing since we left our base, "Fort" Hercules, a barge anchored on the Saudi side of the Persian Gulf not far from Iranian waters. We'd operated off barges in Vietnam, and it worked well in the Persian Gulf. We had leased two mobile offshore drilling platforms from oil companies in the region and converted them to support our operations. The "Hercules," the first one finished, supported Group Two forces. The other barge, farther south in the gulf, supported Group One forces.

By early October, Hercules, under the command of Lieutenant Commander Paul Evancoe, was on station, and patrol boats were searching day and night. Tall, well-built, with a dark mustache that gave him an imposing air, Paul had commanded one of our group's special boat units in Little Creek and had deployed with the force we sent in August. He was a well-respected, aggressive ex–enlisted officer with Vietnam experience. Commander Dick Flanagan, a superb SEAL officer who had a lot of combat experience and was in charge of all our forces in the Persian Gulf, gave Paul the necessary "top cover" to carry out innovative operations in the northern gulf.

Paul really had a joint force on board Hercules. For helo support he had a detachment of Army AH-6 helicopters, the same gunships I'd worked closely with when I commanded Six. He had a Marine Stinger detachment for air defense, and Air Force communicators to augment the mobile communications team from Group Two. And civilians from one of our fellow agencies were helping in intelligence support. It was a good setup, which epitomized synergism. Every unit on the barge contributed to the success of the mission.

There were two patrol boats (PBs) in our patrol this night, each supporting the other. The boats looked impressive, sixty-five-foot battleships, and it was no wonder the Iranians were afraid of them. They had a 40mm gun forward and 20mm guns aft, with .50-caliber and 7.62mm machine guns mounted on both sides and a 40mm automatic grenade launcher amidships. The PBs bristled with weapons. At general quarters, ten of the twelve men in the crew manned weapon stations, making the boat a fearsome sight.

In early August 1987, I had deployed this force of SEALs and boats to the Persian Gulf, where we were to assist other Navy forces involved in Earnest Will, the military operation to keep the oil-shipping lanes in the Persian Gulf free from Iranian interdiction. Our part of the mission was to protect the U.S. Navy mine sweepers as they kept the channel to Kuwait clear of mines, specifically in the area around Farsi Island in the northern gulf. We deployed our forces within four days after receiving orders—incredibly fast, given the relaxed alert status we in Little Creek were on at that time. But when I got the order, the men responded. They knew they were going to war.

I was confident in our firepower on this patrol. In addition to the two PBs, two "Killer Eggs"—Army AH-6 helicopter gunships, nicknamed for their egg-shaped fuselage—were on alert on the barge should we need them. I knew the crews—we'd worked together before. In a previous encounter with two Iranian Boghammer speedboats, the Iranians had learned the meaning of American might.

Soon after Hercules arrived in the northern Persian Gulf, Paul received information that the Iranians were going to lay mines in the shipping channel near Farsi Island. The area was a stronghold for the Iranians and supported nearby mine-laying operations. The PBs were conducting routine patrols in the area, supported by the AH-6 gunships. Paul and his intelligence people noted that whenever the Iranians had laid mines earlier, the mine layer had been protected by Boghammer speedboats. Purchased from Sweden, the Boghammers had machine guns and were fast enough to cause problems for our destroyers and cruisers escorting oil ships from the Straits of Hormuz to Kuwait City. The Iranians had proven to be good seamen. So when our guys noticed that the Boghammers routinely met at a sea buoy off Farsi Island, they decided to see if they could catch a mine layer in action.

Paul sent two patrol boats and the AH-6 helos to the general area of the buoy. They got lucky. The AH-6s spotted two Boghammers milling around the buoy, as if waiting for something. The Killer Eggs flew closer to observe. As they did, one of the Boghammers launched a U.S.-manufactured Stinger—a shoulder-fired ground-to-air missile—at the helos. That was a bad move. The helos were too close for the Stinger to acquire them, so it zinged past harmlessly and the helos immediately opened fire, sinking one Boghammer and seriously damaging the other. The PBs arrived on the scene, captured some Iranians, and recovered the damaged Boghammer, towing it back to the Hercules for intelligence exploitation.

So far, on this patrol, we hadn't been as lucky as Paul's guys had been in October. We had seen nothing since we left the Hercules at 2100 on November 10. Our plan was to patrol south from the barge for about ten miles, then head east for about fifteen miles until we were just outside Iranian territorial waters, and finally go north about thirty miles to a point just off Farsi Island.

The Iranians' tactic was to launch the mines in the northern Persian Gulf and let them drift south with the prevailing currents. Floating mines had been found out in the Arabian Sea 200 miles to the south. Some hadn't gotten that far before they made contact with oilers or with ships from our own Navy. We weren't looking for mines tonight, though. Our boats didn't have mine-hunting gear. Finding the mine layers before they had a chance to do their thing was our mission.

Of course, that meant we were unprotected. I figured we'd know about any mine only after we found ourselves blown a hundred feet or so into the air. That is, if we weren't vaporized immediately; the old Russian mines were sized to sink large ships. A sixty-five-foot boat would never know what hit it. We assuaged nervousness by saying our boat was too small to detonate the mines, but deep down all of us knew that was BS. The men on the patrol boats had been doing this nearly every night, and they had developed the fatalistic attitude most fighting men develop when they have to operate around mines. Our little force controlled the waters around us. In time, Hercules had laid claim to the entire northern end of the gulf. But we couldn't control a mine that had been secreted off the stern of some Iranian boat weeks before and a hundred miles away.

Seas were out of the north, ranging from six to eight feet—significant for a boat our size—as we continued to cut through the dark waters of the northern Persian Gulf. The crews on both boats had become veterans of many patrols in the month they had been operating from Hercules. But this was my first night out in the Persian Gulf, and my adrenaline was pumping as it always did when I went in harm's way. Patrolling at about ten knots, we looked for signs of Iranian boat activity. Until we got to the northern end of the patrol zone, we saw nothing remarkable.

At about 0100, we spotted a blip on the radarscope. It headed south toward us. I didn't know what it was, but from the size of the mark on the Furuno screen we knew it was a good-sized craft, probably a large Arab dhow. Dhows have plied the waters of the gulf since the beginning of recorded history. They are mostly cargo vessels and fishing boats, but more recently some have become mine layers. We laid to just off the track of the suspected dhow. As the boat approached we saw no running lights, but that wasn't unusual for a dhow.

Our boats eased slowly toward the contact, dim gray shapes moving stealthily through the swells. The men had all manned their battle stations, since we didn't know what we were stalking. I stayed outside the pilothouse, just to the side of one of the .50-caliber machine-gun positions. The expectation of going into combat again made my senses ever more alert. I watched as the superbly trained crew went through their approach procedures. The coxswain behind the wheel was peering intently through the boat's windshield, straining to get a glimpse of the contact. The patrol officer, a young lieutenant, was moving back and forth in the bridge area, being careful not to interfere with the boat officer, a young petty officer first class, as he directed the PB.

The patrol officer sent our other PB to take station astern and to our port side, reminding the other boat officer of the fields of fire each boat would have if the contact proved hostile. I watched as the other PB maneuvered into position. We approached the mystery boat's line of travel from its starboard quarter and reduced our speed as the radar showed the contact was 500 meters from our port bow, traveling at ten knots. If it was a dhow, it wasn't under sail.

The gun crew manned the 40mm cannon forward on our boat. I heard them slide the first round quietly into the gun's breech. Other gunners were doing the same with the .50-caliber machine guns and the MK-19 automatic 40mm grenade launchers. The crew was all in battle dress, armored vests cinched tightly against their camouflage fatigues, helmets pulled down tight on their heads. I was wearing a vest and my 9mm Baretta 92 SF pistol in my right hand. If it came to a shoot-out, I was going to be shooting.

The patrol officer handed me his portable night-vision scope. He himself used the large night-vision device mounted on the boat. Through the eyepiece I saw the familiar green glow. Because our PB was rolling heavily in the sea swell, I couldn't get my scope fixed on where the contact should be, but the stabilized boat scope was cooperating better. The patrol officer grabbed my shoulder and pointed toward our port bow. Putting my handheld scope up to my eye, I saw a shape headed south, about 300 meters away.

We could identify the boat, a large dhow about seventy feet long. Both PBs now turned slowly to starboard. The patrol officer told me he intended to bring us parallel to the track of the dhow and slowly close in to have a good look. We increased our speed to match the dhow's. I looked through my scope again but couldn't see anyone or anything on the dhow's deck. Nor did we see any evidence of mines. The dhow's skipper wasn't reacting; clearly he had no idea we were there.

Our two boats were now abeam of the dhow, about 250 meters out and closing in. The dhow was getting larger and larger in my scope. Still I saw no activity on board that would suggest the crew knew they were being stalked.

When we were about 100 meters from the dhow, one of our men fired an illumination flare. Immediately we increased speed to twenty knots and closed to within fifty meters. Illuminating the contact was standard procedure. If they were up to no good, they would probably panic and either start shooting or haul ass.

The flare hovered over and in front of the dhow at about 200 feet, then drifted slowly toward the water, suspended under its parachute. It lit up the dhow like Christmas. It also lit us up. At once the dhow decreased speed, and we slowed as well. The moment of truth was upon us.

At first there appeared to be no one on deck. Then a man emerged from the small deckhouse and looked at us. What he saw must have been frightful. The boats had all weapons trained directly at the dhow. Our other boat was about fifty meters aft of us, their weapons, too, bristling in the white glow of the illumination flares.

The man turned and yelled at someone back inside. I could almost feel our gunners' fingers tightening on their triggers. They were well disciplined, and I knew there would be no shooting unless someone on the dhow threatened us. Would those on the dhow be stupid enough to fight? As the flare floated down just above the sails of the dhow, another appeared overhead.

At that instant more men emerged from the deckhouse and ran around on deck. Were they running to man hidden weapons? We didn't know, but I had my Baretta aimed directly at the fellow yelling instructions to the crew.

It soon became apparent they weren't running to man weapons. They began pointing at the fishing nets attached to the rigging to show they were harmless. They knew who we were, and they were scared to death of us. The patrol officer moved our PB closer to the dhow and told the other to maintain station aft. The dhow's crewmen were all manning their starboard rail, with their hands held high in the air over their heads. If they were getting ready to fight, it was the strangest battle formation I'd ever seen. The man who appeared to be in charge started waving his hands in a friendly gesture.

We stayed alongside the dhow while our guys got a good look. All we could see was fishing nets.

The patrol officer turned to me and said, "Nothing on this one, boss."

I said something like, "At least not on deck."

There was no way we could really tell what they had below, but the dhow was riding high in the water. It certainly looked like nothing more than a fisherman. I remembered, though, some "innocent fishermen" from Vietnam, who had AK-47s hidden just below the gunwales of their sampans, waiting for one of our SEAL ambush patrols to relax. I still didn't completely trust what I saw in front of me.

I turned to the patrol officer. "Why don't we board her and look below?"

"We can't—the commander would have our asses if he ever heard about it." He went on to explain that our rules of engagement didn't allow us to go on board to inspect. In fact, as I later learned, we were pushing the rules by threatening the dhow close aboard.

The patrol officer said, "I'm going to let her pass. She appears to be nothing more than Arab fishermen from Kuwait." He turned to the boat officer and gave the order to break off.

The PB pulled slowly away from the dhow but stayed parallel course until we were about a hundred meters out. Our trail boat sped up and moved to our starboard beam. I looked at the Furuno scope and watched the blip move slowly away.

Since the dhow was headed in the direction of Hercules and we were on the last leg of our patrol, we fell in a couple of hundred meters astern and followed. We all relaxed. I could feel the adrenaline draining from my system. Even though we didn't get to do any shooting, I felt good about what I'd seen. The boat crews were very professional. While acting within the rules of engagement, they were conducting aggressive patrols; no wonder the northern Persian Gulf was quiet. The Iranians would have been stupid to take on our guys.

When I returned to my headquarters in Little Creek, I began touting that little joint force to all in my chain of command. My guys would not have been able to do the job in the Persian Gulf without forces from the other services. For example, the Navy didn't have any helicopter gunships on active duty, and its two reserve squadrons of Vietnam-vintage

Seawolves didn't have nearly the capabilities of the Army AH-6s, and they weren't available to us SEALs.

Unfortunately, everyone above me considered the barge operations to be strictly Navy, with "a little support" being provided by the other services. I knew the real story, and I knew having one commander for all special operations forces would mean that future missions would have the same good chance of success as our work in the Persian Gulf.

From 1988 to 1990, I was the senior SEAL on the Chief of Naval Operations staff in the Pentagon. I spent 90 percent of my time ensuring that the migration of SEALs from Navy control to the special operations command went as smoothly as possible. When I got there, Weinberger's decision to transfer SEALs to SOCOM still stuck in the craw of many senior naval officers. My primary concern was that the flow of operating money not be interrupted by some bureaucratic accountant with a chip on his shoulder. Fortunately, the continued excellent performance of our forces in the Persian Gulf made it increasingly difficult for anyone to contest the efficacy of joint special operations forces. I was finally able to show that SEALs could better support the Navy under the watchful eye of a CINC whose only concern was the care and upkeep of all special operations forces.

During my time in the Pentagon, political infighting was intense. The day I checked in I ran into General Al Gray, the commandant of the Marine Corps. We'd worked together when he commanded all the Marines in the Atlantic and I commanded all the SEALs in the Atlantic.

He asked, "Bob, what the hell are you doing in Washington?"

I said, "General, they finally trapped me for a Pentagon tour."

"A bit of advice," he said. "Get a dog—that's the only friend you'll have in this zoo."

He was right about the "friend" part, but to my surprise, I enjoyed my tour in the zoo. I was there during a watershed time for our defense structure and the special operations community. We solidified a new way of doing business that has worked very well. SEALs have never been better funded, trained, and supported. They have new boats, for example, that we old guys would have loved when we were protecting shipping in the Persian Gulf. They are masters of their own fate, fully responsible for their own destiny. Instead of being buried at the bottom of the Navy structure they have the ear of a four-star general, charged by Congress to make sure they are well cared for. That's a good way to do business.

EPILOGUE: CEASE-FIRE—LOCK AND LOAD

In August 1990, Saddam Hussein's forces overran Kuwait. Desert Shield and Desert Storm, the military operations that held the line in Saudi Arabia and then retook Kuwait, captured the emotions of the country.

At the end of August 1990, I transferred to SOCOM at MacDill Air Force Base in Tampa, Florida, and became the Deputy Director of Simulations and Analysis. I had the task of overseeing the analysis that would determine special-operations-forces funding into the next century. It was not the most exciting work I'd ever done, but the Iraqis helped make my assignment more interesting. During Desert Storm, I was in charge of the SOCOM liaison to the U.S. Central Command (CENTCOM), getting more SOCOM forces employed in the war and helping the CENTCOM commander, General Norman Schwarzkopf, meet terrorist threats outside the combat area. For me, Desert Storm was simple: I went, we conquered, and I came home.

I'd decided to retire from the Navy two days before I got tapped to go to Saudi Arabia. It was time for me to leave. I was too old and too senior to ever again command SEALs, and I knew I wasn't going to be promoted to admiral. General Carl Stiner, for whom I'd worked in the past, was the commander in chief of SOCOM. In January 1992, when I left the Navy, he and Rear Admiral Chuck LeMoyne, an old swim buddy from UDT-22 days then assigned to SOCOM, gave me a rousing send-off. At a larger retirement ceremony than I had wanted, Stiner awarded me a "good-bye medal," which I promptly noted should have gone to Becky for putting up with me for so many years. Becky and I were "piped over the side" to civilian life and left Tampa the next day. I haven't been back and I haven't looked back.

I became an independent consultant on security and other related matters. One of my clients has been my old Mekong Delta buddy Satch Baumgart. Satch got contracts to transport humanitarian aid—food—from the Russian Black Sea port of Novorossisk, by air to Yerevan, Armenia. I helped him set up the process and establish the security needed to ensure the cargo got to its destination.

The first time I went to Russia, I didn't know what to expect. I found a country that in many ways reminded me of what America must have been like in the early 1900s. Communications were terrible. Roads, outside of Moscow, were all two lanes. It could take up to five hours to place a telephone call to a town twenty miles away—if you spoke Russian. It was a country in decay. Things have improved since my first visit. Two types of Russians have emerged: the ones who couldn't shake their ties to the old way, and those who have become prosperous entrepreneurs, taking advantage of the "wild west" opportunities. There are a lot of rich Russians in Moscow now.

But there's been a price for their new freedom. Out of the rubble of the former Communist Party the organized crime elements, popularly called mafias, have taken over business enterprises and aligned themselves with international crime organizations. Drugs, not a great problem under the old regime, have been flowing into Russia as a result. And the decentralization of political power has not only contributed to the rise of the mafias but also eroded the power the old Soviet Union had over its constituent republics. Decentralization has made Russia vulnerable to a force being increasingly discussed in the West: Islamic fundamentalism.

Ironically, the same two forces—drugs and fundamentalist Islam—now threaten the security of both the West and its former ideological competitor.

* * *

In Kazakhstan, Uzbekistan, Turkmenistan, Kyrgyzstan, Tadzhikistan, and all former Soviet republics, lie deep-seated resentments toward the Russians for occupying and subjugating their people. These nations are fertile breeding grounds for the Islamic fundamentalist movement, and the movement is there in force. Additionally many of the republics within the Russian Federation have the same demographics and the same hatreds. Chechnya is the most visible of these, having already begun its war for independence; though the fighting has now stopped, the war is not yet over. Dagestan and North Ossetia could be next. I'm not sure that the Islamic fundamentalist movement had a hand in starting the fighting in Chechnya, but they certainly supported it with men and arms. Though this region has enormous mineral reserves, including large oil deposits, the economies are near collapse. As conditions worsen there will be more pressure to get rid of the people now running the countries, most of whom are former Communist Party members. The area is ripe for the fundamentalist picking.

Why worry about something that's taking place on the other side of the world? Simple answer: oil. The reason we went to war with Iraq in the Persian Gulf. Another reason to worry lies right here in the United States. A growing segment of our population is suspicious and resentful of the government that runs our country. I'm convinced we still don't know all those behind the terrible bombing of the federal building in Oklahoma City. Though all evidence seems to point toward a domestic, anarchist fringe element, who knows? Could they have pulled off that bombing without international help? Who was the mysterious dark-haired, dark-complexioned John Doe who has not yet been identified? For years, international terrorist organizations have been cooperating. The bombing of the World Trade Center in New York was not homegrown.

The wellspring of the fundamentalist movement is Iran, whose rulers consider Western culture inimical to their own. They have shown the will and the means to use force to further their movement. Things will get worse. When we supported the mujahedeen fighters in their struggle with the Soviets in Afghanistan, we created a well-armed, combat-experienced force for the fundamentalists. In Afghanistan, many Muslim countries saw an opportunity to rid themselves of their radical fundamentalist elements. They were happy to send "freedom fighters" to the aid of the mujahedeen. The problem was, those fighters weren't all killed by the Soviets as expected. They won! And then, well armed with U.S. Stinger missiles and other Western arms, they went home. Now they are causing real problems and will continue to do so.

As the Islamic fundamentalist movement becomes more widespread and more energetic it will seek to deflect Western interest from their actions in the East. What better way to do that than to use domestic fringe elements to conduct acts of terrorism in the U.S., thereby focusing our attentions inward while the fundamentalists seek to take control of such eastern Islamic nations as Egypt, Saudi Arabia, the United Arab Emirates, and Bahrain? Three years ago, this scenario might have sounded far-fetched. Today, it's not. We have to be ready. What can we do?

First, we ought to use Iraq as a counterbalance to the fundamentalist movement—a counter to Iran, right at the heart of the movement. To do that we have to start to bring Iraq back into the world's political arena. George H. W. Bush may have been thinking the same thing when he ordered the cessation of Desert Storm. In the aftermath of the war many pundits chastised him for not going all the way to Baghdad and occupying the country. In a famous radio transmission, the commander of one of the 18th Airborne Corps units said, "I'm at the Basra road [the main road to Baghdad from Kuwait] and meeting no resistance. Should I turn left [toward Baghdad] or right in accordance with the plan?" Schwarzkopf told the commander to turn right. That was the correct answer, just as stopping the war when we did was the correct decision. Iraq, personified by Saddam, was the enemy of the moment.

But Iraq is not the real enemy for posterity. The Iranians occupy that lofty position, because they are the fount of the real enemy of Western goals in the region: Islamic fundamentalism. Fostered by Iran, the movement has spread throughout the Middle East and the former Soviet

Union. If that trend continues (and I think it will), in the not too distant future we will see a large Islamic empire stretching east through the central Asian republics to the border of China, and west along the southern Mediterranean to the Atlantic Ocean. The empire will include Pakistan, which has a nuclear capability now, and Iran, which will probably have one soon. And the empire will control much of the world's oil.

Second, the United States needs to develop better means to deal with one of the tools: fundamentalists' international terrorism. The actions urged by President Clinton in the aftermath of the Oklahoma bombing are exactly what terrorists want. When we start pushing more control mechanisms on our society, we are helping the bad guys. More controls will mean more dissatisfied citizens and further unrest. More infringement on our historical liberties is not what's needed.

We need to develop new strategies to deal with terrorism inside our borders. We have to get our heads out of the sand. The key to stopping a terrorist act is to know about it beforehand. Intelligence is the key to foiling terrorists, but getting good intelligence is not easy. All terrorist organizations are set up in cells—otherwise they don't last long. It's not impossible to infiltrate cells, but it's difficult. It takes a lot of time and money. And it's the only sure way to discern terrorists' intentions. We can gather a lot of information electronically, but the bad guys know we're listening so they routinely spread disinformation. We have to have brave, dedicated people inside the terrorist cells, as close to the organizational leaders as possible. Only by "looking the terrorists in the eyes" can we hope to stop them before they act.

Outside our country, the ingredient that's all too often been missing is the political will to use force early enough. Many times I've sat in forward bases with highly trained and dedicated troops, waiting for the signal to go, only to be kept on a string until it was too late. Our political leadership calls the shots on the use of military force. I wouldn't have it any other way. But we have to recognize that talking will get us only so far with people whose thinking is so unlike ours as to seem insane. We must be willing to "thump them on the heads" before we talk, instead of after. The

United States has the best-trained commando forces in the world. They all volunteered for the chance to fight our country's enemies. I know that's what they want—I was one of them. But they should be employed wisely so they don't become cannon fodder for well-intentioned but procrastinating politicians. They should be committed to action when the element of strategic surprise is in their favor, not after all else fails and the bad guys are just waiting for them to appear. Conducting raids on terrorist facilities by aircraft flying at 10,000 feet is not the best way to get their attention. We have to put forces on the ground and have them send the terrorists to meet their makers. We have to terrorize the terrorists in their sanctuaries, doing unto them before they do unto us. This strategy will also work against another of our national threats: drugs.

Drugs are as threatening to our national society as Islamic fundamentalism. Our streets are battlegrounds for drug gangs waging war on each other. Competition is intense among the gangs, intent on infecting the youth of America with their deadly product. I first got into the antidrug business by default in 1988 while I was in the Pentagon. Another division had primary responsibility for Navy counterdrug operations. When pressure started to build in Congress and elsewhere to involve our special operations forces on the ground in Central and South America and in the Pacific, I decided my shop needed to get involved.

DoD wanted no part of the antidrug effort. Military leaders reasoned correctly that the "war on drugs" really wasn't a war and that eliminating the demand was the real solution to the problem. The military had been doing that internally, with fair success, but had neither the charter nor the means to do it for the entire country. Pentagon leaders figured any increased military involvement in combating the supply side—interdicting the drugs before they got into the United States—would come at the expense of readiness. The war-fighting ability of our forces would diminish. And if the military took responsibility for the "war on drugs," it would be scapegoated when the war proved unwinnable given the Rules of Engagement.

Personally, I wanted to involve special operations forces to a greater extent than that envisioned under government policy, which provided for advising and training selected military units in Central and South America under the aegis of the Drug Enforcement Agency (DEA). DEA agents are good and brave guys but not well versed on special operations tactics. Properly employed, our special operations forces could have made a major contribution, and our guys wanted to be involved. It was something real and that's why all of us are in the business—we want to be involved in combat.

I floated a proposal up to my bosses, recommending that special operations forces target and eliminate drug lords in their safe areas. Nothing would make them give up the business as fast as knowing they were going to die if they didn't. Capturing them and turning them over to their host countries wasn't working. Bringing them back to our country for prosecution wasn't working, either—we couldn't get them extradited. Drug lords have too much money and influence; they routinely escape prosecution by hiring high-priced legal "gunslingers" to get them off. The only way to pressure them is to make them fear for their lives.

Not surprisingly, my bosses said, "Great idea, Bob—no." The Secretary of Defense and the service chiefs were afraid of being dragged so far into the war that DoD would be held responsible for the outcome. Even though what I was suggesting would involve only intelligence and special operations, it was too far out to be accepted.

In the end, we developed a policy that protected our guys on the ground as much as possible. If they weren't going to be used effectively, I wanted them used minimally. Anyway, the real solution from the beginning was on the demand side. We had to reduce drug usage in the United States. Someday we may get our national testosterone level high enough to do what's required to eliminate the supply side. Maybe the problems drugs cause our society aren't yet big enough to force our leaders to do the right thing.

Islamic fundamentalism, terrorism, and drugs—these are the enemies of democracy in the twenty-first century. We must deal harshly with them.

Maybe deadly force sounds outlandish because these three evils haven't been viewed as a real problem by the average American; each has always been perpetrated on the other guy. But not anymore. Like the drug scourge, international terrorism sponsored by Islamic fundamentalists has invaded our country. It's time that our national leadership stop viewing drugs and international terrorism in America as simply law enforcement issues—the problems are more complex and far-reaching.

Special operations forces are well suited to meet the challenges of terrorism and drugs. Existing posse comitatus laws preclude the routine use of military forces against domestic threats. Congress enacted those laws to ensure, among other things, that our military structure could not be exploited for internal political gain. That reason remains valid. But there is also a provision in the law for the president to authorize certain military forces to carry out specific missions. In the past, presidents have waived the law to combat situations that threatened national security. I was involved in executing one such waiver, the details of which I will not discuss. International terrorism and the continuing flow of drugs into our society are real threats to our national security. Our special operations forces have talents and capabilities not possessed by even the best-trained domestic law enforcement organizations. Our special operations forces should eliminate international terrorists and drug kingpins, wherever they live. Either Congress should modify the Posse Comitatus Act, or the president should issue a standing waiver, to allow our Special Operations Forces to enter the fray.

Those are my concluding thoughts. But though the final section of this book has been written, the final chapter of Bob Gormly's life has not. I've dodged many bullets of all types and survived. I've been "dinged" in combat and punished by my many years of rigorous and dangerous SEAL training—and after-hours activities. I'm not unique. Anyone who's survived nearly thirty years in the SEAL business will understand what I mean. We all have the same aches and pains. I tell people that had I known, when I was younger, that I would live this long, I'd have taken much better care of myself. As the doctor who performed my retirement physical explained to me after viewing my head-to-foot X rays, "Your problem, Captain, is not that you have the body of a sixty-five-year-old man. Your problem is that you still have the brain of an eighteen-year-old."

No problem—lock and load.

GLOSSARY

AC-130—U.S. Air Force gunship designed to interdict targets on the ground and provide close air support. The aircraft is a basic C-130 modified with special weapons and electronics.

ACU-2—An organization in the Atlantic Fleet that operates specialized craft employed during amphibious landings.

AH-6—U.S. Army light attack helicopter. Hughes 530 variant, affectionately dubbed "Killer Egg" because of the shape of the fuselage and the numerous weapons the helo can carry.

AN PVS-2—Vietnam-era Night Vision Device (NVD). Commonly called the "Starlight Scope" because it used ambient light to provide a magnified image, much as a telescope would do during the day. Newer versions are binocular.

APD—Converted World War II destroyer designed to carry underwater demolition teams.

auger stake—Device with a helix-twisted bottom, commonly used to anchor dog chains in the backyards of America; UDT adapted them to anchor survey lines during submerged reconnaissances.

barilyme—Carbon dioxide–scrubbing chemical used in the Emerson closed-circuit scuba.

Blackhawk—UH-60 helicopter. The basic troop-carrying helo for the U.S. Army.

Boat Support Unit—During the Vietnam era, the organization that ran most SEAL boats. The organizations are now called Special Boat Squadrons.

BTR-60—Russian armored personnel carrier. The BTR-60PB version is equipped with a ZPU-1 heavy machine gun.

BUDS—Basic Underwater Demolition SEAL. Present-day organization that runs basic training for all who seek to become SEALs. When I went through it, it was called UDT Replacement Training. Before that, it had other names, but it's always had the same purpose: to provide only the best-qualified men to the Seal Teams.

bunker works—System of bunkers, connected to allow movement through the system.

Capewell—MC-1 military static-line parachute canopy-release system. Located where the two canopy risers attach to the jumper's harness, capewells have a two-trigger assembly for each riser; the triggers must be pressed simultaneously to detach the riser from the harness and are often difficult to press when there is tension on the canopy.

CINC—Commander in chief; a four-star officer from any of the services, in command of a major DoD organization comprising forces from more than one service. Examples are CINCPAC, CINCLANT, and CINCSOCOM. In the chain of command, CINCs report directly to the Secretary of Defense.

Claymore mine—Antipersonnel mine used extensively in Vietnam. The ball-bearing-covered explosive is "shaped" so that it can be aimed toward the enemy.

closed-circuit scuba—Underwater breathing apparatus that emits no bubbles as the combat swimmer breathes. Designed for clandestine operations in enemy waters. The diver is a part of the system. The system uses a carbon-dioxide scrubber to keep the breathing medium pure oxygen. Two types of closed-circuit rigs have been used by the Teams since 1963: the American-manufactured Emerson and the German Draeger.

combat swimmer—Navy SEAL. The term is used to differentiate between standard Navy divers, who normally conduct noncombat missions, and members of a SEAL Team, whose mission involves swimming into combat.

compass board—Clear plastic board with a compass mounted in it, used to keep one's bearings underwater. Watches and swimmer reels may be attached.

CTF-116—Commander, Task Force-116. The U.S. Navy organization whose mission included interdicting Vietcong operations in the riverine areas of the Mekong Delta and the Rung Sat Special Zone. SEALs, PBRs, and Seawolf light helo fire teams operating in those areas were under the command of CTF-116.

davit—Cranelike device installed on most Navy ships, used for stowing the ship's boats and getting them in and out of the water.

DEFCON—Defense Condition. Denotes a graduated alert system used by the U.S. Military. DEFCON 5 is the normal, peacetime condition. DEFCON 1 is the highest state of alert, meaning war is imminent.

Desert One—The unsuccessful 1980 operation to free American Embassy personnel held hostage by the Iranians.

dry run—Very dangerous helo maneuver, making a strafing run without firing, in order to scare the enemy into keeping their heads down—usually attempted *after* the helo has used up its ammunition.

DZ—Drop zone. The area on which parachute jumpers land. For SEALs, it is often a spot in the ocean.

E & E—Escape and evasion. Used to describe specific training provided American military people who, by nature of their assignment, are more vulnerable to capture by the enemy. All combat aviators and SEALs receive some form of this training. SEALs have a primary role in establishing E & E networks designed to rescue downed aviators.

free-fire zone—In the Vietnam War, a geographic area in which U.S. forces were allowed to open fire without having first received fire. Normally, any area so designated was under the control of the enemy.

frogman—Analogous to "combat swimmer." Originally, a term designating any member of an Underwater Demolition Team. Now often used by Team members to denote one of their own who is a good operator.

"Green Team" training—SEAL Team Six slang for the period of time every new member spends learning to do things that other SEAL teams don't do.

gun target line—The line of bearing between the gun and the target. Naval guns, though very accurate on bearing (direction), are notoriously inaccurate on range (distance), so being near the GTL is risky.

Hagensen pack—Pack specifically designed to carry twenty pounds of explosives.

H-hour—Term used to describe the precise time to begin military operations.

H & I fire—Harassment and interdiction fire, usually done by ground-based artillery. An indiscriminate method of bothering the enemy. Used extensively in Vietnam to unsettle Vietcong and North Vietnamese Army units in their sanctuaries.

hot-refuel—Refueling without shutting down the engines. This is done only under combat conditions.

IBL—Inflatable Boat Large. An eleven-man rubber boat formerly used to transport UDT swimmers.

joint—Term that describes multiservice actions or organizations—e.g., "joint operations"; "joint commands." Operation Urgent Fury was a joint operation in Grenada. SOCOM is a joint command.

Junk Force—South Vietnamese organization that operated wooden-hulled indigenous craft called junks. In the Mekong Delta, some junk force units fought hard and distinguished themselves.

K-Bar knife—Basic tool and last line of defense for SEAL swimmers. Used by frogmen (and U.S. Marines) since World War II. The K-Bar's sturdy seven-inch steel blade has been used in combat and for more mundane purposes such as opening tin cans. Through the years, it has become a symbol of the SEALs and a highly treasured item for SEAL "wannabes."

LANTCOM—Atlantic Command. Historically commanded by a Navy admiral or Marine general (CINCLANT), it's responsible for all U.S. military operations in the Atlantic theater.

LANTFLT—U.S. Atlantic Fleet. The Navy organization charged with carrying out naval operations within a prescribed geographic area that includes the Atlantic Ocean. With the "CINC" preceding it, the acronym refers to the commander in chief of the Atlantic Fleet.

LCPL—Landing Craft Personnel Large. A thirty-six-foot steel-hulled boat formerly used by UDT to transport swimmers from their host ships to an amphibious landing beach.

Lizard Line—Long rope (the length can vary) used to keep a large number of SEALs together during submerged swims. Sometimes, double loops are woven into the line at staggered intervals so swim pairs can hang on as they swim.

LSSC—Light SEAL Support Craft. Vietnam-era boat.

LZ—Landing zone; short for "helicopter landing zone." Area designated for landing helos. Usually describes an area free of obstructions but could be anywhere a helo can land.

MC-1—Military static-line parachute system. Jumpers attach their static lines to a cable inside the aircraft. When they jump, the static line deploys the parachute. The "round" canopy is modified to allow the jumper to turn into the wind before landing.

MT-1—Military free-fall parachute system used by SEALs and special forces. Highly maneuverable "square" canopy acts much like an aircraft wing, allowing jumpers more maneuverability and forward speed than the MC-1 system.

Mike Force—American Special Forces—commanded unit composed of Vietnamese or Cambodian troops; operated throughout South Vietnam.

MX-300/360 radio—Small handheld UHF or VHF radio used by SEALs for short-range communications. Manufactured by Motorola.

NAVAIRLANT—Naval Air Forces, U.S. Atlantic Fleet. With the letters "COM" preceding it, the acronym refers to the commander of the force.

NAVFORV—Naval Forces Vietnam. This organization, based in Saigon, commanded all naval forces operating within the prescribed military boundaries of Vietnam. With the letters "COM" preceding it, the acronym refers to the commander of the force.

NAVOPSUPGRU—Naval Operations Support Group. The forerunner of Naval Special Warfare Groups. Commanded UDTs, SEAL Teams, and Boat Support Units.

NAVPERS—Bureau of Naval Personnel, the organization responsible for assigning all Navy officers and enlisted.

NAVSPECWARCOM—Naval Special Warfare Command. The naval-component command of the U.S. Special Operations Command. Commanded by a rear admiral, NAVSPECWARCOM is responsible for the care and feeding of all naval special warfare forces.

NAVSPECWARGRU—Naval Special Warfare Group. Commanded by a SEAL captain, it's the organization responsible to COMNAVSPECWARCOM for the command and control of SEAL Teams.

northern gun line—Geographic area off the coast of northern South Vietnam, patrolled by U.S. Navy ships that provided gunfire support for Marines in the I Corps, as well as interdiction fire into Vietcong base areas.

NVD—Night Vision Device. Commonly called a "Starlight Scope," it uses ambient light to provide nighttime images much as a telescope would during the day.

OIC—Officer in charge.

OPNAV—Acronym used to identify the staff of the Chief of Naval Operations.

P-3—Land-based antisubmarine-warfare aircraft, the four-engine P-3 Orion was a superb hunter of Soviet submarines.

PACFLT—U.S. Pacific Fleet. The Navy organization charged with carrying out naval operations within a prescribed geographic area that includes the Pacific Ocean. With the letters "CINC" preceding it, the acronym refers to the commander in chief of the Pacific Fleet.

PACOM—Pacific Command. Historically commanded by a Navy admiral (CINCPAC), it's responsible for all U.S. military operations in the Pacific theater.

PBR—River patrol boat. Thirty-two-foot fiberglass boat widely employed on the rivers in Vietnam. Twin .50-caliber machine guns forward plus a single .50-caliber and M-60 machine gun (among other weapons) aft made this a formidable craft for river interdiction. SEALs often used PBRs as insertion craft.

PHIBLANT/PHIBPAC—Amphibious Force U.S. Atlantic/Pacific Fleet. With the letters "COM" preceding it, the acronym refers to the commander of the force.

platoon—Normally the largest operating entity in a SEAL Team. During Vietnam a SEAL platoon contained up to two officers and twelve enlisted men. Present SEAL platoons comprise two squads of one officer and seven enlisted.

point man—First person in a combat patrol. In a SEAL patrol the point man is responsible for ensuring that the patrol does not walk into an enemy ambush. He is also the first man to encounter any mines or booby traps. After the patrol leader, the point man bears the most responsibility for the safety of the patrol. During Vietnam, SEAL point men were some of the best in their platoon or squad.

Popular Force—Irregular South Vietnamese organization formed to protect villages from the Vietcong. Popular Force units seldom operated beyond their villages and hamlets.

PRC-25—Man-portable VHF radio. The basic field radio for SEALs in Vietnam.

OPAREA—Acronym for "operating [or "operations"] area." Refers to an area in which military operations are conducted. "Area of operations" and "AO" are interchangeable terms.

rig—Term commonly used by SEALs to refer to scuba equipment. "How about taking the rig off my back?" one SEAL might say to another after coming out of the water.

rumor board—SEAL slang for intelligence maps. "Rumor board" was usually a more accurate description of the information found on them.

SATCOM—Man-portable satellite radio used by SEALs for long-range voice or data communications.

SEAL Team—Sea, Air, Land Team. Navy organization established in 1962 to conduct clandestine maritime special operations. In the beginning only two SEAL Teams were formed, one in the Atlantic Fleet and one in the Pacific Fleet. Now there are nine, assigned to the U.S. Special Operations Command.

Seawolves—Nickname given the Navy light attack helicopter squadron four, which often supported SEAL operations in the Mekong Delta.

SECDEF—Secretary of Defense.

SECNAV—Secretary of the Navy.

Secret Zone—During the Vietnam War, a term given to a geographic area considered to be completely under the control of the enemy. Anyone living there was considered to be enemy. In the Mekong Delta, the Secret

Zones were mostly mangrove swamps. Originally, not much was known about these areas. SEALs changed that.

semi-closed-circuit scuba—Mixed-gas diving rig used by SEALs when the mission will call for exceeding the depth-time limits for a closed-circuit scuba, and clandestine approach to a target is not an overriding concern. Semi-closed-circuit scubas emit a small trail of bubbles each time the diver exhales. Otherwise, they operate much like a closed-circuit pure-oxygen rig.

slick—Military jargon for a helicopter that is not a gunship. Usually signifies a troop-carrying helo armed only with machine guns at each door.

SOCOM—Special Operations Command. Established by the U.S. Congress to command, control, and resource special operations forces from all the services. Commanded by a "CINC," a four-star officer nominated by the president and confirmed by the Senate.

SOP—Standard operating procedure. The "playbook" for a SEAL organization; a series of tactical maneuvers performed routinely. In a SEAL tactical briefing the patrol leader might say, "Patrol order of movement in accordance with SOP."

Stoner machine gun—5.56-caliber machine gun used extensively by SEALs in Vietnam. Popular with SEALs because it used lighter ammunition than the standard M-60 light machine gun also used during that era.

swimmer reel—Deep-sea fishing reel containing a light nylon line; attached to the underside of a compass board, it is used to log distances underwater.

Team(s)—Term used by SEALs to refer to the SEAL community. One SEAL may ask another, "When did you come into the Teams?" or "What Team are you in now?"

UDT—Underwater Demolition Team. The forerunners of the SEAL Teams, UDTs were first formed during World War II to provide hydrographic reconnaissance for the amphibious forces in the Pacific campaign. In 1983 all UDTs became either SEAL or SEAL Delivery Vehicle Teams; the latter operate wet submersible mini-submarines used by SEALs.

ZPU—Russian antiaircraft weapon. A 14.5mm heavy machine gun, the ZPU-1 was the standard armament in a BTR-60PB.

ZU-23—Russian antiaircraft weapon. A 23mm cannon capable of being mounted in the cargo bed of a truck. The Grenadans had the two-barrel ZU-23-2 model.

SELECT BIBLIOGRAPHY

Though I have relied mostly on my recollections in writing this book, the works listed below refreshed my memory.

Bonds, Ray, ed. *The Vietnam War: The Illustrated History of the Conflict in Southeast Asia*. New York: Crown Publishers, Inc., 1979.

Bosiljevac, T.L. *SEALs: UDT/SEAL Operations in Vietnam*. Boulder, CO: Paladin Press, 1990.

Emerson, Steven. *Secret Warriors: Inside the Covert Military Operations of the Reagan Era*. New York: G.P. Putnam's Sons, 1988.

Ezell, Edward Clinton. *Small Arms of the World*. 12th ed. Harrisburg, PA: Stackpole Books, 1983.

Fall, Bernard B. *Street Without Joy: Insurgency in Indochina, 1956–63*. 3rd ed. Harrisburg, PA: The Stackpole Company, 1963.

Halberstadt, Hans. *U.S. Navy SEALs*. Osceola, WI: Motorbooks International, 1993.

Kelly, Orr. *Never Fight Fair: Navy SEALs' Stories of Combat*. Novato, CA: Presidio Press, 1995.

Kelly, Orr. *Brave Men Dark Waters: The Untold Story of the Navy SEALs*. Novato, CA: Presidio Press, 1992.

Marcinko, Richard with John Weisman. *Rogue Warrior.* New York: Pocket Books, 1992.

Martin, David C. and John Wolcott. *Best Laid Plans: The Inside Story of America's War Against Terrorism.* New York: Harper & Row, 1988.

Sheehan, Neil. *A Bright Shining Lie: John Paul Vann and America in Vietnam.* New York: Random House, 1988.

Spector, Ronald. *After Tet: The Bloodiest Year in Vietnam.* New York: The Free Press, a division of Macmillan, Inc., 1993.

Stubblefield, Gary with Hans Halberstadt. *Inside the U.S. Navy SEALs.* Osceola, WI: Motorbooks International, 1995.

Waller, Douglas C. *The Commandos: The Inside Story of America's Secret Soldiers.* New York: Simon & Schuster, 1994.

INDEX

About the Author

Captain Robert A. Gormly, USN (Ret.), served twenty-nine years as a Navy SEAL. His awards include the Silver Star, three Legions of Merit, three Bronze Stars (two in combat), the Defense Meritorious Medal, and a Purple Heart.

Captain Robert A. Gormly, USN (Ret.), served twenty-nine years as a Navy SEAL. His awards include the Silver Star, three Legions of Merit, three Bronze Stars (two in combat), the Defense Meritorious Medal, and a Purple Heart.